NO PLACE LIKE HOME

NO PLACE
LIKE HOME

Wealth, Community, and the Politics
of Homeownership

Brian J. McCabe

OXFORD
UNIVERSITY PRESS

OXFORD
UNIVERSITY PRESS

Oxford University Press is a department of the University of Oxford.
It furthers the University's objective of excellence in research, scholarship,
and education by publishing worldwide. Oxford is a registered trade mark of
Oxford University Press in the UK and certain other countries.

Published in the United States of America by Oxford University Press
198 Madison Avenue, New York, NY 10016, United States of America

© Oxford University Press 2016

Library of Congress Cataloging-in-Publication Data
McCabe, Brian J., author.
No place like home : wealth, community, and the politics of homeownership / Brian J. McCabe.
pages   cm
Includes bibliographical references and index.
ISBN 978-0-19-027045-2 (hardcover : alk. paper) — ISBN 978-0-19-027046-9 (pbk. : alk. paper)
1. Home ownership—United States.   2. Community development—United States.
3. Wealth—United States.   I. Title.
HD7287.82.U6M385   2016
333.33'80973—dc23   2015030574

9 8 7 6 5 4 3 2 1

Printed in Canada on acid-free paper

Typeset in Scala Pro

Printed by WEBCOM, Inc.

To my parents, Bonnie and John

CONTENTS

ILLUSTRATIONS AND TABLE

Figures

Table

ACKNOWLEDGMENTS

In one important way, writing a book is like buying a home—you accrue a lot of debt(s). This book would not have been possible without the friendship, advice, and support of countless people, and I wish to acknowledge them here.

This book began as my dissertation in the Department of Sociology at New York University. The department provided a nurturing space for the development of my sociological imagination, and I am grateful to colleagues at New York University who helped guide my growth as a sociologist and a scholar. Vicki Been, Neil Brenner, Vivek Chibber, Dalton Conley, Issa Kohler-Hausmann, Colin Jerolmack, Eric Klinenberg, Johanna Lacoe, Amy LeClair, Mike McCarthy, Peter Rich, Pat Sharkey, Amy Ellen Schwartz, Florencia Torche, Mark Treskon, and Larry Wu were incredibly helpful in this process, in ways both big and small. Many of them read chapters, offered encouragement, and advised on the process of securing a contract and writing a book. Others were more distant from this project but were critical to my formation as a sociologist. I would especially like to thank Max Besbris and Ruth Braunstein for their close, careful read of the near-final manuscript.

While studying as a graduate student at New York University, I also worked as a doctoral research fellow at the Furman Center for Real Estate and Urban Policy. There, I found an unmatched community of scholars concerned about housing and urban policy, and I consider myself fortunate to be a part of the Furman Center team. While on leave from Georgetown University to complete portions of the manuscript, I was welcomed back to the Furman Center with open arms and once again found an incredibly supportive space to write about housing and talk about urban policy. On this visit, Fadi Hanna opened up his home to me as I took refuge in New York City, and I remain deeply indebted to Fadi for his unmatched hospitality (and for sharing one of my favorite homes with me).

Several people at New York University deserve special mention. First, Jeff Manza chaired my dissertation committee and has been an untiring advocate for me throughout this process. He has been an invaluable mentor and friend, and I am deeply grateful for the opportunity to work so closely with him. Second, Ingrid Ellen has contributed immensely to my growth as a policy researcher and urban scholar. Her thoughtful guidance of my professional development and continued support of my research endeavors continue to be deeply formative, and I am thankful to her for taking me under her wing as a part of the Furman Center family. Both Jeff and Ingrid have been incredibly influential to my professional development in ways that far exceed the pages of this book. Finally, Jen Heerwig—the better half of my Roadshow—went above and beyond what should reasonably be expected of anyone in a non-marital relationship. Jen read countless drafts of this manuscript, often on unacceptably short notice, and always pushed me to write a better book. She has been a critical, engaged, and thoughtful part of this process from start to finish. This book is better—and completed—in no small part to having Jen as a close colleague, coauthor, and friend.

In the Department of Sociology at Georgetown University, I have found a collegial group of colleagues to whom I owe a great deal of thanks. José Casanova, Bill Daddio, Margaret Hall, Leslie Hinkson, Becky Hsu, Kathleen Guidroz, Dennis McNamara, Bill McDonald, Hanadi Salih, Sarah Stiles, and Tim Wickham-Crowley have created a supportive, nurturing environment for young scholars committed to both teaching and scholarship, and I am grateful to work with such a supportive group of people at my alma mater. In Washington, DC, I have also found a tremendous scholar and friend in Katie Wells, who took an interest in my research and has been an invaluable resource in the final stages of completing the book.

The research in this book was supported with a handful of grants, and I would be remiss not to mention the incredible opportunities they provided. While completing my dissertation, I traveled to the Herbert Hoover Presidential Library to research the early efforts to promote homeownership. I am indebted to Patricia Hand, the Academic Programs Coordinator at the Herbert Hoover Presidential Library Association, and Matthew Schaefer, a research librarian at the Library, for their assistance during my trip to West Branch, Iowa. I also had an opportunity to continue this research with a trip to the Hoover Library at Stanford University with a grant from Georgetown University. Frederik Heller, the manager of Virtual Libraries and Archives at the National Association of Realtors, assisted with gathering archival materials on the Own Your Own Home campaigns. Tom Sander, the Executive Director of the Saguaro Seminar on Civic Engagement at Harvard's Kennedy School of Government, was instrumental in providing access to the Social Capital Community Survey. At various points, my dissertation research was funded with grants from the Horowitz Foundation for Social Policy, a Doctoral Dissertation Research Grant from the U.S. Department of Housing and Urban Development, and the generous Dean's Dissertation Grant from the Graduate School of Arts and Sciences at New York University.

Over the years, I presented parts of this research at the Eastern Sociological Society meeting and the annual American Sociological Association conference. I have presented pieces of this work at colloquia and seminars, both at Georgetown and beyond. I am grateful to participants in seminars at the Metropolitan Policy Center at American University, the Government Department at Georgetown University, the America's Initiative at Georgetown University, the National Center for Smart Growth Research and Education at the University of Maryland, the Metropolitan Institute at Virginia Tech, and the Department of Sociology at New York University for their critical feedback at various points along the way.

At Oxford University Press, James Cook and Amy Klopfenstein were incredible guides in the process of publishing this book. In particular, James took an interest in this project at an early stage and has been a generous and thoughtful steward at each step along the way.

My friends in New York and Washington, DC, rarely tired of hearing about the civic benefits of homeownership, and when they did, they rarely showed it. To befriend a Ph.D. student, and especially one writing a dissertation and applying for jobs, must be exhausting—perhaps as exhausting as befriending an assistant professor working to complete a book manuscript. Their friendship was—and remains—invaluable. Soon, I look forward to talking with them about anything other than homeownership.

And finally, but also most important, I owe my deepest thanks to my family, and particularly to my parents. For more than thirty years, they have nurtured my curiosity and supported my pursuits with absolutely unconditional support. Without them, I would never have had the courage to embark on this project or the perseverance to finish it. My parents encouraged the creativity and critical engagement with the world that led me to the types of questions at the heart of this book. They were enthusiastic about my career choices, and patient as I embarked on the long road of writing this book. They are deeply responsible for the sense of social justice and critical inquiry that, I hope, are reflected in my research. With my sincerest love and gratitude, this book is dedicated to my parents, Bonnie and John.

NO PLACE LIKE HOME

1

INTRODUCTION

WEALTH, COMMUNITY, AND THE POLITICS OF HOMEOWNERSHIP

A couple of days before her fortieth birthday, Helen Butler bought her first home in the suburbs of Washington, DC. For years, Helen had dreamed of owning her own home. Although she held an upper-middle-class job and earned a steady income, she had never been able to save enough for the down payment to buy a house. Still, investing in homeownership seemed like the logical next step in strengthening her financial footing. Like many homebuyers in the years before the housing crisis, Helen was able to secure a mortgage that would allow her to buy a home without many up-front costs. She took out a loan for $465,000, found a nice community within driving distance of the city, and purchased her piece of the American Dream.

For Veronica Fischer and her husband, Paul, buying a home had long seemed a distant dream. For more than a decade, their family lived in a two-bedroom rental house in Portland, Oregon. Each month, Veronica worried that the landlord would sell the property, forcing them to find a new home in a different neighborhood. Even worse, as the family paid the monthly rent, Veronica and Paul felt like they were throwing away money on rent rather than investing in the future of their family. When they discovered a program to buy a home with the help of a local community organization, they jumped at the chance. After years of saving and sacrificing, they were finally able to purchase a home of their own.

And in Camden, New Jersey, Alyson Wilson, a single mother of two children, purchased her first home. A lifelong resident of Camden, Alyson had spent most of her life renting apartments throughout the city. As rents rose and landlords sold their properties, she never knew how long she would be able to stay in each neighborhood. Sending her teenage daughters to school—and encouraging them to make friends in the neighborhood—had become increasingly difficult as they moved around the city. But after years of searching for an affordable home to buy, she finally found one in an up-and-coming neighborhood on the east side of the city. Although she was eager to start building equity, moving into a home of her own wasn't just a financial investment for her family. As a homeowner, Alyson would start to put down roots in her community. After years of moving from place to place, she would finally be able to build the long-term relationships in her neighborhood that she had been unable to sustain as a renter.

As they purchased their homes, Helen Butler, Veronica Fischer, and Alyson Wilson joined the majority of Americans in fulfilling one of the core pieces of the American Dream. By the end of the twentieth century, as opportunities for low-income and minority Americans to buy a home expanded, the national homeownership rate had soared to historic highs. By 2006, with nearly seven out of ten Americans living in homes of their own, more people owned their homes than at any other point in American history.[1]

These historically high rates of homeownership reflect the continued importance of owning a home to many Americans. According to recent public opinion polls, the overwhelming majority of homeowners report being satisfied with their ownership decisions, and most renters aspire to own a home of their own at some point in the future. In fact, homeownership remains one of the few goals to unite an increasingly diverse and polarized American public. As James Surowiecki recently wrote in the *New Yorker*, "Americans may disagree about nearly everything, but few contest the idea that owning your home is a good thing." Across nearly every segment of society—old and young, conservative and liberal, homeowner and renter—Americans remain deeply committed to the promise of owning a home.[2]

While there are many reasons why Americans prefer ownership to renting, the stories of Helen Butler, Veronica Fischer, and Alyson Wilson highlight two of the central motivations for buying a home in the United States. On one hand, owning a home is often the best way for households to save money and generate wealth to pass along to their children. Homeownership helps families climb the economic ladder, and it is a critical resource as they save for retirement, send children to college, and work to build a small nest egg. Today, Americans hold more wealth in their homes than they do in any other asset, making housing wealth the centerpiece of economic mobility and financial independence.

On the other hand, buying a home often deepens social bonds in local communities by rooting people in their neighborhoods. Throughout much of the twentieth century, as federal housing policies created new opportunities for Americans to own their own homes, policymakers pointed to the important role of homeownership in strengthening communities, building better citizens, and encouraging people to engage in the routine practices of civic life. Homeowners often take a more active role in local politics and community affairs than renters, and this civic engagement is used to justify public investments in homeownership.

But in this book, I argue that these core ideas about homeownership—on one hand, the importance of building wealth through housing and on the other hand, the role of ownership in strengthening communities—are not nearly as straightforward as common accounts suggest. The growing importance of housing as a tool for building wealth has transformed the ways citizens participate in public life, upending long-standing ideas about the role of homeownership in strengthening communities and building better citizens. While homeowners perform many of the textbook acts of civic engagement at higher rates than renters—attending community meetings, voting in local elections, and joining neighborhood groups, for example—they often do so as a way to protect their property values. This participation contributes to patterns of segregation and social exclusion in their neighborhoods, raising doubts about the benefits to communities that come from active, engaged citizenship.

Structured around the enduring importance of owning a home for building wealth and the way it transforms communities, I wrestle with this important paradox about homeownership in this book. Although public policies encourage ownership as a tool for building citizenship and strengthening communities, I show that the financial importance of homeownership changes the way citizens participate in community life. While deepening patterns of residential stability often does help to build stronger communities, I argue that the importance of owning a home for building household wealth can have the opposite effect. Weaving together both a historical analysis of housing policies with a contemporary account of the politics of homeownership, I conclude that owning a home is not the infallible tool for building communities and strengthening citizenship that proponents often claim.

Strengthening Communities through Homeownership

When Alyson Wilson moved into her new home, she felt settled in her community for the first time in her life. As a thirty-six-year old resident of Camden, Alyson was used to moving from neighborhood to neighborhood with her two teenage daughters. Moving put a strain on her family, though. It was hard to

build relationships with her neighbors or encourage her daughters to befriend other kids in the community when her family moved so frequently.

After years of moving from one apartment to another, Alyson was finally
able to purchase a home in a neighborhood that had been struggling for
many years. Over the previous decade, the Camden Housing Authority had
started renovating rundown houses on the east side of the city and selling
them to Camden residents. Using federal funds allocated through the
Neighborhood Stabilization Program, a program designed to help revitalize
blighted urban neighborhoods, the city was reinvesting in some of the
Camden's poorest communities. As the housing authority repaired abandoned homes and sold them to first-time homebuyers, city leaders hoped that
a new class of homeowners—people like Alyson Wilson—would bring stability to the area, becoming anchors in the community. In a home of her own,
Alyson would finally be able to start forging the social connections in her
community that had been difficult to maintain as a renter.[3]

Today, many low-income homeowners, like Alyson Wilson, benefit directly
from federal programs to buy a home. They take advantage of down payment
assistance programs or reap the rewards of neighborhood investment initiatives, like the Neighborhood Stabilization Program. But it isn't just low-income
buyers who benefit from federal investments in homeownership. Every year,
millions of households claim the mortgage interest deduction, taking advantage of a tax deduction that disproportionately benefits high-income homeowners. They benefit from a mortgage finance system that supplies credit
cheaply to American homebuyers through a government guarantee against
the risk of default. These benefits are part of an elaborate infrastructure that
encourages citizens to buy their own homes by lowering the cost of borrowing.

While contemporary justifications for these policies often focus on the
financial benefits of owning your own home, that wasn't always the case. In
fact, historic efforts to expand homeownership opportunities rarely acknowledged the financial rewards to individual citizens, as owning a home
was not the great investment vehicle it is today. Instead, when they set out
to buy their homes, early twentieth-century homebuyers typically saved *for*
homeownership rather than saving *through* it. They joined savings and loan
organizations, making monthly contributions to these local lending institutions and borrowing from these pooled funds to purchase their houses.
And unlike contemporary mortgage loans, which offer low down payments
and amortize over thirty years, mortgage loans in the early twentieth century required a much higher down payment and typically came due within
a decade.[4]

Instead of promising that homeownership would provide a brighter financial future, proponents argued for a civic promise of homeownership. Building a nation of homeowners would do the difficult work of strengthening democratic life and building better communities. Homeownership tied people to their neighborhoods by creating shared identities and encouraging households to work together to solve local problems. By uniting citizens behind a collective concern for their community, homeownership promised to transform everyday citizens into protectors of the American way of life.

The transformative power of homeownership to build better citizens and unite the citizenry behind a shared set of values reflected the long-held American belief in the power of property ownership. At the beginning of the republic, the founders linked property ownership to political citizenship by tying the right to vote—the central right of political membership—to the ownership of real property. This vision of propertied citizenship was embodied in Thomas Jefferson's vision of a nation of yeoman farmers—an agrarian country populated by self-sufficient citizens concerned about the places where they lived. These citizens would be uncorrupted by the polluting influence of city life and would uphold the independence and civic virtues critical to a functioning democratic process.

Initially, every state in the union had suffrage requirements linking property ownership to political participation. Citizens in Virginia were required to own at least fifty acres of land to be eligible to vote, and those in Massachusetts had to own property in the same town where they cast their votes for their representatives in the U.S. House. While these suffrage requirements were formally eliminated across states by the mid-nineteenth century, they left a legacy that persists today, shaping the way Americans think about property ownership, citizenship, and civic life.[5]

In early America, the importance of property ownership as a marker of political citizenship reflected several key ideas about the transformative power of property to invest citizens in community affairs. Explaining the historical interconnectedness of property ownership and citizenship, historian Alexander Keyssar argues that these ideas extended a legacy inherited from the British. On one hand, early American political leaders believed that the ownership of real property forced citizens to take a heightened interest in the affairs of their communities and their country, particularly on issues of taxation. As property owners, they cared about how decisions were made and how those decisions would affect their holdings. On the other hand, political leaders believed that property owners were independent citizens ready to participate in democratic politics. They were unencumbered by external influences and therefore capable of evaluating policies and making decisions without relying on others. Citizens who failed to acquire property lacked an investment in the future of their country and were dismissed as undeserving of the rights and responsibilities of membership in the political community.[6]

While contemporary efforts to encourage homeownership often center on the importance of owning a home for economic mobility, political leaders continue to lean on these historic arguments to claim that homeownership anchors citizens in their neighborhoods, generates shared interests in those places, and fortifies the social bonds that are central to safe, vibrant communities. Exemplifying the continued importance of citizenship to federal homeownership efforts, President George W. Bush invoked the rhetoric of citizenship as he worked to expand opportunities for Americans to buy homes. Each year of his presidency, Bush issued a proclamation declaring National Homeownership Month. While he noted the financial self-sufficiency that would come from owning a home, he also acknowledged the broader civic improvements that would result from increasing the number of homeowners. "Where homeownership flourishes, neighborhoods are more stable, residents are more civic-minded, schools are better and crime rates decline," he remarked in announcing National Homeownership Month. In his announcements, he underscored the power of homeownership to generate shared concerns for local neighborhoods. "The benefits of homeownership extend to our communities. Families who own their own homes have a strong interest in maintaining the value of their investment, the safety of their neighborhoods, and the quality of their schools." While recognizing the importance of homeownership for building wealth, Bush also pointed to the importance of building communities through investments in homeownership.[7]

And while conservative leaders are deeply committed to the rhetoric of an ownership society, they are not the only ones to describe homeownership as a tool for anchoring citizens in their communities and investing them in the responsibilities of upstanding citizenship. In a 2003 Senate hearing about expanding homeownership opportunities for low-income and minority Americans, Democratic senator Paul Sarbanes described the civic promise of homeownership. "We talk a lot about homeownership...and I want to spend just a moment reminding us why we put so much effort into achieving this very important goal," he noted, drawing on familiar themes about citizenship and community life. "Homeownership is an asset-building engine for families and neighborhoods, indeed for society as a whole. When a family buys a home, they are buying more than brick and mortar. They are really buying into the neighborhood. With each homeowner, we create another anchor in a community, another advocate for better schools, safer streets, small business development. Common sense tells us and the evidence actually confirms that homeowners are more engaged citizens and more active in their communities."[8]

Building Wealth through Homeownership

Veronica Fischer immediately felt a sense of relief when her family moved into their home. For the first time in her life, Veronica owned a home—a sixteen-hundred-square-foot house with four bedrooms and two bathrooms, as well as a laundry room upstairs. Asked whether she was glad to be a homeowner, she suggested "thrilled" would be a better word. "It was like receiving a windfall or perhaps winning the lottery," Veronica said. "One month you're living in a house that leaks every time it rains, a basement that floods when it rains.... And then suddenly you're moving into a brand-new, four-bedroom house."[9]

As she talked about her new home, Veronica pointed to all the benefits that would come from the opportunity to own a home. As a renter, her monthly payments increased periodically, rising to $900 a month by the time she moved. But in a home of her own, she would have the security of stable monthly payments. She wouldn't have to ask anyone before making improvements to the house—painting walls, remodeling the kitchen, or fencing in the yard, for example. And homeownership would allow her family to gain a better financial footing. "One of the best things about homeownership is the chance to build a future for my extended family, and to build equity in my home, which will mean more security," Veronica noted. With the equity she expected to build, she could start thinking about sending her children to college and planning for her own retirement. Buying a home meant more than just finding a place to live. For Veronica Fischer—and for millions of Americans like her—homeownership was her best shot at becoming financially stable and climbing into the prized middle class.

While the importance of homeownership as a tool for strengthening communities continues to justify federal investments in ownership, the power of homeownership for building wealth has come to dominate the way many Americans approach their decision to buy a home. Asked to explain their preference for ownership over renting, Americans often point to the financial independence of owning a home or the promise of economic mobility. Recently, respondents in the National Housing Survey, a monthly survey conducted by Fannie Mae, were asked to identify the reasons to buy a home. Eighty-five percent noted that owning a home was a good way to build wealth to pass along to their children (fig. 1.1). About 80 percent reported that

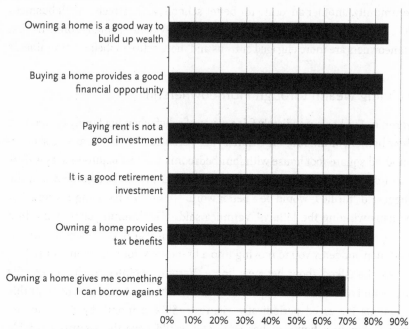

FIGURE 1.1. Support for financial reasons to buy a home. In the National Housing Survey, respondents were read each of the statements shown and asked whether it was a major reason, a minor reason, or not a reason to buy a home. Shown here is the percentage of respondents who reported that each statement was either a major reason or a minor reason to buy a home.

buying a home was a good financial investment and that homeownership was important in saving for retirement. About 70 percent acknowledged the importance of homeownership as an asset against which they could borrow money. Like Veronica Fischer, Americans strongly believe that buying a home is a good way to build wealth and that the equity they build through their homes will help them climb the economic ladder.[10]

Corroborating the findings of the National Housing Survey, a growing number of public opinion polls report that the financial benefits of ownership are the *most* important reasons Americans report a preference for ownership. Although owning a home comes with substantial lifestyle benefits—it is an important marker of social status, and it often leads to a heightened sense of independence—fully half of Americans identify the financial incentives of ownership as the most important reason to buy a home. Today, more than four out of five citizens agree that buying a home is the best investment a household can make. Nearly nine out of ten Americans—including three-quarters of renters—believe that owning makes more financial sense than renting.[11]

This commitment to homeownership as a financial investment reflects a single, important fact. Americans hold more wealth in their homes than in any other asset, making housing the most important economic tool for millions of citizens. The average homeowner reports more than twenty times the wealth of the average renter, according to a recent analysis by researchers at the Federal Reserve Bank. And middle-class and minority households are more invested in housing than high-income, white households. While the average homeowner in the United States holds about 25 percent of his or her wealth in his or her home, the average African-American or Hispanic homeowner holds more than 40 percent (fig. 1.2). Homeowners in the bottom two income quartiles hold about half of their wealth in housing. While most American homeowners concentrate their wealth in their homes, building equity through homeownership is a particularly important tool for wealth creation for low-income and minority households.[12]

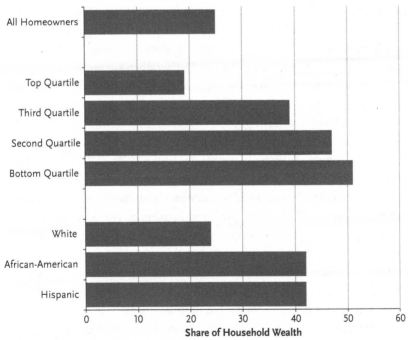

FIGURE 1.2. Housing equity as a share of household wealth. Data from analysis of 2007 Survey of Consumer Finance in Christopher E. Herbert, Daniel T. McCue, and Rocio Sanchez-Moyano, "Is Homeownership Still an Effective Means of Building Wealth for Low-Income and Minority Households?," in *Homeownership Built to Last*, edited by Eric S. Belsky, Christopher E. Herbert, and Jennifer H. Molinsky, 50–98 (Washington, DC: Brookings Institution Press, 2013), table 1.

It is important to acknowledge that housing is a distinctive type of financial investment. Like other investments, including stocks or bonds, owning a home can help citizens to generate wealth and save money. Homeowners build wealth through housing as they pay down their mortgage debt and build equity in their homes. Yet, in many ways, owning a home is unlike other types of investments. It creates substantial use value because it provides shelter that citizens would otherwise get by renting. Households cannot diversify their housing investments to maximize financial gains or minimize exposure to risk. And while homeowners can gain access to their housing wealth through home equity loans, this wealth is often less easy to access than other types of investments.

Despite the distinctiveness of housing as a financial investment, the opportunity for economic mobility in the United States rests on the investments citizens make in their homes. To build wealth through homeownership, households often rely on the equity they build in their homes—in other words, the difference between the value of their home and the remaining money they owe on their mortgage. One way to increase equity is to pay down a mortgage loan. Each month, as homeowners pay off a portion of their debt and lower the principal on their mortgage, they are building more equity in their homes. Against the common notion of "throwing away" money through rent—a sentiment expressed by Veronica Fischer when she rented her Portland home—homeownership forces households to build wealth with their monthly mortgage payments, creating the "forced savings" program championed by proponents of homeownership.

But for the last two decades, the promise of building wealth through housing rested increasingly on rising home values. In the 1970s and 1980s, housing values rose slowly in the United States, providing only modest gains for American homeowners. But in the two decades before the Great Recession, housing values began to skyrocket. This rapid growth in housing prices contributed to the growing appeal of homeownership, confirming for many Americans that homeownership was the best investment they could make.[13]

Still, the financial investment in homeownership depends on a range of factors, including the type of mortgage loan a household uses, the neighborhoods where they live, and the length of time a family stays in their home. Housing values appreciate more slowly in poor neighborhoods and neighborhoods of concentrated disadvantage. But even in neighborhoods with robust housing markets, building equity often means enduring short-term shocks to the housing market. Families who were forced to sell during the recession often experienced substantial losses on their homes, while those who weathered the economic downturn survived the worst of the crisis when property values started to rise again. Often, simply staying put—living in a home for a long period of time—is one of the best strategies for building wealth.

Perhaps most important, the promise of generating wealth hinges on the type of mortgage instrument households use. When they opt for traditional mortgages, like the thirty-year fixed-rate loan, and pay off the principal with regular monthly payments, homeowners build equity by paying down their debt. However, many of the mortgage instruments pioneered in the run-up to the housing crisis lacked this forced saving component. Loans without down payment requirements enabled households to enter into homeownership without any equity in their homes, and interest-only loans encouraged home-buyers to make monthly payments without paying down the principal of the loan. These risky mortgage products created obstacles for homeowners looking to build wealth through housing and raised doubts about whether buying a home would continue to be the best tool for building wealth.

Still, even on the heels of the housing crisis, most social scientists concur that under the right circumstances, owning a home remains a good strategy for building wealth. In one study, researchers at the Joint Center for Housing Studies at Harvard University used the Panel Study of Income Dynamics to track the relationship between homeownership status and household wealth. They accounted for a range of factors that influence whether or not a household owns their own home, and they controlled for baseline differences between homeowners and renters that are likely to impact the ability of a household to generate wealth. Even after adjusting for the fact that homeowners tend to have higher levels of education, make more money at their jobs, and build up savings more effectively than renters, homeowners still come out on top. Consistent with the results from more than a decade of research, their findings confirm the basic intuition of most Americans. Under the right conditions—good neighborhoods, sound mortgage products, and a long-term commitment—owning your own home remains a durable strategy for building household wealth, even for low- and middle-income households.[14]

Wealth, Community, and the Housing Crisis

When Helen Butler bought her home in the suburbs of Washington, DC, she pointedly noted that buying a home was the best financial investment she could make. After all, for nearly two decades, home prices had been steadily climbing across the country, solidifying the financial importance of owning a home. But for Helen Butler, like for so many other Americans, homeownership wasn't everything she had hoped. Lured by rising home values, Helen was caught off guard when housing prices started to plummet in 2007. She quickly found herself deeply underwater, owing more on her home than the home was worth.[15]

As Helen looked around her community, she noticed that similar houses on her block were selling for less than half of what she had paid. Although Helen valued the safety of her community and the friendliness of her neighbors, she watched as some of them walked away from their homes rather than continuing to make monthly payments on a mortgage worth more than the value of the home. She was left to ponder whether homeownership was, in fact, the right tool for climbing the economic ladder. Like many other homeowners during the housing crisis, she considered walking away from her investment, realizing that abandoning her home meant leaving behind not just the investment that she had made but also the community where she lived.[16]

As homeowners, like Helen Butler, wrestled with the future of housing as a financial investment alongside a new set of challenges to the stability of their communities, the housing crisis launched a public conversation about the topics at the center of this book. At least momentarily, Americans began to ask questions about the place of homeownership in American life, wondering whether buying a home would continue to be a reliable vehicle for economic mobility or a guaranteed way to strengthen community life. As Jennifer Molinsky, Eric Belsky, and Christopher Herbert, scholars from the Joint Center for Housing Studies at Harvard University, recently noted, the crisis forced Americans to wrestle with the core benefits associated with buying a home in America. "Questions now center on whether homeownership still has the same wealth-building potential that benefited homeowners in the past…[and] whether it is a preferred path to stronger communities and better social outcomes," they wrote.[17]

By now, the contours of the housing crisis are widely known. By the end of the twentieth century, the national homeownership rate had started to rise at a remarkable clip, driven by the entry of millions of low-income and minority Americans into the ranks of homeownership. Low interest rates made mortgage credit available to these households, many of whom had previously been excluded from ownership opportunities, and a robust economy helped to usher in the quickest expansion of homeownership in decades. The enduring belief that owning a home would help families climb the economic ladder convinced millions of Americans to buy homes of their own.[18]

Although they aspired to own their own homes, many first-time homebuyers faced obstacles in qualifying for traditional, fixed-rate mortgages, including low credit scores and high down payment requirements. Without access to credit on the prime market, they often turned to the subprime market to borrow money to buy a home. By 2005, the subprime market accounted for more than 20 percent of all mortgage originations in the United States—up from only 6 percent five years earlier.[19]

While loans made on the subprime market created ownership opportunities for first-time homeowners—and enabled millions of existing homeowners to refinance at lower rates—they also carried substantial risk. Often these loans lacked the forced-savings components that historically made homeownership such an attractive financial investment. Many borrowers took out adjustable-rate mortgages that included an initial "teaser" interest rate, while others purchased their house without a down payment, embarking on ownership with no equity in their homes. Rather than steadily paying down the principal of their loan, homeowners increasingly relied on rising home prices to build wealth through housing.[20]

Soon, though, the American economy began to slow. After nearly two decades of growth in housing prices—growth that confirmed for many Americans the financial importance of owning a home—the housing market started to tumble. Housing sales leveled out, and property values began to fall. Struggling to keep up with monthly payments, countless American households faced the possibility of foreclosure. They would be forced to leave their communities—the places where they had built social ties and were involved in local organizations and institutions—as they struggled to pay their mortgages. Homeowners also watched helplessly as their housing values tumbled. During the crisis, the net worth of the median family plummeted nearly 40 percent as home prices fell—a devastating blow to families who had bet their economic futures on the housing market. The largest expansion in homeownership since the 1950s had led to the worst economic crisis since the Great Depression, sending shockwaves through the global economy.[21]

Critical to the story in this book, the expansion of ownership opportunities in the run-up to the housing crisis was built, in large part, on an enduring ideology of homeownership that presented homeowners as better neighbors, citizens, and Americans. Buying a home would be a tool for social inclusion—a way to integrate citizens into the norms and expectations of citizenship. As sociologist Anne Shlay noted, the expansion of homeownership for all Americans had become the "hallmark of US housing policy, *sine qua non*," largely synonymous with efforts to build better, safer housing for American families.[22]

Yet, as millions of families lost their homes to foreclosure, and millions more watched the value of their housing investments collapse, the crisis exposed the way Americans accepted this ideology of ownership as a social good without critically engaging with the challenges and risks of owning a home. In fact, the public construction of ownership as a social good created a cover for banks and lending institutions to push homeownership, regardless of these dangers. They often touted the benefits of ownership for crafting stronger communities and building better citizens as they peddled mortgage products to first-time homebuyers on the subprime market.[23]

As the ideology of homeownership shielded banks and lending institutions from scrutiny, the housing crisis exposed the dominant economic narrative of owning a home. While millions of Americans entered into homeownership with the expectation of building wealth and saving for retirement, the expansion of mortgage-backed securities fueled a financial instrument tied to the fortunes of homeowners. As mortgages were repackaged and sold around the world as mortgage-backed securities, global investors looked to profit from the housing decisions made by individual households. The transformation of homeownership into a global financial commodity exposed the myriad of actors—from realtors to bankers, investors to builders—whose fortunes rose and fell with those of American homeowners—an important observation as we begin to unravel the ideology of ownership in the United States.

Yet the housing crisis served as a powerful reminder that owning a home is not exclusively a tool for building wealth. Although the storylines of risky mortgage lending, plummeting housing wealth, and the global recession quickly came to dominate our public discourse about the crisis, the years since the crisis have also been a stark reminder of the importance of studying homeownership as a social phenomenon rather than simply as a series of economic transactions. Buying a home continues to hold deep social meaning for most Americans. It shapes the way citizens interact in their communities, and it substantiates claims to citizenship. And while we often describe owning a home as a marker of social inclusion, homeownership also creates unique forms of social stratification and contributes to the politics of exclusion. In this book, I offer a critical reappraisal of the ideology of homeownership on the heels of the housing crisis, highlighting the social relations inherent in owning a home.

Laying the Foundation

In the wake of the housing crisis, I offer an analysis in this book that untangles the ideological roots of our commitment to homeownership and asks about the ways our housing investments shape patterns of community participation. While contemporary discussions privilege housing as a tool for building household wealth, the long-standing American commitment to homeownership rests largely on the important role that owning a home has played in strengthening communities. Bringing together these central ideas about homeownership, I argue that the financial promise of owning a home mediates the possibilities that homeownership holds for building stronger communities. Armed with new evidence on the civic habits of homeowners, I offer a distinctly sociological framework for thinking about wealth, civic engagement, and the politics of homeownership in America.

The story begins nearly a century ago, during a remarkable and irreversible demographic shift. At the beginning of the twentieth century, Americans were moving to cities. As urbanization upended local communities, political leaders struggled to recreate the social bonds of these communities in growing urban centers. Reformers searched for solutions to the perceived decay of social life across the urban landscape. They sought to combat fears of political radicalism, end disruptions in the workplace, and fight the decline of social mores in an increasingly diverse and plural country.

Against the backdrop of this urban transformation, chapter 2 investigates the ways political leaders, civic reformers, and business elites mobilized behind the idea of homeownership for resolving the crisis of citizenship. Owning a home would moor citizens to their communities, they argued, and would help to overcome the challenges of social unrest in American cities. I use this chapter, structured around two early twentieth-century campaigns to promote homeownership, to investigate the ways civic leaders translated the long-standing American commitment to property ownership into a belief in the transformative power of owning a home. By reframing the personal housing choices made by individual Americans into acts imbued with distinctly political and social meaning, the chapter lays the historic foundation for understanding homeownership as a tool for building community and strengthening citizenship.

Although the campaigns successfully defined homeownership as a political and social act, they offered few solutions to the growing housing shortage in the post–World War I period. Instead, building a nation of homeowners required a sustained commitment by the federal government to overcome the obstacles to buying a home, especially in American cities. In chapter 3, I dig into the federal housing policies that contributed to the remarkable growth in homeownership over the course of the twentieth century. Beginning with the origins of federal housing policies during the New Deal, I investigate the policies that created opportunities for Americans to own their own homes by lowering the barriers to entry into homeownership, expanding the availability of mortgage credit, and facilitating the private development of owner-occupied housing. Only on the back of these extensive interventions—interventions aimed at making homeownership cheaper and more accessible to millions of citizens—were the majority of Americans able to achieve the dream of home-ownership in the post–World War II period.

Yet the expansion of homeownership opportunities during the twentieth century created lasting forms of social exclusion. African-American house-holds had far fewer opportunities to own their own homes, and these inequal-ities in ownership contributed to enduring patterns of social and economic stratification. Extending research on residential segregation, I point to the im-portance of tenure stratification—the separation of homeowners and renters—as a meaningful dimension for the study of social inequality.

While political leaders argued that homeownership would reengage Americans in their communities, they did not foresee how the financial en-tanglements of homeownership would shape Americans' civic engagement. By the end of the twentieth century, Americans had come to see their homes as a tool for building wealth, and their involvement in public life would focus on protecting their financial investments in housing. The growing impor-tance of homeownership to the wealth portfolio of millions of citizens created new incentives for homeowners to become involved in their communities.

In chapter 4, I investigate the civic habits of homeowners, asking how homeowners build social relationships and participate in the political life of their communities. While owning a home creates financial incentives for civic participation, I also use the analysis in this chapter to evaluate the role of residential stability in driving citizens to engage in public life. In doing so, I highlight the importance of considering the multiple mechanisms linking homeownership to claims of enhanced citizenship. The analysis challenges an oversimplified narrative that paints homeowners as better citizens and more engaged members of their communities. Instead, I show that the finan-cial importance of owning a home leads citizens to participate in a narrow set of political activities as they work to protect the most important investment they own—their homes.

While homeowners are more engaged in a limited set of community ac-tivities than renters, the analysis in chapter 4 reveals little about the impact of their participation on the communities where they live. While we tend to think of active, engaged citizenship as the backbone of strong, vibrant neigh-borhoods, I investigate what happens when civic engagement is driven by the self-interested need to protect property values. Against classic accounts of community participation, which suggest that communities are stronger when citizens engage in public life, I use chapter 5 to ask about the ways homeowners contribute to patterns of segregation and social exclusion as they become involved in local politics and community affairs.

Chapter 5 relies a handful of case studies to investigate the ways homeowners engage in the politics of exclusion. I argue that as homeowners work to protect their wealth portfolios, they often adopt a defensive posture, working to create communities narrowly aligned with their interests as property owners. They elevate concerns of property owners above other community interests and justify their own participation in public life by highlighting their position as taxpayers. Often the language of property values creates a thinly veiled cover to exclude renters from the political dialogue. While homeownership can contribute to the creation of stronger communities, I show that higher levels of civic engagement resulting from the demands of property ownership can also lead to the formation of neighborhoods that are more fractured and polarized.

In chapter 6, I return to an analysis of the federal subsidies targeted at American homeowners. Through a critical engagement with a series of federal tax deductions and exemptions, I ask how federal tax subsidies incentivize ownership by encouraging Americans to see their homes as a vehicle for building wealth. Through an analysis of the mortgage interest deduction, one of the costliest subsidies in the tax code, I argue that these policies increase the investment value of housing. In doing so, they deepen the politics of exclusion, contributing to the central puzzle in this book.

While reviewing the ways the federal government subsidizes homeownership, I use chapter 6 to ask a broader question about whether federal housing policies should favor ownership over renting. Beyond the financial returns to homeowners, what benefits are derived from favoring homeowners in the tax code? While proponents of these policies often justify these tax expenditures by appealing to the public benefits of homeownership—the way it helps to strengthen neighborhoods or to build stronger communities—I contend that subsidizing ownership by increasing the investment value of housing exacerbates the politics of exclusion. As an alternative to the mortgage interest deduction, I propose policies to subsidize residential stability. Drawing on the evidence from chapter 4, I argue that many of the community benefits commonly associated with ownership are, in fact, the result of increased stability within neighborhoods rather than the result of the financial investments citizens make in their homes.

Finally, in the conclusion, I revisit the core themes of the book, laying out three key lessons for our continued engagement with homeownership. Specifically, I encourage readers to consider the study of homeownership as a social phenomenon, pushing back against the dominant economic approach to studying homeownership. The study of homeownership as a social phenomenon also counters the narrative of ownership as a set of independent, individual decisions, showing instead that social forces shape people's housing choices and these choices in turn impact social relationships in local communities. The conclusion highlights the contrast between the inclusionary rhetoric of ownership and the exclusionary politics of it. It encourages readers to separately identify the importance of residential stability in the study of homeownership.

Taken together, these chapters offer a historically grounded, empirically informed critique of America's long-standing ideology of homeowners as better citizens and active members of their communities. I ask readers to pay careful attention to the way Americans' ideas about homeownership are shaped by broader social structures—for example, the way ideas about citizenship and property ownership intersect in the home; the growing importance of housing as a vehicle of wealth creation; and the complicated and often contradictory ways that homeowners engage in their communities. Ultimately, through the analysis in this book, I show that homeownership is not always the marker of social inclusion that proponents claim. By elevating concerns about property values over other issues, owning a home often contributes to patterns of social exclusion in local communities. Through an investigation of the powerful political and social forces behind the ideology of homeownership, I craft a more nuanced analysis of the way homeowners engage in their communities and the consequences of their participation for civic life.[24]

2 SELLING THE CITIZEN HOMEOWNER

THE CIVIC ROOTS OF THE AMERICAN DREAM

On September 15, 1931, President Herbert Hoover announced his plans to hold a national conference on the state of housing in America. Since World War I, the country had been coping with a growing housing shortage, leaving millions of Americans in substandard housing conditions. The war efforts had diverted building resources from homebuilding, and the lack of national standards in the building industry contributed to the high cost of housing. Hoping to address the challenges to building high-quality, affordable housing, Hoover convened experts from across the country for a four-day conference on the state of homebuilding and homeownership.[1]

For much of his career, Hoover had worked tirelessly to improve housing quality and lower the cost of homeownership, noting the importance of sound housing to the national welfare. In his announcement of the upcoming conference, he underscored the important role that decent, affordable housing played for millions of families. "Adequate housing goes to the very roots of the well being of the family, and the family is the social unit of the nation," Hoover remarked, impressing on conference attendees the importance of the task ahead. "It is more than comfort that is involved, it has the important aspects of health and morals and education.... Nothing contributes more to social stability and the happiness of our people than the surrounding of their home. It should be possible in our country for anybody of sound character and industrious habits to provide himself with adequate housing and preferably to buy his own home."[2]

The President's Conference on Home Building and Home Ownership marked the culmination of Hoover's efforts to improve housing conditions in the United States. In the 1920s, Hoover served as the inaugural secretary of commerce, using his national prominence to advance his vision for a nation of homeowners. He worked to lower the cost of construction materials and standardize homebuilding practices. He galvanized the resources of the federal government to support civic groups and private enterprise in promoting homeownership, serving as the chief spokesman for the Better Homes in America movement. Under his leadership, the department published a booklet, *How to Own Your Own Home*, that educated more than 300,000 homebuyers on the intricacies of owning a home.[3]

But soon after Hoover won the presidency in 1928, the country faced an economic crisis that worsened the housing situation for millions of Americans. The collapse of the stock market on Black Tuesday sent the economy into a downward spiral, forcing millions of Americans out of work and marking the beginning of the Great Depression. At the height of the depression, the unemployment rate climbed to nearly 25 percent. As more Americans lost their jobs, they were unable to keep up with their monthly housing payments, creating an unprecedented housing crisis in communities across the country. Foreclosures skyrocketed, and housing construction virtually ceased, raising doubts about the future of homeownership in the United States.[4]

Recognizing the importance of housing to the growing economic crisis, in 1931 Hoover convened a diverse coalition of citizens to engage in a national conversation on the future of housing and homeownership. Conference invitees included representatives from organizations directly involved in the homebuilding process, including the National Association of Real Estate Boards, the U.S. Building and Loan League, and the National Housing Association. Acknowledging the reach of housing into other social issues—and specifically, the way housing shaped families and strengthened communities—he invited representatives from the National Conference of Parents and Teachers, several national women's magazines, and the American Civic Association. For months, attendees prepared for the conference, drafting proposals to increase the supply of housing and ease the pathway to homeownership. As they began putting together recommendations, Hoover tasked them with considering both the short- and long-term consequences of their participation. While the conference would focus on the immediate housing challenges Americans faced, it would also identify the long-term obstacles that kept hardworking people from buying homes of their own.

Bringing the conference attendees together at Constitution Hall in Washington, D.C., President Hoover reminded them about the many benefits that would result from their efforts to provide better housing to the American people. With radio networks carrying the proceedings of the conference into living rooms nationwide, he stressed the urgency of the discussions taking place in the nation's capital. "You have come from every State in the Union to consider a matter of basic national interest," Hoover told the audience. In the short term, reviving the homebuilding industry would steer the country out of the Great Depression. Stimulating home construction would help to provide employment opportunities for millions of unemployed workers in the building and construction trades—one of the industries hit hardest by the economic collapse. Their efforts to lower the barriers to homeownership would contribute to resolving the crisis of unemployment and lifting the nation from the depths of the Great Depression.[5]

But as he welcomed conference participants to Washington, DC, Hoover encouraged them to take the long view of their participation in the historic conference. Beyond the immediate benefits of promoting homeownership, the president underscored the importance of building a nation of homeowners to America's long-term viability and health. Homeownership made for better family life, greater social stability, and improved citizenship, he reminded the delegates. It would recommit citizens to the promise of democracy and serve as the foundation of American patriotism. Conference participants, as they devised solutions to the obstacles Americans faced in buying homes, were helping to ensure that the aspiration for homeownership was a realistic, achievable one for millions of citizens. "This aspiration penetrates the heart of our national well-being," Hoover told the delegates. "[Homeownership] makes for happier married life, it makes for better children, it makes for confidence and security, it makes for courage to meet the battle of life, it makes for better citizenship. There can be no fear for a democracy or self-government or for liberty or freedom from home owners no matter how humble they may be." To hear the president tell it, the very future of the country rested on this commitment to building a nation of homeowners.[6]

The President's Conference on Home Building and Home Ownership capped nearly two decades of work by civic leaders to expand homeownership opportunities in the United States. While the conference emerged from the economic crisis of the Great Depression, it was preceded by a series of homeownership campaigns crafted in response to a period of social instability and unrest in American cities. In this chapter, I focus on two campaigns for homeownership in the beginning of the twentieth century—the Own Your Own Home movement and the Better Homes in America campaign—to explain the origins of the ideology of homeownership as a tool for building communities and strengthening citizenship. In the context of a major demographic shift in the United States, I argue that early twentieth-century political leaders and civic advocates recast homeownership as more than simply a personal housing decision. They crafted ideas about homeowners as better citizens and more loyal Americans.

The early twentieth-century campaigns to promote homeownership emerged in response to social unrest and political disruptions in American cities. Building from the legacy of property ownership as the hallmark of political citizenship, which I discussed in chapter 1, civic leaders pursued homeownership as a strategy for resolving the tensions of urban life. They organized local events and staged model homes, arguing that the decision to rent or buy contributed to the development of good citizenship and served as an antidote to transient communities. In publicity material distributed for the campaigns, homeowners were recast as upstanding patriots and better Americans. Only they were capable of defending the American way of life against the dangers of radical politics, urban unrest, and disruptions to the system of industrial capitalism. Buying a home was not simply a neutral choice among types of shelter but was instead inscribed with deep political significance. As Hoover later made clear to the conference attendees, the future of the country rested on the decision each and every American made to rent or buy his home.

Urbanization and the Crisis of Citizenship

By the time Hoover convened the conference delegates, the United States had undergone an irreversible demographic shift: millions of Americans had moved to cities. The Industrial Revolution had arrived on American shores midway through the nineteenth century, having transformed the landscape on the other side of the Atlantic Ocean. Soon, the transcontinental railroad connected both sides of the vast country. As steel mills and manufacturing plants rose up in growing urban centers, the center of the American economy shifted from farms to cities. Manufacturing replaced agricultural production as the engine of the economy, drawing countless Americans into employment opportunities in rapidly expanding industrial cities.

Typical of this transition was the city of Chicago. From its position on the shores of Lake Michigan, the city emerged as the center of the growing transnational railroad system. Raw materials were shipped to Chicago, where they were processed and transported back through the country on an extensive freight network. Manufacturing jobs in commodity production—everything from meat processing to lumber manufacturing—made Chicago an epicenter of population growth by the late nineteenth century. Barely 100,000 residents in 1860, Chicago grew to more than 1 million inhabitants in just thirty years, with population growth continuing unabated for decades to come. By the turn of the century, 1.7 million people lived in Chicago; by 1920 the population exceeded 2.7 million.[7]

Although it was spectacular in its size, Chicago was typical in its trajectory. Across the United States, Americans were discovering new work opportunities in the industrial factories dotting the urban landscape. They were joined there by millions of European immigrants. By the turn of the century, Brooklyn had grown to more than 1.1 million citizens, up from fewer than 100,000 only fifty years earlier. Philadelphia was a city of 121,000 people in 1850; by 1900, nearly 1.3 million people had settled there. And in Cleveland, a population of only 17,000 people grew to nearly 400,000 by the turn of the century. By 1900, nearly forty American cities had populations exceeding 100,000 people. Just fifty years earlier, only six cities could lay claim to populations of that size.[8]

Rapid urbanization in the United States triggered a remarkable set of political and cultural shifts that would fundamentally alter the American way of life, disrupting Jefferson's vision of a nation rooted in the shared bonds of property ownership. Outside the cities, community ties were constructed largely around the shared interests that property owners held in their communities and towns, creating the glue of American citizenship for more than a century. But urbanization uprooted citizens from their communities, as they searched for work in industrial factories. This movement to cities disrupted norms of community life, untangling the threads of property and place that generated social cohesion throughout the American countryside. Instead of putting down roots, urban citizens were more transient, focusing on securing steady employment rather than building social networks.

This migration to cities ushered in a period of social instability and political unrest. In urban factories, labor disruptions threatened the stability of the emergent system of industrial capitalism, and threats of political radicalism—both at home and abroad—provided new challenges to the sanctity of democratic governance. These challenges grew increasingly acute as the urban population grew more diverse. By the beginning of the twentieth century, millions of European immigrants had joined migrants from the countryside, creating a mosaic of customs, practices, and political views in urban America. Urbanization generated the roots of labor unrest, provided the conditions for social instability, and fostered the formation of political radicalism, setting the stage for a crisis of citizenship in American cities.

Describing the movement to cities, historian Robert Wiebe recounted the growing uncertainty and instability that new migrants encountered. Their inability to plant roots in the modern city was the cause of growing disorder, and many people living in cities abandoned the rituals of citizenship as they focused on their own economic security. "The thousands recently arrived, the thousands more moving about, concentrated narrowly on their own security," Wiebe wrote. "Men struggling to learn new skills or to preserve old ones in a rapidly changing economy could not afford to think about citywide issues. Without stability at home or on the job, the civic spirit had no place to take root." In the rural communities they had come from, Americans took pride in their towns and developed shared concerns about the places where they lived, but the instability of city life forestalled the possibility of an active citizenry in urban America.[9]

As the number of Americans living in cities climbed, the number of American homeowners fell. In 1920, the U.S. Census reported that, for the first time in American history, the majority of Americans lived in cities. The same year, the Census reported that the national homeownership rate had fallen to an all-time low. Fewer than 46 percent of American households lived in homes they owned, down from nearly 48 percent three decades earlier, when the Census first recorded the national homeownership rate. Noting that many of the challenges of urbanization resulted from the rise of tenancy—Americans living in apartments they did not own rather than in homes of their own—Herbert Hoover often remarked that a nation of tenants would not make for a stable country.[10]

For those able to secure homes in cities, their ownership presented an opportunity to boost industrial wages or grow their sense of independence, but rarely did property ownership create the shared sense of community common outside the cities. Although urbanization did not foreclose the possibility of property rights entirely, as the historian Margaret Garb notes in her history of homeownership in Chicago, it did shift the social meaning of ownership for citizens who were able to buy their own homes. Industrial urbanization demanded that workers relinquish control of their labor, giving up the small-scale production and independence of rural America. Buying a home allowed workers to augment industrial wages by renting rooms to boarders and offered an opportunity for independence in the industrial city. However, as they worked to survive in industrial cities, urban migrants rarely viewed homeownership as a means of developing shared interests with fellow citizens.[11]

The Imperative of Homeownership: Campaigning to Own Your Own Home

Reformers across the country searched for solutions to the perceived decay of social life simmering across the urban landscape. How could political leaders combat fears of political radicalism? What could factory owners do to ensure that workers performed their tasks without disruption? How could civic reformers combat the perceived decline of social mores in an increasingly diverse and plural country? Reformers relied on two approaches for tackling the instability and disorderliness of American cities. One approach focused specifically on addressing individual-level behaviors and family relations. Concerned about the moral order of urban America, religious and other organizations promoted temperance movements and religious education to offset the perceived moral decay in the country. By reforming individuals' behaviors, charitable efforts hoped to transform urban masses into respectable, honorable citizens.[12]

An alternative approach focused on the environmental influences shaping the country's moral character rather than on individuals' behaviors themselves. Urban dwellers weren't inherently depraved or morally bankrupt, these reformers argued. Instead, the conditions in which they lived—the squalid housing, run-down neighborhoods, and windowless workplaces—led people to behave in ways that ran counter to the norms that social reformers expected. Instead of focusing on individuals' behaviors, they sought to reshape the types of places where citizens lived. They lobbied for the construction of expansive parklands and playgrounds, hoping that a redesign of the urban landscape would result in a subsequent realignment of the nation's moral bearings. Especially in the largest cities, reformers lobbied to change tenement laws, providing access to proper sanitation and ventilation for citizens living in crowded industrial cities.[13]

These efforts to reform urban housing conditions coincided with a movement to promote homeownership in cities across the country. Just before World War I, political leaders, civic organizations, and businessmen began to rally around a series of campaigns to encourage Americans to own their own homes, hoping that homeownership would combat the moral decay, social unrest, and political radicalism in American cities. The campaigns served multiple purposes. Taking their cues from mid-nineteenth-century efforts to redesign the American home, campaign leaders argued that owning a home would reinforce traditional gender roles and strengthen family bonds. They highlighted the importance of homeownership in solidifying the single-family, detached home as the central aspiration of middle-class Americans.[14]

But beyond the importance of homeownership for stable families, the campaigns also engineered homeownership as a response to the threats posed by rapid urbanization, selling homeownership as the answer to growing instability and social unrest in American cities. First, by tying citizens to their communities, campaign leaders hoped that expanding homeownership opportunities would reinforce the norms of property ownership as the centerpiece of a democratic society. Rooting people in their communities would serve as an antidote to urban unrest and a solution to social instability. Next, the campaigns argued that the norms of upstanding citizenship were taught largely in the owner-occupied home. Citizens learned the national value of thriftiness, for example, when they lived in homes of their own. And finally, the campaign leaders presented homeownership as a way to end labor radicalism and recommit workers to the system of industrial capitalism. They billed homeownership as the choice of the true patriot and the model American citizen. Owning a home was the unequivocal retort to threats posed by political radicalism in the early-twentieth century.[15]

By linking homeownership to the norms of citizenship, the campaigns argued that buying a home was more than just a choice of shelter. It was a decision imbued with deep social significance, helping to create common values and unite an increasingly diverse country behind a shared vision of citizenship. Before investigating the ways the campaigns promoted these ideas about citizenship and community, I provide a brief background to the Own Your Own Home campaign and the Better Homes in America movement; then, drawing on brochures, speeches, publications, and other materials from these campaigns, I argue that they presented homeownership as a tool for deepening residential stability in communities, reinforcing the norms of citizenship and democracy, and fending off political radicalism in early twentieth-century America.

The National Association of Real Estate Boards and the Own Your Own Home Campaign

One of the earliest efforts to promote homeownership was launched by Hill Ferguson, an enterprising young realtor in Birmingham, Alabama. Born and raised in Birmingham, Ferguson was an ardent community enthusiast, described by his biographer as both a civic statesman and an up-and-coming businessman. After graduating from the University of Alabama, he churned through a handful of careers—briefly as a lawyer, a newspaperman, and a salesman in New York City—before eventually turning his attention to real estate. Back in Alabama, Ferguson joined the prestigious Jemison Realty Company and launched a successful career buying and selling homes in his hometown. In 1914, he launched the first citywide campaign in the country to encourage citizens to buy their own homes.[16]

As Ferguson entered the real estate industry, the profession itself was undergoing a remarkable period of professionalization. Real estate men were wrestling with a public reputation marred by images of unscrupulous and dishonest practices. Their business thrived on buying and selling property— a commodity laden with deep social and political meaning in the United States. They were often accused of prioritizing financial gain over the concerns of communities and billed as unethical, immoral, and shortsighted in their practices.

Determined to shake their reputation as greedy salesmen and recast their profession as the vanguard of community interests, a group of real estate professionals came together in Chicago in 1908 to found the National Association of Real Estate Boards. While the real estate industry had a clear financial stake in these efforts to expand homeownership opportunities, the professionals gathered in Chicago presented themselves as the defenders of community interests, capable of reigniting the civic spirit against the backdrop of the disruptive migration to cities. In fact, according to Jeffrey Hornstein, a historian of the real estate industry, their inaugural gathering in Chicago focused largely on the contribution that realtors, as an organized profession, could make in addressing the social challenges of early twentieth-century America. "The real estate men developed a vision of themselves as part of a larger cohort of men and women whose cooperative work in balancing various interests would redeem American civilization and mitigate the harsh impact of rapid industrialization and haphazard urban development," Hornstein writes. "Real estate men…envisioned themselves as part of an emerging stratum of public-spirited men and women to whom was delegated, by virtue of their innate ability and learned skill, the role of uplifting society." As Hill Ferguson—and thousands of other realtors from around the country—worked to promote homeownership, they leaned heavily on this new-found image of a real estate profession committed to projects that would better the nation.[17]

The National Association of Real Estate Boards quickly recognized the potential for a national homeownership campaign to advance their vision of real estate professionals as protectors of the civic spirit. Soon, Ferguson was appointed secretary of the Association and charged with overseeing a nationwide effort to expand the Own Your Own Home campaigns. From his position in Washington, D.C., Ferguson orchestrated local realtors across the country in their work to encourage Americans to own their own homes. Mimicking the success of the Birmingham campaign, the movement spread rapidly in the early twentieth century. From Oakland to Indianapolis, local committees opened storefront offices and printed thousands of cards advertising the importance of homeownership. By 1917, eighty-one cities nationwide had formed local Own Your Own Home committees, according to the *National Real Estate Journal*, the industry magazine. A year later, the number of cities engaged in campaigns to promote homeownership had climbed to 137.

Leaders of the Own Your Own Home campaign took to the *National Real Estate Journal* to articulate their vision for a nation of homeowners. They outlined the types of committees and subcommittees that campaigns should establish, including a cooperation committee to secure the participation of local organizations and an advertising committee to spread the word about the benefits of homeownership. Organizers focused on the goals of the campaigns, often noting the importance of homeownership to various aspects of community life. In one article, campaign organizers outlined the benefits of the movement, which included "making the community a better place in which to live; making a better and more intelligent community interest in public affairs; a general improvement in community morale, as exemplified in church and school support and attendance; ... [and] placing the community, throughout, on the sound financial basis inherent in homeownership."[18]

Although they believed that the success of their Own Your Own Home campaigns would help to solidify the professional place of realtors in the United States, deepening their own commercial interests, organizers were careful to emphasize the social contribution of their work to promote homeownership. Campaign materials noted that realtors were historically "found in the vanguard, more often than not, when it is a matter of community welfare." Fearful that the movement would undermine itself if it looked like a commercial boon to the industry, executives from the National Association of Real Estate Boards warned local leaders against appearing overtly involved in these efforts to promote homeownership. H. P. Haas, president of the Association, encouraged realtors to remain in the background, avoiding the appearance that commercial gain, rather than civic duty, drove their efforts. Thus, real estate professionals could focus on solidifying their image as protectors of the civic spirit and vanguards of the national welfare.[19]

But soon, efforts to promote homeownership ran up against the priorities of a country at war. With the nation engaged in World War I, political leaders pleaded with the National Association of Real Estate Boards to cease their campaigns for homeownership. Although the country faced a growing housing shortage, national leaders requested that building resources be transferred to the wartime efforts. "Home building is an excellent thing in normal times," wrote treasury secretary William McAdoo, "but at present, unless there is a real shortage of houses for War workers, I strongly advise that materials, valuable labor and credit be not utilized for this purpose." Yielding to pleas from national leaders, the Association halted their efforts to promote homeownership. They promised to remain prepared to resume their patriotic duties as the vanguards of community life once the war ended.[20]

While the Own Your Own Home campaigns lasted only a couple of years, they helped to reframe the way Americans thought about housing and homeownership. Although the campaigns offered few solutions to the obstacles that prevented Americans from buying homes of their own, they refocused attention on the ideology of housing in America. They painted homeownership as a moral imperative for citizens concerned about the well-being of their communities and emphasized the important role that homeownership played in fulfilling the obligations of citizenship. As they recast individual housing choices with profound social and political significance, campaign leaders enthusiastically heralded homeownership as a response to disengaged community life.

Herbert Hoover and the Better Homes in America Movement

Although the National Association of Real Estate Boards ceased their Own Your Own Home campaigns during the war, renewed efforts to address the housing situation in America emerged soon after the war. In 1922, Marie Meloney, the editor of the *Delineator*, an American women's magazine, embarked on a new housing campaign. Concerned about the declining quality of housing in the country, Meloney launched the Better Homes in America movement to educate Americans about the importance of well-managed, owner-occupied homes.

Like the Own Your Own Home campaigns, the Better Homes in America movement relied on local affiliates to promote homeownership and encourage proper homemaking techniques. In communities across the country, local civic leaders came together with business groups and community organizations to run educational campaigns, emphasizing the importance of well-managed homes. These groups often constructed a model home and used it to display the features of properly maintained housing. When new homes could not be built, local committee leaders found outstanding homes in their communities to demonstrate the ideas behind the movement. Often communities held home improvement contests or asked schoolchildren to enter writing contests about housing and homeownership. They put on pageants, offered lectures, and encouraged active discussions of housing and homeownership in American communities. Citizens were presented with information about the benefits of good housekeeping, proper upkeep, and the value of financial thrift as they toured their town's model home. Through annual demonstration weeks, these groups helped affirm the single-family, detached home as the aspiration of millions of American households.

While local businesses in each community were quick to join the Better Homes in America committees, the movement emphasized their noncommercial focus. "The organization is entirely educational," noted one campaign brochure. "It works for the good of others and has no commercial products to sell." Although business groups, including electric and gas companies, lumber manufacturers, and appliance wholesalers, were eager to benefit from the flurry of construction activity that would result from widespread efforts to promote homeownership, campaign materials emphasized the movement's focus on the civic promise of the campaign, fearing that the involvement of these groups would derail their core message.[21]

Soon after incorporating the Better Homes in America movement, Marie Meloney approached Herbert Hoover about aligning the nascent movement with federal efforts to expand homeownership opportunities. As secretary of commerce, Hoover had created the Division of Building and Housing, hoping to leverage the resources of the federal government to address concerns about the cost of construction material and inefficiencies in the building industry. But his vision for the Division of Building and Housing—and, more generally, for the Department of Commerce—was even broader. Hoover imagined a role for the federal government coordinating between private businesses and charitable organizations to address the challenges the country faced. By bringing together civic groups and private enterprise concerned about the housing shortage, the Department of Commerce could help to improve the housing situation for millions of citizens. The Better Homes in America organization provided an opportunity for Hoover to advance this housing agenda, and at the request of Meloney, he accepted the group's invitation to serve as their chair, advocating through its network of local affiliates for the expansion of homeownership across the country.

With Hoover at the helm, the movement quickly gained support from a large cross-section of civic organizations and government leaders. Funding from philanthropic sources, including the Rockefeller family, helped the movement build an impressive list of sponsoring civic organizations, including the American Child Health Association, the American Red Cross, and the Girl Scouts of America, as well as federal agencies, including the Department of Agriculture, the Department of Labor, and the U.S. Treasury. With the movement formally incorporated by the end of 1923, Harvard professor James T. Ford agreed to serve as the organization's executive director.[22]

Each year, the national committee awarded prizes to communities exhibiting the best model homes. In one of the earliest demonstration weeks, civic leaders in Port Huron, Michigan, a community of 30,000 people, won the praise of national leaders. High school students planned and built a model home, furnishing the house and planting the grounds around it. Built for $5,000, the house was suitable for an industrial worker and was eventually sold at the end of the week. They ran a publicity campaign, attracting more than 8,000 residents of Port Huron to visit the home. The campaign brought together more than seventy-five local commercial and civic organizations, each of which sponsored or participated in the demonstration week. Secretary Hoover awarded a prize to the Port Huron campaign, recognizing the important civic contribution the group had made by spreading the message of homeownership and proper homemaking techniques in their community.[23]

In cities like Port Huron, the Better Homes in America movement spread quickly. Local chapters multiplied, marking the success of an organization that relied almost exclusively on local, unpaid committees. Organizers published an annual *Plan Book for Demonstration Week* that clearly spelled out the link between homeownership and homemaking on one hand and the benefits to families, communities, and the nation on the other. In the first demonstration week following the organization's incorporation, 770 local chairs organized campaigns nationwide. Within eight years, the number of local chairs had grown to 9,772. Between 1924 and 1932, the number of houses on display grew from 108 to 831. As the movement expanded, leaders from across the country offered their support for the Better Homes in America movement, acknowledging the importance of homeownership to stable families, strong communities, and the health of the country. While the campaigns helped to reinforce traditional family norms, promoting specific practices of domesticity and solidifying the single-family home as the central aspiration of middle-class Americans, they also worked to spread ideas about citizenship and patriotism, promoting single-family, owner-occupied housing as a tool to strengthen communities and the country.[24]

Community, Citizenship, and Patriotism: Recasting the Promise of Homeownership

Through their campaign materials, including newspaper advertisements, brochures, and speeches, leaders of the Own Your Own Home and Better Homes in America movements recast the decision to buy a home as an important one for communities and the country. On one hand, the campaigns emphasized the importance of homeownership to resolving the crisis of way-ward community life and social unrest in American cities. They contrasted the rootedness of homeownership to the listlessness of tenancy, suggesting that owning a home would generate a shared concern for community life.

On the other hand, the campaigns hammered home the importance of strengthening citizenship through homeownership. Prospective homeown-ers had to sacrifice and save, both values that were important to the prosperity of the country, and the children of homeowners learned important civic les-sons from living in owner-occupied homes. The campaigns presented home-ownership as the tenure choice of the true American patriot, arguing that owning a home was incompatible with radical, antidemocratic political beliefs. Against the backdrop of growing unrest in American cities, I show in this section how these campaigns depicted the decision to rent or buy as a matter of national importance. It was a choice marked with a deep social sig-nificance, especially for a country recovering from war and grappling with the challenges of major demographic changes.

Community Life and Social Stability

When he awarded the town of Port Huron the annual Better Homes in America prize in 1923, President Hoover touted the wide range of benefits from these locally organized campaigns. Writing to congratulate the local leaders on their success, he stressed the importance of housing to the health of local communities. "The home is the foundation of the society and of our institutions, and is the pledge of contentment and satisfaction," Hoover told the citizens of Port Huron. "It is the conclusive reply to every threat against the fundamental principles upon which our Government is based. To raise the standard of the American home is, therefore, to raise the standard of the American people." Housing was the cornerstone of community life, and ef-forts to improve the housing situation would inevitably reverberate throughout local communities.[25]

When the campaigns emphasized the promise of single-family homes, they often framed it as an alternative to life in the crowded urban tenements. Especially in the country's largest cities, including New York and Chicago, housing reformers believed that tenements posed a serious threat to the foun-dation of civic life. Reports on tenement life, including those by the roving Dutch photographer Jacob Riis, captivated audiences, exposing the squalor of American cities. The campaigns emphasized that tenancy was antithetical to the ideal of a propertied citizenry and that the growth of tenement housing discouraged Americans from engaging deeply in their communities. As Hoover congratulated leaders of the Port Huron campaign and lent his voice to countless other efforts nationwide, he repeatedly noted that tenement life stood in the way of the nation's deep yearning for homeownership.[26]

The promise of homeownership to strengthen communities was grounded in the importance of housing for investing Americans with a sense of civic purpose. "The home owner puts down roots in the community," claimed one pamphlet by the Girl Scouts of America, one of the lead sponsors of the Better Homes in America movement. "Through the relation of his home to its neighborhood and to the city government, he acquires a keener civic interest and a greater sense of civic responsibility." Acknowledging the challenges of community engagement in early twentieth-century cities, campaign material highlighted the ways that homeownership drove participation in local affairs and ignited the bonds of social connectedness central to vibrant communities. Campaign leaders emphasized that homeowners were direct taxpayers, drawing on century-old arguments about the relationship between property ownership and political citizenship.[27]

But the campaigns weren't the only groups to pick up on ideas about homeownership and community life. Newspaper outlets and business groups promoted similar messages about the importance of homeownership to social stability. In 1924, the *Buffalo Courier* published a series of editorials and cartoons decrying the rise of tenancy in American cities. Like many other cities, Buffalo was experiencing an enormous population shift. In just thirty years, the population had nearly doubled, reaching more than half a million citizens by 1920. Concerned about the rise of tenancy, the editors of the *Buffalo Courier* published a two-panel cartoon caricaturing the typical homeowner and the typical renter. One panel depicted a beleaguered renter carrying a suitcase labeled "Hard Times." He was presented opening the door to his rented home with a bubble above him showing a pile of rent receipts. The other panel depicted a man sitting atop his own home, joyfully smoking a pipe. The accompanying text presented the homeowner as a respected member of his community, living a carefree life in a home of his own. "The man who OWNS HIS OWN HOME...is looked-up to and respected and has a much better standing in his community; and, there is no gainsaying the fact that, the more homeowners there are in a community the more prosperous that community is," read the text below. As the Better Homes in America campaign gained momentum in the 1920s, editorials like the one in the *Buffalo Courier* helped to disseminate ideas about homeownership nationwide.[28]

While the Better Homes in America campaign emphasized the noncommercial nature of the movement, many in the business community viewed efforts to promote homeownership as germane to their interests as well. Building from the emphasis on ownership as an antidote to social instability, American businessmen capitalized on the promise of owning a home as a tool for overcoming threats of labor unrest. In industrial cities, American workers had launched a series of crippling strikes that demonstrated the potential for an organized workforce to disrupt the levers of industrial production. With steel and textile workers striking across the Northeast, factory owners increasingly feared the economic disruption that would result from labor instability. The construction of owner-occupied housing, business leaders hoped, would contribute to the creation of a docile, stable workforce, ending unrest in American factories.

In cities like Chicago, business leaders took the initiative to promote the virtues of better housing for tying citizens to their communities. In 1919, the Chicago Chamber of Commerce applauded plans to build owner-occupied houses for the city's working class, focusing on the importance of well-designed homes for the city's growing immigrant population. "The hope and the ambition of those who are supporting the undertaking are to make better Americans, more healthful, more contented and more prosperous, out of many of the foreign-born who now live in squalid neighborhoods in different parts of Chicago," wrote leaders from the Chamber of Commerce. "Stabilize the workers by supplying them with homes and the restlessness which now characterizes many will be eradicated, it is believed, and a constant supply of manpower created." By offering workers a material stake in the economic system, homeownership would create a stable workforce in American cities.[29]

Citizenship and Civic Benefits

While campaign leaders expected homeownership to increase social stability by tying Americans to their communities, residential stability formed only part of the rationale for these growing efforts to promote homeownership. When leaders from the National Association of Real Estate Boards took to their professional publication, the *National Real Estate Journal*, to spread the gospel of homeownership, they often pointed to the myriad of civic benefits that would come from the opportunity to own a home. Chief among them, homeownership meant thriftiness, as households scrimped and saved toward the promise of buying a home. In 1917, Fred Reed, the chair of the Own Your Own Home campaign in Oakland, California, wrote a letter sharing the

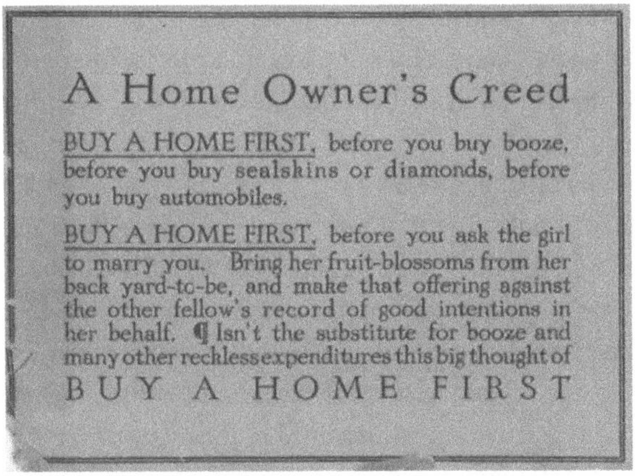

A Home Owner's Creed

BUY A HOME FIRST, before you buy booze, before you buy sealskins or diamonds, before you buy automobiles.

BUY A HOME FIRST, before you ask the girl to marry you. Bring her fruit-blossoms from her back yard-to-be, and make that offering against the other fellow's record of good intentions in her behalf. ¶ Isn't the substitute for booze and many other reckless expenditures this big thought of

BUY A HOME FIRST

FIGURE 2.1. A Home Owner's Creed, *National Real Estate Journal*. Reproduced from *National Real Estate Journal*, April 1917.

successes of his local efforts. After remarking on the importance of thrift to the strength of the nation, Reed included a simple creed urging Americans to consider buying a home before spending money on other luxury goods (fig. 2.1). "Before you buy booze, before you buy sealskins or diamonds, before you buy automobiles," read the creed, "Buy a Home First...Isn't the substitute for booze and many other reckless expenditures this big thought of Buy a Home First."[30]

Across the country, the value of thriftiness became a rallying cry for proponents of homeownership. They emphasized how saving for homeownership contributed to the sacrifices that Americans were making for a country on the brink of war. As potential homebuyers saved through building and loan associations, the campaigns celebrated their efforts as a productive investment in the future of the country. The campaign materials noted the importance of thrift and the spirit of cooperation, arguing that the decision to save for homeownership reinforced distinctly American values. "The family which wishes to acquire a home must curtail wasteful spending or useless expenditures. The building of good homes for this reason increases national wealth and well-being," noted movement organizers in a pamphlet prepared for a local Better Homes in America campaign.[31]

But it wasn't just in the process of buying a home that citizens learned key American values and contributed to the strength of the country. Promotional material for the campaigns emphasized the ways that homeowners learned the practices of citizenship by living in a well-maintained, owner-occupied home. For decades, efforts to link the design of single-family homes to the promise of upstanding citizenship were intended to influence the way Americans thought about their homes. In the mid-nineteenth century, Andrew Jackson Downing had published a series of pattern books promoting specific designs for country housing in the United States. These publications presented residential architecture as the incubator of good citizenship, advocating for a style of architecture that reinforced core ideas about independence, hard work, and family life to generations of American citizens. In the mid-nineteenth century, when Downing presented these designs, the question of ownership was rarely in doubt. Most Americans lived in homes they owned outside urban centers. Now, in the early twentieth century, with the American commitment to homeownership threatened by the movement to cities, housing advocates stressed the importance of ownership alongside their emphasis on housing design and upkeep.[32]

Especially for children, they said, the owner-occupied home helped to teach civic values necessary for maintaining the political order. Children's first encounter with the contours of democratic citizenship would be in the well-managed home. One Better Homes in America brochure called attention to the civic values taught in the American home. "The home should also be a laboratory for the development of good citizenship.... The home should teach habits of obedience, respect for rightfully constituted authority, and the rights and property of other people—in a word, boys and girls should have their first knowledge of a sanely organized community, and law, and government, in the home, long before they study these things formally from a text book." These core principles, conveyed through the owner-occupied home, were the foundations on which the practices of citizenship were built.[33]

A 1924 ad in the *Baltimore Sun* pointed to the importance of homeownership for fostering good citizenship, especially among children. "The family that owns the home it lives in takes greater pride in civic achievement and the children are apt to grow up with greater love for their community and their country," the ad noted, identifying the civic benefits along with the importance of building stronger families through homeownership. "Owning your home makes you more thoroughly appreciate the advantages of American citizenship."[34]

To further engage young citizens, local Better Homes in America committees often ran competitions, encouraging schoolchildren to talk about the benefits of owning your own home. An ad in the *Charleston Daily Mail* on February 28, 1926, announced an essay contest for local students. Interspersed with reminders from national leaders about the importance of homeownership as the foundation of civilization, the ad asked students to write an essay explaining why people should own their own homes. Students considering the virtues of homeownership were reminded of the promise it held. "Homeownership provides the very best assurance of true happiness...and the social prestige, economic independence and good citizenship of its owner," the ad read. As the Better Homes in America movement expanded to thousands of communities across the country, these types of advertisements served as constant reminders of the important place of homeownership in American life.[35]

Patriotism and Democracy

Still, the emphasis on good citizenship was not just about teaching good values and tying Americans to their communities. The promise of homeownership included the guarantee that citizens who owned their own homes would not succumb to the radical politics that threatened the United States at the beginning of the twentieth century. On the heels of World War I, the country endured a brief Red Scare—a fear that political radicals were infiltrating the country, disrupting its stable political order. Campaign leaders invoked threats of unrest from the Russian peasantry as a tool for promoting homeownership, often arguing that the root cause of Bolshevism stemmed from the housing situation of the Russian people. "One great reason why Russia is now in a state of such complete unrest is that thus far no way has been found to give each peasant a home, where he may work out his living and his destiny in peace and quiet," wrote one realtor in the *National Real Estate Journal*. The campaigns capitalized on fears of Bolshevism and political radicalism from abroad to promote homeownership at home, often claiming that the best defense against these threats was to build a nation of homeowners. "Every assistance should be extended to enable our people to build or buy homes. Where there is a community of homeowners, no Bolshevists or anarchists can be found," noted Senator William M. Calder of New York, drawing on rhetoric popularized through the homeownership campaigns.[36]

While radical ideologies would find no place to take root in a nation of homeowners, expanding opportunities for Americans to own their own homes would also serve as the foundation of civic pride. After all, the home was a storied American institution. Homeowners were praised as independent citizens capable of defending American democracy through their active involvement in the process of governing. Because of their deep commitment to their communities and the country, they displayed more nationalism and civic pride, campaign leaders often argued. Reflecting these beliefs about ownership and citizenship, one editorial in the *National Real Estate Journal* reminded real estate professionals that a "man will put very little energy or enthusiasm into singing, 'My Country: 'Tis of Thee,' when he don't [*sic*] own a foot of the country and when he knows that his landlord can any day drive him and his family from under the roof that shelters them."[37]

Reframing the decision to rent or buy a home as a choice laden with stark political consequences, the *National Real Estate Journal* devoted scores of columns

The Best Citizen

Which is the best citizen—the home-owner or the renter?

Scott Nearing, sensationalist, Socialist, I. W. W. leader and whatnot, recently declared that the man who rented was the best citizen.

What better argument for the "Own Your Own Home" campaign?

In these trying times, when every man and woman is putting forth the best effort, seeking to accomplish something that will mean something to the country in a tangible way, why shouldn't the real estate operators of America come forth with a slogan like this:

BE PATRIOTIC! BUY A HOME!

Who contributes most to the upbuilding of a nation? The home-owner or the renter?

The home-owner, of course, because he realizes that upon the future depends the result of his investment; because he knows that he is more responsible than the fellow who pays out the monthly stipend.

The home-owner is the fellow who wears tailored clothes; the renter is the one who gets his duds off the shelf. The first man gets what he wants; the second gets what some other fellow thinks he wants.

Be a tailored man! Own your own home.

Realtors: You have a definite duty. Aside from your natural wish to dispose of property on your lists, you have a patriotic call.

The nation looks to you for education! Put a shoulder to the wheel! Get into the human side of present conditions. Teach the nation that there is one duty none should shirk.

Convince the nation that it will become greater when it owns its own home!

FIGURE 2.2. The Best Citizen Column, *National Real Estate Journal.* Reproduced from *National Real Estate Journal,* February 1918.

to reminding realtors that buying a home was the responsible choice for upstanding citizens. One column offered an explicit comparison of homeowners and renters, creating archetypes of each to emphasize the links between patriotism, citizenship, and buying a home (fig. 2.2). Titled "The Best Citizen," the column asked rhetorically about the role of homeownership in fulfilling civic obligations: "Which is the best citizen—the homeowner or the renter?" The column went on to promote the role homeowners played in strengthening the country and building the nation. Like many other vignettes and stories in the *National Real Estate Journal*, the vignette focused on convincing real estate professionals to fulfill their patriotic duties by emphasizing the importance of homeownership in their communities. "Convince the nation that it will become greater when it owns its own home!" the vignette concluded.[38]

Beyond the Ideology of Homeownership

With their rhetoric of citizenship, patriotism, and community, the Own Your Own Home and Better Homes in America campaigns had a profound impact in early twentieth-century America, transforming the way citizens viewed their homes. No longer were housing decisions simply personal choices made by individual households. Instead the decision to rent or buy was imbued with stark political importance. Through their newspaper advertisements, their campaign pamphlets, and the strong endorsements of national political leaders, the campaigns helped to recast the American homeowner as the guardian of liberty and defender of the American way of life. They argued that owning a home shaped the way citizens engaged in their communities and reflected the commitments citizens made to uphold core American values. For nearly two decades, from the inauguration of the Own Your Own Home campaign in 1914 to the shuttering of the Better Homes in America movement in the 1930s, the campaigns worked to present the decision to rent or buy in overtly political tones, underscoring the importance of homeownership in a country struggling with deep demographic shifts. They laid the groundwork for the ideology of homeownership that is central to this book's story: an ideology linking homeownership to citizenship and civic life that persisted throughout the twentieth century.

Yet, despite their soaring rhetoric about the promise of homeownership to strengthen citizenship and build communities, these campaigns did little to lift the national homeownership rate. Although political elites and civic leaders worked tirelessly to remind Americans about the importance of owning a home to the prosperity of the country and the vitality of local communities, recasting homeownership as the civic obligation of the American patriot and the certified response to concerns of social unrest, the obstacles to owning a home remained formidable. Housing conditions in industrial cities kept citizens from fulfilling the obligations of citizenship, and the costs of buying a home remained prohibitively high. Building materials were expensive, and mortgage financing was scarce. Although the campaigns solidified homeownership as the tenure choice of the true American citizen, they were largely ineffective in helping more Americans to buy homes of their own.

In 1931, as President Hoover gathered delegates for the national conference on housing and homeownership, he hoped to move beyond the rhetoric of the last two decades, offering a way forward that would enable more Americans to own their own homes. While he continued to emphasize the value of homeownership to citizens, communities, and the country, he tasked conference participants with creating national standards that would enable more Americans to own their own homes. "That our people should live in their own homes is a sentiment deep in the heart of our race and of American life. We know that as yet it is not universally possible to all," he noted. "We know that many of our people must...live under other conditions. But they never sing songs about a pile of rent receipts. To own one's own home is a physical expression of individualism, of enterprise, of independence, and of freedom of spirit."[39]

After fifteen months of planning and preparation, participants in the conference produced an eleven-volume report. Drawing on the expertise of architects, civic leaders, builders, and bankers, it laid out a broad agenda for the future of housing in America. One volume examined construction practices in the country, looking at ways to end the inefficiencies that limited the supply of housing. It suggested national standards for home construction that would lower the cost of housing. Another volume addressed issues of housing finance, acknowledging concerns about the availability of credit across the country. The parochial system of housing finance, which would be at the center of reform efforts over the next decades, kept millions of Americans from securing the loans they needed to purchase their homes. The report addressed everything from the minutiae of housing layouts and kitchen designs to the more comprehensive details of planning residential districts. It pushed for the decentralization of urban slums, recognizing how cramped living conditions limited the possibilities for strong citizenship, and encouraged continued efforts to promote homeownership nationwide.

Closing the conference, Ray Lyman Wilbur, the secretary of the interior, reminded participants that their work had just begun. He told conference attendees that their service, as ambassadors of well-maintained, owner-occupied homes, extended beyond the four days they spent in Washington. "You are enlisted for further service which will not stop until every American home is clean, convenient, wholesome, sanitary, and a fit place for a mother and father to bring to maturity young citizens who will keep our Nation strong, vigorous and worthy." The campaigns and the conference had outlined the reasons that expanding homeownership was critical to building communities and strengthening citizenship. Now, with fewer than half of American households living in homes they owned, it was time for the federal government to begin the important work of building a nation of homeowners.[40]

In the next chapter, I show that the federal government took a more active role in promoting homeownership in the decades after the President's Conference on Home Building and Home Ownership. Tracing the history of federal homeownership policies over the twentieth century, I identify the ways that federal policies ensured the availability of capital for mortgage lending in local markets and lowered the cost of buying a home. With these interventions into the housing finance system, the number of American homeowners grew at a remarkable clip, especially in the post-World War II period. When Hoover left office in the early 1930s, barely 40 percent of Americans lived in homes they owned, but by the end of the twentieth century that number had risen to nearly 70 percent. Yet these high rates of ownership masked persistent disparities in the homeownership rate, generating a new set of challenges to truly building a nation of homeowners.

3 BUILDING A NATION OF HOMEOWNERS

FEDERAL HOUSING POLICY IN THE TWENTIETH CENTURY

In 1945, John P. Dean, a sociologist at Queens College in New York City, wrote one of the earliest critiques of homeownership in America. Examining the forces shaping the American preference for homeownership, Dean asked whether homeownership was, in fact, a sound housing decision for millions of American households. In his book, he acknowledged the confluence of forces pushing households toward homeownership, from the cultural importance of property ownership to the pressures from real estate professionals to buy homes. And while he acknowledged many of the benefits that come from owning one's own home, he also pointed to many of the challenges that households faced in buying homes of their own, including the complicated financial decisions that went into doing so.

Still, Dean recognized what countless scholars, political leaders, and ordinary citizens have long acknowledged—that Americans overwhelmingly preferred owning to renting. Citing a series of early public opinion polls showing a strong preference for homeownership, he reminded readers that owning a home remained one of the bedrock aspirations of the American public. Although most citizens were tenants, "if wishes were houses," he wrote, "a clear majority of Americans would be homeowners."[1]

The publication of Dean's book came at a critical moment in the history of homeownership in the United States. A decade after the President's Conference on Home Building and Home Ownership, the 1940 Census revealed that the number of American homeowners had dropped to an all-time low. Only 43 percent of American households lived in homes they owned, a number that had declined decennially since the Census started reporting the homeownership rate fifty years earlier. But while Americans had fewer opportunities for homeownership, they remained convinced of the importance of owning one's own home. Given the choice, nearly 90 percent of Americans preferred homeownership to renting, according to one poll cited by Dean. As chapter 2 showed, political leaders and civic groups had mounted a series of campaigns pointing to the importance of homeownership for healthy families, strong communities, and national prestige. While the campaigns worked to solidify owner-occupied housing as the preference of the majority of Americans, promoting homeownership as the choice of the true patriot and the upstanding citizen, fewer than half of American households were able to live in homes they owned. What kept Americans from owning their homes in the first half of the twentieth century? Despite their deep preference for homeownership, why were so few Americans able to achieve this cornerstone of the American Dream?

For most Americans, the largest obstacle to buying a home was the parochial system of housing finance—a system that raised the cost of credit and kept capital for mortgage lending scarce. In the current era of global capital mobility, it is difficult to imagine the housing finance system homebuyers faced a century ago. Today, capital for mortgage lending is part of a vast financial network that spans the globe. When households want to buy a home, they get a mortgage from a bank or lending institution, like Bank of America. These mortgage loans are typically repackaged and sold in groups to investors around the world. Mortgage loans that originated in Topeka, Kansas, for example, are packaged in a mortgage-backed security with loans originated in other cities. Investors in Hong Kong, Moscow, or New York City purchase these securities, holding them in their investment portfolio as they would other investments, like stocks and bonds. The securitization of mortgages into global financial instruments ensures that money is available for mortgage lending in communities around the country.

Against this picture of a global system of mortgage lending, the system of home finance at the beginning of the twentieth century was a distinctly local affair—an affair perhaps best captured in the public imagination by the character George Bailey in the 1946 film *It's a Wonderful Life*. Working-class homebuyers joined building and loan associations—commonly known as thrifts—to save for homeownership. They purchased shares in these thrifts and paid monthly installments to them. In turn, the thrifts lent funds from these pooled savings to members exclusively for the purpose of buying homes. And although thrifts functioned primarily as financing organizations, they also served important social purposes. By keeping mortgage lending local, they helped to generate bonds of reciprocity in their communities, bringing citizens together behind the shared goal of owning a home. Especially in neighborhoods made up largely of recent immigrants, thrifts attracted investors by highlighting the American values learned by saving for homeownership.[2]

Over the course of the early twentieth century, the number of thrifts grew tremendously, creating the cornerstone of the housing finance industry. By the 1920s, as Herbert Hoover assumed the leadership of the Department of Commerce, more than 10 percent of Americans were members of thrifts—four times the number at the start of the century. And while these institutions were not the only places Americans could turn for mortgage financing, they originated more than half of all institutionally held mortgage loans in the United States. Commercial banks and insurance companies also provided loans to homebuyers, although the terms of their loans typically favored wealthier homebuyers who had already amassed substantial savings for a down payment.

This system of housing finance created several major obstacles to expanding homeownership opportunities in the early twentieth century. Perhaps most important, owning a home was often more expensive than renting one. The loans originated by thrifts amortized fully within a decade, while those originated by other lending organizations, including commercial banks and insurance agencies, were typically partially amortizing loans with balloon payments due at the end. Homeowners would need to secure a secondary loan when the first mortgage period ended to pay off the balance of the loan. And unlike today's mortgage loans, which typically require modest down payments, those from commercial banks and insurance companies required homebuyers to make a down payment of up to 50 percent of the purchase price. The fully amortizing, long-term loans with low down payments common today were not among the financing options available to early twentieth-century homebuyers.[3]

While the terms of mortgage lending were often unfavorable to homebuyers, the localized system of housing finance limited the availability of capital for mortgage loans. Because thrifts collected and distributed funds locally, they were often unable to meet the demand for financing within their communities. In the early twentieth century, there was no system to recapitalize these institutions—to provide additional capital when the demand for mortgage financing outstripped the supply of money to lend. While their emphasis on citizenship, solidarity, and patriotism positioned local thrifts as anchors in the community, these foci could not save them from the limitations of the localized system of housing finance. The scarcity of capital available for mortgage lending made credit expensive and difficult to obtain for many homebuyers.

Building a nation of homeowners would require a serious, sustained commitment by the federal government to lower the costs of homebuying and transform the housing finance system. Although earlier advocates, like Herbert Hoover, promoted homeownership as the solution to social challenges facing early twentieth-century America, the federal government had done remarkably little to sway the housing decisions citizens made. But in the 1930s, following the President's Conference on Home Building and Home Ownership, the federal government began to intervene in the housing market, changing the way Americans bought and sold their homes. Congress passed several major pieces of legislation during the New Deal that would rechart the course of twentieth-century housing policy, solidifying a new role for the federal government in helping Americans to own their own homes.[4]

This chapter tells the story of the federal interventions that led to the dramatic expansion of homeownership in the twentieth century. By increasing access to mortgage credit, facilitating the private construction of owner-occupied housing, and providing direct assistance to American homebuyers, the federal government created opportunities for millions of Americans to own their own homes. As the number of American homeowners skyrocketed in the second half of the twentieth century, building a nation of homeowners would emerge as one of the most important success stories in post-World War II America.

Most of these twentieth-century policies designed to encourage homeownership did not center on building wealth through investments in owner-occupied housing—one of the core justifications for policies designed to expand ownership opportunities today. While housing values now make up the most important piece of the wealth portfolios of many American households, as I noted in chapter 1, these policies were not originally predicated on the importance of owning a home for building household wealth. In fact, the earliest homeownership policies were part of the largest expansion of the welfare state in American history. They were passed alongside programs, like Social Security, that foretold an expanded role for the American government in protecting citizens against economic insecurity. Only later in the twentieth century, as more citizens bought their own homes, would Americans come to recognize the importance of homeownership as a tool for building wealth.

Instead, as they worked to build a nation of homeowners, federal policymakers acted on the belief that expanding ownership opportunities was important for solving the social, political, and economic challenges the country faced. As I noted in chapter 2, promoting homeownership was intended to solidify the norms of citizenship and tie people to the neighborhoods where they lived. It would resolve the political challenge of assimilating an increasingly diverse population into the norms of democratic society. And homeownership was an engine of economic growth. Stimulating the demand for ownership would serve as a tool for strengthening the American economy.

While proponents advocated expanding homeownership opportunities as a way to solve a set of social problems, the growth of homeownership would also create new challenges for the country. Critically, the rhetoric of home-ownership as a deeply inclusive institution masks the way these programs erected new forms of social exclusion. Although programs like the Home Owners Loan Corporation (HOLC) and the Federal Housing Administration (FHA) created opportunities for millions of Americans to own their own homes, they also contributed to the persistence of racial and residential segregation. By supporting the financing of homeownership in homogenous neighbor-hoods outside central cities, federal housing policies limited opportunities for African-Americans to buy their own homes, erecting barriers to residential integration that would endure throughout the century. By highlighting the contribution of these federal policies to patterns of segregation and social exclusion, I set the stage for my analysis of tenure segregation and the politics of exclusion later in the book.[5]

A New Deal for American Homeowners

The challenges American homebuyers encountered at the beginning of the twentieth century worsened during the Great Depression. The rising unem-ployment rate forced more and more homeowners to default on their mort-gage payments, tripling the number of foreclosures between 1926 and 1932. During the same period, the demand for new housing construction virtually ceased, bringing the construction industry to a standstill. Annual residential permits for new housing units dwindled as the demand for housing collapsed, worsening the unemployment crisis as jobs in the building trades disap-peared. There were no programs to assist struggling homeowners in meeting their mortgage responsibilities, and the existing system of housing finance was unable to reignite the demand for homeownership. As housing construc-tion stopped and foreclosure activities climbed, the United States faced the worst housing crisis in the nation's history.[6]

In the 1930s, the federal government laid the groundwork for a housing finance system that would address many of the limitations of the existing system. Specifically, federal policymakers were tasked with two challenges to improve the housing situation for millions of Americans. In the short term, the federal government needed to assist homeowners struggling to make their mortgage payments. Already, with foreclosure rates on the rise and persistent unemployment keeping millions of homeowners from repaying their loans, the Great Depression threatened the foundation of homeownership in the United States. To build a nation of homeowners, the federal government would first need to prevent existing homeowners from losing their homes. But in the long term, the government would need to overcome the parochial system of housing finance that limited the availability of funds for mortgage lending. Redesigning the housing finance system would increase the availability of capital for mortgage lending and create new opportunities for Americans to own their own homes.

The first major piece of housing legislation to expand liquidity to local building and loan associations was the Federal Home Loan Bank Act in 1932. With this legislation, Congress created a network of twelve home loan banks to recapitalize local lending institutions. While loans from building and loan associations offered mortgages with lower down payments and higher loan-to-value ratios than commercial banks, they were often unable to meet the demand in their communities. When the demand for homeownership outstripped the supply of funds for lending, these local organizations had nowhere to turn. Before the New Deal, there was no system for addressing imbalances in the supply of capital and the demand for it by shifting capital from one community to another. But with the introduction of the federal home loan banks, the government took a more active role in ensuring the availability of capital to meet the needs of homeowners. These banks could borrow from the federal treasury to infuse capital into local financial institutions, integrating the housing finance system into broader circuits of capital. The Federal Home Loan Bank Act began the steady march away from the local system of housing finance by recognizing the need for capital to flow across different regions of the country to meet the specific needs of local communities.[7]

Although the home loan banks addressed immediate concerns about liquidity in the mortgage market, they offered little assistance for homeowners struggling to meet their mortgage obligations. Recognizing the need to provide direct relief to American homeowners during the Great Depression, Congress passed the Home Owners Loan Act, establishing the HOLC the following year. The HOLC refinanced individual mortgages and advanced cash to homeowners for necessary home repairs. Although the HOLC was short-lived, lasting only four years, the program helped to refinance more than a million mortgages, benefiting 40 percent of eligible households. By lending more than $3 billion to assist delinquent homeowners in repaying their taxes, making immediate home repairs, and refinancing existing mortgages, the HOLC provided direct assistance to American homeowners.[8]

The HOLC also left a legacy that would jeopardize opportunities to expand homeownership to nonwhite households for decades to come. To determine the suitability of neighborhoods for housing investments, the HOLC created a color-coded series of maps in the 1930s. These maps identified neighborhoods according to their lending risk. In neighborhoods that were stable, homogenous, and mostly white, appraisers deemed there to be little risk in lending through the HOLC. These neighborhoods were colored green and identified as safe for housing investments. But in racially mixed neighborhoods or those perceived to be in decline, appraisers feared that government investments were riskier. African-American neighborhoods were deemed to be higher risk for federal housing investments as appraisers evaluated the declining quality of housing in these undesirable neighborhoods. They considered the racial composition alongside the physical conditions of neighborhoods, codifying race into the system of mortgage lending. Private lenders relied on these guidelines established by the HOLC, developing a system of redlining that would continue to shape housing investments. Decades later, the FHA continued to rely on this scheme of color-coded neighborhoods to indicate the safety and stability of federal housing investments.[9]

While the HOLC assisted individual homeowners with direct subsidies, it offered nothing more than a wobbly seawall against the persistent levels of unemployment. By the time President Roosevelt took office in 1933, nearly one-quarter of American workers remained unemployed. And while the federal home loan banks provided immediate liquidity to the housing finance system, they offered little by way of updating the outdated mortgage loans used by most American homebuyers. Addressing the twin challenges of an imperiled housing finance system and persistently high levels of unemployment, especially in the construction and building industries, President Roosevelt called for a more robust intervention into the housing market. As part of the package of New Deal legislation, Congress passed the National Housing Act of 1934, establishing the FHA and charting a new course for twentieth-century housing policy.

Although largely overlooked in history of the New Deal, the National Housing Act had a profound impact on American society in the twentieth century. With the FHA, the federal government created a system of mortgage insurance to reduce the risk assumed by private lenders. Prior to the creation of the FHA, mortgage lenders independently assumed the risk of default. When homebuyers failed to make their monthly mortgage payments, lenders themselves took the loss. But the mortgage insurance system insulated lenders from this risk, providing an explicit government guarantee for loans that adhered to specific underwriting criteria outlined by the FHA. Gone were the five-year, interest-only loans that required homebuyers to front up to 50 percent of the purchase price of their homes. In their place, Americans would begin buying homes with long-term loans, high loan-to-value ratios, and low down payments.[10]

For loans to be eligible for federal mortgage insurance, the FHA required that lenders make long-term, fully amortizing loans of at least twenty-five years. Increasing the maximum loan-to-value ratio meant that homebuyers could finance a larger portion of their purchase through debt rather than saving for a down payment. Soon, 80 percent loan-to-value ratios became the industry norm, lowering the up-front costs of homeownership and eliminating cumbersome second mortgages from the home buying process. By standardizing the underwriting criteria, the FHA helped to lower the cost of owning a home, eventually opening the doors of homeownership for millions of American families. With fully amortizing loans backed by the federal government, the opportunity to buy a home was often more affordable than the option to rent one.[11]

While the National Housing Act helped to lower the cost of housing, providing a pathway for millions of Americans to own their own homes, the legislation was predicated on the importance of homeownership to national economic growth rather than the importance of building individual wealth through housing. As Marriner Eccles, the chair of the Federal Reserve Board under President Roosevelt, testified before Congress, providing a boost to the construction industry was critical to the overall economic recovery efforts during the Great Depression. "The significance of a new housing program that could revive the economy was not lost on President Roosevelt. He knew that almost a third of the unemployed were to be found in the building trades, and housing was by far the most important part of that trade," Eccles noted. "A program of new home construction, launched on an adequate scale, not only would gradually help put these men back to work but would act as a wheel within the wheel to move the whole economic engine."[12]

The mortgage insurance program in the National Housing Act was geared at commercial banks and insurance companies, many of which had substantially larger stores of capital than local building and loan associations. The federal mortgage guarantee would enable those institutions to lend funds at lower interest rates, increasing the availability of capital in the mortgage markets. By encouraging private lenders to make more money available for homebuying, the National Housing Act led to a remarkable uptick in housing construction. Housing starts increased quickly by the end of the 1930s, reflecting a construction industry buoyed by federal involvement. By 1941, on the verge of World

War II, the number of new housing starts had risen by more than 600 percent from a decade earlier.[13]

While the advent of mortgage insurance standardized the underwriting criteria for mortgage lending and lowered the cost of homeownership, the National Housing Act also established a secondary mortgage market in the United States. Congress authorized the establishment of national mortgage associations to purchase mortgage loans from private lenders that met the standards established by the FHA. Several years later, the Federal National Mortgage Association—or Fannie Mae—became the first government-sponsored agency to purchase FHA-insured loans. The creation of the secondary mortgage market allowed local lending institutions, instead of holding mortgage loans on their books, to pass along their loans to investors. The secondary mortgage market provided capital to replenish the supply of funds available for lending in local communities. Through the advent of the secondary mortgage market, Fannie Mae helped to increase liquidity in housing markets and ensure that local lenders had money available to lend to homebuyers.

Together, the provisions of the National Housing Act changed the way Americans bought and sold their homes. In setting minimum standards for housing construction and assuming the risk of default, the FHA enabled lenders to loan money at lower interest rates and expand their lending activity. As a result, the cost of homeownership fell dramatically, creating more opportunities for Americans to own their own homes. And the establishment of Fannie Mae—and more generally, the creation of the secondary mortgage market—laid the groundwork for today's global system of mortgage finance, eventually leading to the creation of the mortgage-backed securities common in contemporary financial markets. But perhaps most important, beginning with the New Deal, the federal government took an active role in promoting homeownership, moving beyond the rhetoric of the 1910s and 1920s. It didn't simply argue that homeownership was the best housing choice for millions of Americans or that the nation would be stronger when millions of Americans owned their homes. Instead it proactively worked to expand opportunities for homeownership, charting the course for achieving a nation of homeowners.

Suburbanization and the American Dream

As the FHA lowered the cost of homeownership in the United States, the number of Americans buying their homes rose. By 1950, 55 percent of American households lived in homes they owned. Ten years later, the home-ownership rate had risen to nearly 62 percent—an increase of nearly 9 million households living in homes of their own. As they bought their own homes, homeowners increasingly found their way to the postwar suburbs. Soon, this became one of the most important stories of postwar America—the remarkable suburban expansion as Americans took advantage of homeownership opportunities outside central cities.[14]

Suburbanization in the postwar period underscored the continued role of the federal government in shaping the residential choices Americans households made. While the FHA remained officially neutral on the types of mortgage loans it guaranteed, the mortgage insurance program was implicitly biased toward owner-occupied housing in suburban neighborhoods. Before guaranteeing mortgage loans, the FHA required on-site inspections to ensure compliance with standardized construction techniques, ultimately raising the quality of housing construction in the United States.

More important, the FHA required lenders to submit an appraisal to evaluate the riskiness of their housing investment. Lenders accounted for the characteristics of the surrounding neighborhood when they calculated the riskiness of these housing investments, drawing on standards developed by the HOLC in the early 1930s. Neighborhoods with changing economic conditions or racially integrated neighborhoods were deemed high-risk by the FHA. These were often neighborhoods in urban centers. By relying on the standards established by the HOLC, the FHA limited opportunities for African-Americans to buy their own homes, creating racial disparities in access to homeownership that would persist throughout the twentieth century. But outside central cities, there was little risk of economic decline or racial integration. The FHA readily approved loans made on residential units in these growing postwar suburbs, thereby encouraging builders to focus on housing construction outside American cities.

Among the most successful builders in postwar America, William Levitt stands as a legend in the history of suburbanization. Although the Levitt family had constructed wartime housing through government contracts, William Levitt made his name—and transformed suburban residential development—in the construction of a suburban Long Island community. In the 1940s, the Levitt family began construction on a neighborhood in Hempstead, Long Island. To build a neighborhood of suburban ranch houses, Levitt relied on modular construction using prefabricated materials. Most of the materials were put together off-site and then dropped at the four-thousand-acre development. At sixty-foot intervals, homes were constructed in a twenty-seven-step process that the Levitt family had pioneered to lower the cost of construction. As buyers took loans backed by the FHA, these suburban homes were sold for little money down and minimal, consistent down payments. In advertising these suburban communities, Levitt emphasized that buying a house in the postwar suburbs was often much cheaper than renting in the city, putting homeownership within reach of millions of middle-class citizens.[15]

The first suburban communities built by William Levitt were available only to returning veterans, and for good reason. In the Servicemen's Readjustment Act, passed by Congress in 1944, the federal government provided direct assistance to returning service members to purchase a home of their own. Known colloquially as the G.I. Bill, the Act created a series of measures to integrate veterans into middle-class American life. It provided tuition assistance and a cost-of-living allowance for service members to pursue educational opportunities. It offered job training and placement programs and guaranteed a modest unemployment allowance for those unable to find work. But, central to federal efforts to reintegrate veterans into the American way of life, the G.I. Bill provided low-interest loans and down payment assistance programs to millions of returning veterans, creating opportunities for them to purchase their own homes.[16]

Loans backed by the Veteran's Administration made homeownership a simple, risk-free decision for returning servicemen. The loans typically carried an interest rate of 4 percent, and the Veteran's Administration guaranteed them for 50 percent of the value of the loan. Unlike traditional loans, which still required homeowners to save for their purchases, those offered through the Veteran's Administration did not require homebuyers to put forward a down payment, thereby eliminating one of the major obstacles to homeownership for American families. Over the next decade, as returning veterans took advantage of the provisions of the G.I. Bill, the Veteran's Administration guaranteed more than 2 million loans, encouraging families to purchase their piece of the American Dream in suburban communities, like Levittown.[17]

Although the suburbs offered new opportunities for reimagining the contours of citizenship, the benefits of homeownership were not equally shared in these suburban communities. The suburbs Levitt constructed were homogenous in both their housing stock and their racial composition. Homes in Levittown were only available to white households. Mindful of the communities he was creating, William Levitt acknowledged the realities of the housing situation in postwar America. "As a company, our position is simply this," Levitt noted. "We can solve a housing problem, or we can try to solve the race problem, but we cannot combine the two." Many of the new postwar suburbs included racial covenants that limited homeownership opportunities to white households. While racial restrictions ensured that the FHA would guarantee mortgage loans in these suburban communities, they also ensured that African-American households would have little access to homeownership opportunities during this period of suburbanization. Although the suburbs foretold a major demographic shift in the United States, they also created growing boundaries of social exclusion and marginalization.[18]

While the reconfigured system of housing finance hastened the decline of central cities and spurred the growth of the American suburbs, changes introduced in the National Housing Act of 1934 were not solely responsible for suburbanization in the postwar period. In the 1940s and the 1950s, the federal government commenced a program of urban renewal that cleared urban neighborhoods for redevelopment. These programs pushed households from central cities, contributing to the process of white flight in the postwar period. At the same time, massive highway construction opened up land for residential development, paving the way for private builders to construct suburban residential communities within commuting distance of the city. Soon, Americans were able to live in these suburban neighborhoods but continue to hold their jobs in the city, reconfiguring the landscape of housing and work in the twentieth century.

The inaugural program of urban renewal came with the Housing Act of 1949, the first major piece of housing legislation in the postwar period. In it, Congress authorized federal funding for slum clearance and urban redevelopment, marking the first widespread federal intervention into the remaking of American cities. The Housing Act of 1949 set aside $1 billion in federal funds for cities and municipalities to acquire slums and blighted land, based largely on the belief that urban slums came at great civic costs. "A slum neighborhood that requires more than its proportionate share of health and welfare services is a drain on national as well as local resources, and seriously affects the development of good citizenship and confidence in the values of democracy," congressional leaders noted, returning to the rhetoric of citizenship and democracy in their discussion of housing. Clearing cities of their blighted neighborhoods would facilitate the construction of suitable housing and vibrant communities, proponents of urban renewal argued. Expanding the scope of these programs, Congress created the Urban Renewal Administration five years later with the Housing Act of 1954. In doing so, they cemented the policy of urban redevelopment as the postwar response to the enduring crisis of cities and facilitated the outward migration of homeowners to the suburbs.[19]

As they authorized the redevelopment of "blighted" urban neighborhoods, Congress declared the central goal of postwar housing policy to be the promotion of a "decent home and a suitable living environment for every American family." This language, put forth in the National Housing Act of 1949, was to become the unofficial mantra of housing advocates for the second half of the century. Although officially neutral toward ownership status, the language suggested an inherent bias toward homeownership. For decades, reform efforts had linked homeownership to population health, social welfare, and practices of upstanding citizenship. Although the specific types of homes that would replace urban slums were left to the demands of the market, the problems of urban slums—poor health, declining social mores, and deteriorating citizenship—had historically been addressed by investing households with a stake in their homes and neighborhoods.[20]

While urban redevelopment programs provided a push from central cities, the construction of an interstate highway system continued to pull citizens to the suburbs by making suburban neighborhoods increasingly accessible to American workers. In 1956, Congress passed the Interstate Highway Act to expand the interstate roadway system across the country. The Act authorized more than 40,000 miles of roadway, paid for mostly by the federal government. Although the interstate highway system was originally intended to ease congested roadways, increase automobile safety, and facilitate mobility in the event of a Cold War attack, it had the secondary effect of increasing access to low-cost land beyond the city. By connecting large tracts of land outside urban centers to the cities themselves, the system of highways opened up new tracts of suburban land for residential construction and increased reliance on the automobile as the primary mode of travel. By the 1950s, the number of automobiles in the United States had tripled from three decades earlier, cementing the place of the postwar suburb in the country's residential geography.[21]

Still, opportunities for homeownership were shared unevenly in the postwar suburb. While suburbanization created new ways for Americans to own their own homes, raising the national level of homeownership to historic highs, millions of citizens were excluded from the chance to buy a home. Although more than 60 percent of Americans lived in homes they owned by the 1960s, African-Americans were substantially less likely than whites to own their own homes. Federal mortgage insurance shaped these racial disparities, limiting lending activity in primarily African-American and racially integrated neighborhoods. Without access to mortgage credit, African-American households had few opportunities to purchase a home of their own. Only over the next couple of decades, in the context of the civil rights movement, would the federal government begin to address racial discrimination in the housing and mortgage markets, albeit with limited success.[22]

Closing the Gap: Addressing Inequality in Access to Homeownership

As suburbanization created new homeownership opportunities for whites outside cities, it simultaneously contributed to the growing concentration of African-Americans in urban neighborhoods, exacerbating well-documented patterns of segregation in the United States. These patterns of housing inequality and residential segregation occurred alongside major shifts to the American economy. Although manufacturing had served as the mainstay of urban employment for decades, this sector began to migrate beyond the traditional urban core. Increasingly, American cities were home to a growing population of African-American citizens, marginalized by the changing industrial base and facing few opportunities for economic mobility.[23]

In time, growing social unrest in the United States would refocus attention on the housing situation of African-American households and the limited opportunities that existed for them to own their own homes. In the 1960s, riots broke out in cities across the country, highlighting entrenched patterns of segregation, limited economic opportunities, and persistent injustices in urban communities. As American cities burned, from Washington, D.C., to Oakland, California, the urban riots called attention to the economic and housing situation of the country's poorest citizens.

Responding to the urban riots, President Lyndon B. Johnson convened the Kerner Commission, chaired by Illinois governor Otto Kerner, to evaluate the situation in American cities. The Kerner Commission hoped to tackle the causes of growing social unrest, famously noting the pattern of inequality that had come to plague the United States. "Our Nation is moving toward two societies, one black, one white—separate and unequal," the Commission acknowledged. In their final report, the Commission identified the unsatisfactory housing conditions as an underlying factor that contributed to instability in American cities.

By the 1960s, enthusiasm for public housing had long since waned in the United States, leaving few advocates for expanding public housing to address the root causes of the urban riots. Instead, members of the Kerner Commission recommended the expansion of homeownership opportunities for low-income Americans. "The ambition to own one's own home is shared by virtually all Americans, and we believe it is in the interest of the nation to permit all who share such a goal to realize it," they wrote. "Home ownership would eliminate one of the most persistent problems facing low-income families in rental housing—poor maintenance by absentee landlords—and would provide many low-income families with a tangible stake in society for the first time," the Commission reported. Drawing on rhetoric popularized nearly a half century earlier, the Commission viewed homeownership as a way to invest households with a stake in their neighborhoods, emphasizing the promise of owning your own home as a pathway to stronger citizenship.[24]

In the 1960s, Congress passed a series of laws to increase opportunities for African-American and low-income households to buy a home. While previous legislation, like the National Housing Act of 1934, had increased homeownership opportunities by tying homeownership to broader macroeconomic policy goals, these pieces of legislation worked directly to increase minority access to homeownership. Following the urban riots, Congress authorized the creation of the Section 235 program, a mortgage subsidy program to provide direct assistance to minority homebuyers. Participants in the Section 235 program paid 20 percent of their income toward their housing costs, including mortgage payments and property taxes, and the federal government paid the difference. This direct subsidy program lowered the barriers to entry by limiting the monthly housing costs households paid on their homes. It also shifted housing policy away from supporting low-income Americans through public housing developments, underscoring the deep commitment of the federal government to encouraging access to homeownership. As he embraced homeownership in the 1960s, President Johnson recognized the important role that homeownership played in creating stable urban communities. "Owning a home can increase responsibility and stake out a man's place in his community. The man who owns a home has something to be proud of and good reason to protect and preserve it," he reminded the nation in the wake of the urban riots.[25]

Still, the problem of minority access to homeownership was not just one of resources or wealth. Even when they had sufficient economic resources to purchase a home, African-Americans still experienced discrimination in the housing markets. Banking institutions continued the practice of redlining neighborhoods, and realtors often steered African-American households away from particular communities. Even into the 1960s, the color-coded maps used by the HOLC to identify the riskiness of mortgage lending continued to shape the residential opportunities available to African-American households. As they relied on the racial characteristics of neighborhoods to calculate the riskiness of their investments, the FHA limited the choices available to African-American households. Banks continued to follow the standards set by the FHA for defining reasonable risks, exacerbating the challenges African-Americans faced in buying a home of their own.[26]

During the 1960s and the 1970s, the federal government began to address discriminatory practices in the real estate industry and housing markets. These efforts began with the Fair Housing Act, passed as part of the Civil Rights Act, which prohibited discrimination in financing, renting, and selling homes on the basis of race, religion, and sex. Specifically, the Fair Housing Act prohibited real estate agents from steering clients toward particular properties on the basis of their race. Realtors were forbidden to make false statements to clients with the intent of not selling a property to a specific racial or ethnic group, including telling clients that properties were unavailable when in fact they remained on the market. And the Act prohibited sellers from refusing to sell a property to a potential buyer on the basis of the buyer's race. The Fair Housing Act marked the first intervention by the federal government to address the overtly discriminatory practices that kept African-Americans from owning their own homes.[27]

Although the Fair Housing Act marked an important pivot in federal efforts to address racial discrimination in the housing market, the enforcement of this legislation proved largely untenable. Despite provisions outlawing housing discrimination, the mechanisms for identifying and punishing discrimination were weak. In fact, audit studies, in which pairs of subjects, one black and one white, were sent to inquire about the availability of particular properties, revealed substantial discrimination in the housing market long after the passage of the Fair Housing Act. Not until two decades later, when Congress passed an amended version of it, did the federal government begin to tighten enforcement against housing discrimination.[28]

In addition to addressing overt discrimination, including racial steering by realtors, Congress needed to address the shortage of mortgage capital in segregated, urban communities and the unwillingness of lenders to make loans to African-American households. Citizens living in poor, racially segregated neighborhoods still had very little access to mortgage credit. To increase the availability of credit, Congress passed the Home Mortgage Disclosure Act in 1975. It required mortgage lenders to report the location of home mortgage loans to federal authorities. Later, as federal law mandated that lenders report the characteristics of borrowers and the outcome of mortgage applications, proponents expected that the disclosure of this data would increase transparency in the lending process. Policymakers could track the characteristics of loans made in particular neighborhoods, identifying places that lacked adequate mortgage financing. This transparency, they hoped, would increase the ability of advocates to combat redlining, opening up homeownership opportunities for African-American and low-income households.[29]

While the Home Mortgage Disclosure Act required lenders to disclose the home mortgages made within particular communities, it included no requirement for banks to provide access to credit in those neighborhoods. To complement the transparency requirements of the Home Mortgage Disclosure Act, Congress passed the Community Reinvestment Act in 1977. Under its terms, depository institutions were required to meet the credit needs of underserved communities. In neighborhoods where banks drew deposits, the Act mandated that they also provide mortgage credit for homeownership. Although the effectiveness of the Community Reinvestment Act continues to be the subject of substantial debate, it increased access to mortgage credit in underserved communities, ultimately highlighting efforts by the federal government to directly address racial inequalities in access to homeownership. Increasing the transparency of mortgage loans and ensuring the availability of capital were key strategies to expand homeownership opportunities for African-American households.[30]

Investing in Homeownership

While many American homebuyers started to accumulate assets through housing in the post-War period, federal policies were rarely justified by referencing the importance of housing to building individual wealth. Instead, during the Great Depression, political leaders used housing policies to jump-start a dormant economy, creating employment opportunities for workers in the construction trade. On the heels of the urban riots, they encouraged citizens to buy their own homes as a way of creating stability in urban neighborhoods and stemming the tides of social unrest. And while they touted the widespread benefits that homeownership would bring to the country—stimulating economic growth, encouraging stability in urban communities, and solidifying the best practices of citizenship—they rarely talked about owning a home as a way to build wealth.

Although Americans today are deeply committed to buying their own homes for financial reasons, as I reported in chapter 1, that wasn't always the case. In fact, when John P. Dean wrote about homeownership in the 1940s, he questioned the very wisdom of homeownership as a financial investment. "There is no sure way of telling in advance whether a home purchase will be a good investment," Dean wrote—a statement that would seem anachronistic in late twentieth-century America. However, in the early part of the century, homebuyers were often unclear about the finances of homeownership, and this confusion raised doubts about the long-term value of owning a home. And while historians pointed to the ways urban homeowners used their homes to augment their industrial wages by renting rooms to boarders, their commitment to homeownership grew from the prestige, status, and security of owning a home rather than the promise of profiting from it.[31]

While today's homeowners often point to the importance of homeownership to retiring comfortably and generating wealth to pass along to one's children, housing served a different purpose for homebuyers through much of the twentieth century. When William Levitt built the suburbs, homeowners rarely thought of buying a home and moving to Levittown as a way of weathering economic insecurity or saving for retirement. In fact, in the 1960s, when sociologist Herbert Gans asked families why they moved to Levittown, few identified the investment value of their homes as a reason. Although they acknowledged that the cost of owning was often lower than the cost of renting, the promise of owning a single-family home was driven by media representations of suburban life, the social status of homeownership, and the desire for spacious yards and living space.[32]

What had changed by the end of the twentieth century that transformed homeownership into a core strategy for building wealth? Why did Americans come to view their homes as the best financial investment they could make and the surest route into the prized middle class? One answer lies in the transformation of social welfare policies in late twentieth-century America, and the way Americans started to finance their consumer spending through their housing equity. During the New Deal, when Congress passed the National Housing Act, they laid the groundwork for the modern welfare state. In the 1930s, they passed programs for retirement assistance and unemployment insurance, and they expanded on them with poverty reduction programs and health insurance coverage in the Great Society several decades later. But by the 1980s, with the ascent of political conservatism, the American welfare state had started to shrink. Rhetoric about private responsibility replaced the belief in a robust social safety net, and the resulting legislation shifted much of the burden of economic security to households themselves.[33]

Accounting for changes in the American welfare state, political scientist Jacob Hacker describes the transformation of social policy in his book *The Great Risk Shift*. While Hacker maintains that the bones of the social welfare state remain intact—programs like Medicaid, for example—he argues that many federal and private programs that historically assumed risk have slowly unraveled. "Although most U.S. public social programs have indeed resisted radical retrenchment, the American social welfare framework has also, in crucial areas, offered increasingly incomplete protection against the key social risks that Americans confront," Hacker notes. From unemployment insurance to health care coverage, the politics of risk privatization have shifted the burden of risk insurance away from businesses and governments, placing squarely on individuals and households the cost of covering their own risks. "As a result of this process, many of the most potent threats to income are increasingly faced by families and individuals on their own, rather than by collective intermediaries," he writes.[34]

As social policies have been rolled back, and Americans battle economic insecurities without the collective insurance of a generous welfare state, they increasingly rely on the private accumulation of wealth to protect against risk. Today, as political scientist Herman Schwartz notes, homeownership is the most important form of private insurance available to households. We can think of housing investments as a substitute for a safety net that would otherwise be provided by a more generous state or through employer-provided benefits. "As welfare state opponents succeeded in shifting risk off the fiscal institutions and onto individuals, housing moved to the forefront of individual strategies for attaining economic security. Home equity became a source of current and future consumption, emergency cash, and disguised retirement savings," Schwartz notes. To build wealth—wealth that we use to pay for our health expenses, weather periods of economic insecurity, and, most important, retire comfortably—Americans have invested in their homes, anchoring homeownership as the cornerstone of the wealth portfolio.[35]

The continued importance of homeownership as a financial investment is reflected in the remarkable growth in housing values at the end of the twentieth century. While federal housing policies lowered the cost of ownership, often making it cheaper to own a home than to rent one, the real growth in housing prices solidified the investment value of owning a home. It wasn't just the promise of living mortgage-free into retirement that made homeownership a good financial investment. It was also the remarkable growth of housing prices that occurred at the end of the twentieth century.

To measure the growth of housing prices, social scientists often turn to the Case-Shiller Home Price Index, a measure of real price growth. Figure 3.1 plots housing prices for the twentieth century, indexed to the earliest available level in 1890. While there was some fluctuation in housing prices during the twentieth century, figure 3.1 captures a remarkable rise in housing prices at the end of the century. As prices started to climb at an unprecedented pace, they solidified the promise of homeownership as a tool for building wealth. In fact, until the crash of the housing market, owning a home looked like best financial investment a household could make—a fact that explains Americans' unshakable belief in the financial promise of homeownership.[36]

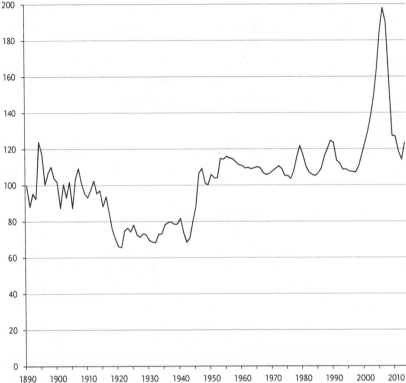

FIGURE 3.1. Historic housing price index in the United States, 1890–2013. Annual housing prices are indexed to housing prices in 1890, the first year for which housing prices are available, to evaluate housing price trends throughout the twentieth century. Historic housing prices data from Robert J. Shiller, *Irrational Exuberance* (Princeton, NJ: Princeton University Press, 2015).

As housing prices climbed, homeowners looked to their homes as a way to finance their consumer spending. Often, they refinanced their homes to extract cash from their housing investment. By borrowing against the rising value of their homes, homeowners can finance their lifestyles and fuel their spending habits by drawing the equity out of their homes. As Bethany McLean recently noted in a column in the *New York Times*, homeowners are using their houses as credit cards to fuel their consumer spending rather than buying homes as a way to save. The expansion of home equity loans—which provide substantial tax benefits—have made it even easier for homeowners to finance their spending with the equity in their homes.[37]

One of the major reasons Americans came to view their homes as a financial investment has to do with the tax benefits associated with buying a home—a set of policies to which I return in chapter 6. Today, the federal government rewards homeowners for their housing decisions through a series of tax exemptions and deductions. While many of the twentieth-century efforts to promote homeownership focused on lowering the cost of mortgage credit and ensuring the availability of capital for mortgage lending, contemporary tax policies have reinforced the importance of building wealth through homeownership.

At the center of these efforts is the mortgage interest deduction—a provision of the tax code that allows some homeowners to deduct the interest they pay on their mortgage loans (and home equity loans) from their taxable income. In the 1980s, the federal government reformed the tax code to prioritize interest paid on mortgage loans above other types of consumer debt—a change that increased the financial importance of buying a home. And while the mortgage interest deduction is the costliest tax subsidy for American homeowners, it is not the only provision of the tax code that provides preferential treatment to them. Under existing federal law, many homeowners don't pay taxes on the money they make—their capital gains—when they sell their homes. The federal tax code allows homeowners to deduct state and local property taxes from their federal tax liability. And unlike owners of rental property, who are required to report rental income as taxable income, homeowners are exempt from taxation on this imputed income. Together, these tax expenditures contribute to making homeownership a more attractive investment than it would otherwise be.[38]

By the end of the twentieth century, as I have noted, buying a home (and building equity in it) had become the most important way to build wealth for millions of American families. The remarkable growth in housing prices fortified confidence in the financial power of owning a home, and tax policies encouraged millions of citizens to recognize the investment value of ownership. Owning a home had emerged as a pillar of economic security, and households relied on their homes as a tool for economic mobility and independence. After decades devoted largely to highlighting the civic virtues of homeownership, Americans had come to embrace the financial benefits of buying a home.

A Nation of Homeowners

Building a nation of homeowners marked one of the greatest accomplishments of America in the twentieth century. Early on, as the country struggled to dislodge itself from the depths of the Great Depression, fewer than half of American households owned their own homes, as reported in figure 3.2. But

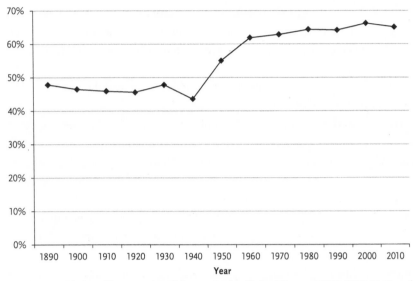

FIGURE 3.2. National homeownership rate in the United States, 1890–2010. National homeownership rate from the decennial U.S. Census.

over the course of the twentieth century, and specifically in the postwar period, the number of American homeowners grew quickly. By the end of the century, the number of American households living in homes they owned reached an all-time high. More than two-thirds of Americans owned their own homes, marking the expansion of homeownership as one of the defining achievements of the century.[39]

But the growth in the national homeownership rate was neither natural nor inevitable. Although Americans have long preferred to own their homes—a fact that John P. Dean acknowledged in his mid-twentieth-century book on the soundness of homeownership—building a nation of homeowners required extensive interventions into the way Americans bought and sold their homes. By assuming the risk of mortgage lending, standardizing underwriting criteria, and ensuring the widespread availability of capital in the mortgage market, the federal government made homeownership affordable to millions of American families.

Still, the remarkable expansion of homeownership described in this chapter contributed to enduring patterns of residential segregation. While federal programs to expand homeownership raised the number of Americans who owned their own home, white households disproportionately benefited from these programs. Critically, as housing emerged as the most important tool for building wealth, the uneven opportunities for African-American households to buy their own homes worsened patterns of economic inequality. One of the legacies of these programs would be the enduring patterns of segregation and social exclusion that persisted as a result of federal policies to build a nation of homeowners.

While we often justify contemporary homeownership policies by pointing to the importance of housing for building wealth, the story told in this chapter serves as a stark reminder of the multiple ways that political leaders expected homeownership to contribute to resolving the social, political, and economic challenges of twentieth-century America. Although the rapid growth of housing prices by the end of the twentieth century solidified the importance of homeownership as a financial investment, the importance of housing as an investment opportunity is relatively new. Through much of the twentieth century, political leaders justified the expansion of homeownership by pointing to the macroeconomic benefits of stimulating housing construction and the micro benefits of reshaping family life. Nearly every policy acknowledged the potential for homeownership to engender stronger citizenship and promote resiliency in local communities. Political leaders believed that owning a home would root Americans in their neighborhoods and deepen their attachment to civic affairs. Even recently, as political leaders have outlined the importance of homeownership for building wealth, they have rarely strayed from the orthodoxy of homeownership as a tool for engaging citizens in their communities.

Despite the historical legacy linking homeownership to the norms of citizenship, there is limited research on the social, civic, or political benefits that emerged from these efforts to expand ownership opportunities and build a nation of homeowners. In the next chapter, I examine these expected benefits of homeownership—the way owning a home ties citizens to their communities, creates social bonds between neighbors, and encourages them to take part in local politics. Although political leaders often turn to the civic promise of homeownership to justify housing policies, we are only beginning to understand how homeownership reshapes the ways citizens participate in their communities, and how the growing financial importance of owning a home mediates this participation. The next chapter investigates whether homeowners are more engaged in their communities—attending political meetings, voting in local elections, or joining neighborhood organizations, for example. In many ways, the answer is surprising. Owning a home drives participation in a limited set of civic activities, but it is not the transformative marker of upstanding citizenship that proponents often make it out to be.

4

BUILDING WEALTH?

PROPERTY VALUES AND THE CIVIC HABITS OF HOMEOWNERS

Soon after winning the presidency, President Bill Clinton launched the National Homeownership Strategy, his signature contribution to the twentieth-century project of building a nation of homeowners. For much of the century, as I described in the previous chapter, political leaders worked to expand opportunities for Americans to buy their own homes. As they lowered the costs of buying a home and transferred the risk of mortgage lending onto the federal government, the number of Americans who owned their own home soared. By the 1960s, more than 60 percent of citizens lived in homes they owned.[1]

But by the 1980s, the homeownership rate had flattened, dipping slightly as the American economy entered a brief recession and interest rates climbed. By the time President Clinton took office, the country faced deep challenges in expanding opportunities to buy homes, especially for low-income and minority Americans. Racial discrimination continued to plague housing markets, and low-income citizens had few resources to buy homes of their own. White households were nearly twice as likely to own their homes as African-American and Latino ones. More than 80 percent of households with incomes above the national median lived in homes they owned, compared to barely half of households with incomes below it.[2]

Standing in the East Room of the White House, the president made the expansion of ownership opportunities the centerpiece of his housing strategy. Flanked by housing leaders and first-time homebuyers, he reflected on the remarkable story of homeownership in the twentieth century. "One of the great successes of the United States in this century has been the partnership forged by the national government and the private sector to steadily expand the dream of home ownership to all Americans," Clinton noted, implicitly referencing many of the policies described in the previous chapter. With the National Homeownership Strategy, he proposed to harness the resources of both the federal government and private businesses in boosting opportunities for Americans to own their own homes. His plan would extend this historic partnership by pushing the national homeownership rate to historic highs, creating 8 million new homeowners by the end of the century.[3]

To expand opportunities for Americans to own their own homes, the National Homeownership Strategy called for increasing the construction of starter homes and encouraging households to consider inexpensive mobile homes. It proposed greater access to education and counseling services, enabling would-be homeowners to make sounder financial decisions. And the plan aimed to reduce the cost of homebuying for first-time homeowners by promoting technological advances that would make purchasing a home quick and easy. Building on many of the policies discussed in the previous chapter, the National Homeownership Strategy leaned heavily on private organizations to increase access to mortgage credit, lower the barriers to homeownership, and broaden the opportunities for Americans to buy a home.

As he introduced his plan, President Clinton remarked on the importance of homeownership for building household wealth. As I noted earlier, owning a home had become the largest piece of the wealth portfolio of millions of Americans by the end of the twentieth century. Housing equity makes up a disproportionate share of assets for the average homeowner, and economic mobility is often built on the financial decision to buy a home. As the global economy increased employment instability, though, President Clinton acknowledged that homeownership had become one of the most durable strategies for financial independence. "No one...can look at these young people and say, I will guarantee you, no matter what happens in the global economy, you will always have the job you have today, and you'll make more money next year than you did this year.... That's not the way it works anymore," he noted. "But we can guarantee to people that we're going to empower them to help themselves. We'll make homeownership more accessible," he promised, recognizing the economic security of ownership as a form of private insurance against the uncertainty of the global economy.

Beyond the benefits to individual households, President Clinton pointed to the broader macroeconomic benefits that would come from extending homeownership opportunities. Like President Roosevelt, who argued that expanding homeownership would stimulate economic growth, Clinton noted the importance of housing for creating new jobs and fueling consumer demand. "When a family buys a home, the ripple effect is enormous," he noted.

"It means new homeowner consumers. They need more durable goods, like washers and dryers, refrigerators and water heaters. And if more families could buy new homes or older homes, more hammers will be pounding, more saws will be buzzing."

But as he stood in the East Room of the White Housing, laying out the multiple benefits that come from owning a home, Clinton also drew on the historic promise of homeownership for building communities and strengthening citizenship. Standing with Millard Fuller, the founder of Habitat for Humanity, he used language reminiscent of the early twentieth-century campaigns to emphasize the ways that ownership engaged Americans in the practices of citizenship and encouraged them to fulfill the responsibilities of democratic life. "When we boost the number of homeowners in our country, we strengthen our economy, create jobs, build up the middle class, and build better citizens," he noted. Reflecting on his own humble beginnings, he told a story of a woman from Arkansas who lived in the first house built by Habitat for Humanity in his home state. For years, she had been unable to save enough to become a homeowner, but with the help of Habitat for Humanity, she and her family were able to buy their first home. "And it made her a better citizen," he told the crowd gathered in the East Room of the White House. "It made everybody that put a hammer to a nail a better citizen, and it made all of us who saw it unfold better citizens."

Although President Clinton assured his audience that extending homeownership opportunities would engage citizens in their communities, he offered little evidence to show that homeowners were actually more engaged community members than renters. In fact, when he introduced the National Homeownership Strategy, his administration acknowledged that there was actually very little social science research on the civic benefits that come from people owning their own homes. While a handful of existing studies offered preliminary evidence about the ways homeownership shaped civic involvement, proponents of homeownership largely took these benefits as a matter of faith. "The validity of some of these assertions [about the benefits of homeownership] is so widely accepted that economists and social scientists have seldom tested them," acknowledged leaders at the Department of Housing and Urban Development.[4]

Even today—more than two decades after President Clinton introduced the National Homeownership Strategy—we have only a limited understanding of the way homeownership shapes civic engagement and political participation. In fact, the evidence on the activities associated with homeownership is mixed, and explanations about why homeowners engage in their communities are muddled. In this chapter, I ask whether owning a home transforms citizens into more active, engaged members of their communities. Through analyses of several national surveys, I evaluate the types of activities driven by home-ownership and the reasons that owners participate in these activities at higher rates than renters.[5]

Despite the enduring rhetoric that paints ownership as a tool for crafting better citizens, the findings of this chapter are decidedly mixed. Homeowners are more likely to vote in elections, attend community meetings, and work coop-eratively with their neighbors, fulfilling some of the shared responsibilities of civic life. However, across a broader range of social capital and political participa-tion measures, homeowners and renters are actually quite similar. Homeowners are no more engaged in most types of political activities than renters, and although they are more trusting of their neighbors, they are no more likely to report participating in informal neighborly activities in their community.

With the evidence from this chapter, I reject the oversimplified narrative that presents owners as better citizens. Instead, I show that the civic benefits of homeownership are substantially narrower than proponents often claim. Looking at the types of activities in which homeowners engage at higher rates than renters, I argue that it is their interest in protecting their property values that motivates homeowners to become involved in some of these activities, including local politics and community meetings. However, for other types of activities, including socializing with neighbors and volunteering, I show that higher rates of participation are driven by increased residential stability. While proponents of homeownership have long pushed ownership as a way to deepen claims to citizenship, they have largely failed to distinguish the role of resi-dential stability from the financial incentives of owning a home in shaping the way citizens participate in their communities.

Why Do Homeowners Participate in Their Communities?

While President Clinton praised the civic benefits of homeownership, he neglected to identify why he expected homeowners to become more involved in their communities than renters. In fact, despite decades of rhetoric, propo-nents of homeownership rarely identify the reasons why homeownership would deepen community engagement or encourage citizens to take a more robust approach to civic life. Before turning to an analysis of the civic habits of American homeowners, I briefly explain the two main reasons why we might expect homeownership to transform citizens into more active, engaged participants in civic and community life.

One explanation linking homeownership to civic engagement points to the importance of building wealth through housing—a commitment noted by contemporary political leaders as they pushed for new ownership opportunities. As I noted in chapter 1, Americans hold more wealth in their homes than they do in any other asset, including stocks and bonds, their retirement accounts, or other types of property. For millions of families, saving for retirement, building a small nest egg, and climbing the economic ladder rest on their financial investments in housing. Especially for low-income households, many of whom do not have any other tools for building wealth, owning a home is the best opportunity for a stronger, more stable financial future.[6]

Notably, buying a house is a different type of financial obligation from other investments. When citizens invest money in the stock market or put funds in a retirement account, they can move their investments around, making choices to maximize the value of their wealth portfolio. With the click of a button or a call to a broker, an investor can sell a stock or select an alternative mutual fund, shifting the assets in his or her portfolio. Diversifying an investment portfolio helps to hedge against risk. But housing is a nondiversified asset. Although a homeowner can access the wealth built through homeownership by tapping into home equity loans, he or she cannot diversify his or her housing wealth to hedge against the risk that home values will fall. And as the recent housing crisis reminded us, homeownership can be a risky investment—especially for households that concentrate most of their wealth in housing.

One way for homeowners to protect their housing investments from losing value—or to increase the value of their investments—is to become involved in their communities. The characteristics of local communities—everything from the physical condition of neighboring homes to the rate of taxation in a town— influence housing values. Good schools raise property values; high crime rates lower them. Property values are typically higher in historic neighborhoods with architectural amenities or in places with high-quality institutions and services. Meanwhile, houses in impoverished neighborhoods typically sell for less than similar homes in more affluent communities. These neighborhood characteristics are capitalized in home values, meaning that the quality of the surrounding neighborhood influences the ability of homeowners to build wealth through their housing.[7]

As a result, we would expect homeowners to be more involved in their communities than renters as they work to protect and defend their property values. By attending town meetings or contacting their local legislators, homeowners may fight neighborhood changes that lower their property values and support those changes that they expect to raise them. Homeowners might engage in their communities to fend off development projects that they expect to lower their property values, or they may advocate for land-use decisions that they anticipate will increase their housing prices. Recognizing the way community characteristics are capitalized in their property values, homeowners are likely to get involved in their communities to protect their largest investments—their homes.

Expanding on these ideas about property values, housing wealth, and community participation, economist William Fischel coined the *homevoter hypothesis* to explain the way homeownership shapes political participation. On the basis of community observations in Hanover, New Hampshire, Fischel argued that homeowners take an outsized role in their communities because they recognize the way community changes impact their property values. They are mindful of local government decisions—everything from school funding to zoning to the conditions of local roadways.[8]

Yet Fischel, in his book *The Homevoter Hypothesis*, was not primarily concerned with the activities of homeowners themselves. Instead, he sought to show that local governments operate more efficiently and responsively than higher levels of government because they are responsive to the needs and demands of local homeowners. "The reason that local governments perform better is that the benefits and costs of local decision making are reflected in the value of property in the jurisdiction," Fischel wrote, acknowledging the multiple ways that community characteristics are capitalized in housing values. "The homevoter hypothesis holds that homeowners...are guided by their concern for the value of their homes to make political decisions that are more efficient than those that would be made at a higher level of government."[9]

Still, the homevoter hypothesis tells us little about the actual political habits of homeowners—the ways they engage in their communities or the types of activities they use to improve their neighborhoods. In fact, Fischel takes for granted that homeowners recognize the way local amenities are capitalized in their property values and that they are more active in their communities to protect their housing investments. While *The Homevoter Hypothesis* does not provide empirical evidence comparing rates of participation among homeowners and renters, it does lay out a clear set of reasons to expect higher levels of political participation and community involvement among homeowners.

Yet protecting housing wealth isn't the only reason that homeowners are more likely to engage in their communities. In the early twentieth century, during a period of widespread urbanization, political leaders and business elites often encouraged ownership as a way to stabilize communities, as I noted in chapter 2. Homeowners, they argued, are less likely to move than renters and more likely to set down roots in their community. This pathway—the increased residential stability of homeownership—points to the second mechanism linking homeownership to enhanced citizenship. When citizens stay in one place for a long period of time, they may be more likely to participate actively in the routines of citizenship and community life.[10]

Several years ago, sociologist Claude Fischer argued that Americans are increasingly stable, calling us "ever-more rooted Americans." Although it often seems that Americans are constantly on the move, Fischer argued that Americans have become less mobile over the last half century—a period in which the number of homeowners has climbed to record highs. By the late 1990s, barely 10 percent of the population reported moving within a county in any given year, continuing a decline in the mobility rate throughout the twentieth century. Simply put, Americans today are staying put in their communities, moving less frequently than their parents and grandparents did.[11]

While the expansion of homeownership opportunities may not fully explain declining rates of residential mobility, there are several reasons why owning a home makes citizens less likely to move. On one hand, buying a home increases the transaction costs associated with moving. When they sell their homes, homeowners face an array of fees—from realtors to lawyers—that renters do not incur. On the other hand, buying a home often signals the intent of a household to stay in their community. When people expect to live in one place for a long period of time, they are substantially more likely to purchase a home.

Whether homeownership leads to increased stability or the expectation of stability leads people to buy a home, the outcome is the same—homeowners move less frequently than renters. This increased residential stability influences all types of behaviors and outcomes, from finding jobs to completing an education; from making friends to building social capital. Several decades ago, the economist Andrew Oswald proposed that high homeownership rates are associated with higher rates of unemployment. Given the costs homeowners incur with moving to new locations, Oswald argued that homeowners are less likely to follow job opportunities across counties or across the country. The high transaction costs associated with owning a home may keep people from securing the best employment opportunities, as homeownership ties them to a particular place while jobs migrate more freely.[12]

The same forces that restrict homeowners from following employment opportunities, though, may prove to be a boon for civic engagement and community participation. Residential stability in a community helps citizens deepen the social networks and strengthen the interpersonal relationships that are central to active, engaged citizenship. People often become involved in their communities—joining civic groups or participating in volunteer activities, for example—when their friends and neighbors ask them to participate, and staying in a neighborhood may facilitate the development of social bonds that integrate them into community affairs. It may also strengthen the sense of place that Americans feel in their communities, deepening loyalties in a neighborhood and generating a stronger sense of community pride. By tying citizens to their communities, the transition to homeownership may increase civic participation and lay the foundations of upstanding citizenship, even apart from the financial investments that citizens make in their homes.

Measuring Community Participation

While these two mechanisms—the opportunity to build wealth through housing and the way ownership leads to residential stability—explain why homeownership may lead to higher levels of civic engagement, social scientists are left with another puzzle in evaluating the enhanced citizenship claims of homeownership. How do we choose among the countless ways that citizens become involved in their communities to develop a more complete picture of the civic habits of homeowners?

There are scores of ways that citizens can participate in neighborhood and civic life. They can attend town meetings, vote in local elections, and work cooperatively with their neighbors on a community project, just to name a few. Some types of community engagement are simply social or recreational—interacting regularly with neighbors or joining a sports league, for example. Others are inherently political—for example, volunteering on a political campaign or voting in an election. Civic involvement may be goal-oriented, with the aim of making a difference in the neighborhood, or it may simply be a way of building interpersonal relationships in a community. In short, there are multiple dimensions along which social scientists study community involvement to identify the ways that neighbors socialize, build social capital, and advocate for political change in their communities.

To better understand the way homeownership shapes community participation, I draw on the Social Capital Community Survey, one of the most thorough efforts to understand the way citizens build and sustain social capital resources. The Social Capital Community Survey captures a broad range of ways that citizens engage in their communities, including information on the way they perceive their neighborhoods and interact with their neighbors. It includes information on political involvement, membership group participation, and engagement in various types of community activities. (In the appendix, I provide additional information on the Social Capital Community Survey, including details of the regression analyses used in this chapter.)

To supplement the findings from the Social Capital Community Survey, I also draw on the Current Population Survey, a monthly survey conducted by the U.S. Bureau of Labor Statistics. While the Current Population Survey is primarily designed to measure employment trends across the country, several times each year it asks people about their participation in community activities and civic life. For example, it asks about their engagement in local politics and whether they volunteer in their communities. (Again, I provide additional information on the Current Population Survey in the appendix.)

To capture the multiple dimensions of civic involvement, I group the measures used in this chapter into four broad categories: political participation, community engagement, social capital resources, and civic attitudes. The measures of political participation capture the ways that citizens participate explicitly in the political process, asking whether they voted in recent elections, attended a political meeting, or signed a petition. The measures of community engagement include variables capturing whether they volunteered in their communities or joined various types of membership groups, for example. These measures identify how homeowners and renters engage as community actors, although not always with the explicit intention of political change.

To identify whether homeownership helps citizens build social capital resources, I include several measures of neighborliness and social trust. These include measures of informal social interaction within communities, as well as variables identifying levels of trust in particular social groups. Finally, the measures of civic attitudes include a handful of indicators to identify the way citizens feel about their neighborhoods and the communities around them. Respondents were asked whether they feel empowered to change their neighborhoods, and whether they would rank their communities highly as places to live. Taken together, these measures of political participation, community engagement, social capital resources, and civic attitudes allow for a nuanced analysis of the way homeowners and renters build social connections in their communities, and the specific impact of homeownership on civic involvement. Table 4.1 displays the question wording from the Social Capital Community Survey that corresponds with each indicator in this chapter.

For each measure of participation—for example, voting in elections—the analysis includes a pair of graphs (e.g., figs. 4.1 and 4.2). The first graphs (the

Table 4.1 Measures of Civic Involvement

Variable	Question wording
Political participation	
Vote in recent election	Did you vote in the (last) presidential election... or did you skip that one?
Attend a political meeting or rally	In the past twelve months, have you attended a political meeting or rally?
Sign a petition	In the past twelve months, have you signed a petition?
Participate in a protest or march	In the past twelve months, have you participated in any demonstrations, protests, boycotts, or marches?
Community engagement	
Work on a community project	In the past twelve months, have you worked on a community project?
Attend a public meeting to discuss school or town affairs[+]	How many times in the past twelve months have you attended any public meeting in which there was discussion of town or school affairs?
Volunteer[+]	How many times in the past twelve months have you volunteered?
Participate in a neighborhood association	In the last twelve months, have you been involved in a neighborhood association, like a block association, a homeowner or tenant association, or a crime watch group?
Participate in a sports club or league or an outdoor activity club	In the last twelve months, have you been involved in an adult sports club or league, or an outdoor activity club?
Participate in a parents' association or other school support group	In the last twelve months, have you been involved in a parents' association, like the PTA or PTO, or other school support or service groups?
Participate in a service or fraternal organization	In the last twelve months, have you been involved in service clubs or fraternal organizations such as the Lions or Kiwanis or a local women's club or a college fraternity or sorority?

(continued)

Table 4.1 Continued

Variable	Question wording
Participate in an organization affiliated with religion	In the last twelve months, have you been involved in any organization affiliated with religion, such as the Knights of Columbus or B'nai B'rith, or a Bible study group?

Social capital resources

Variable	Question wording
Work with others to fix or improve something in the neighborhood	In the past two years, have you worked with others to get people in your immediate neighborhood to work together to fix or improve something?
Talk or visit with neighbors at least once a week	About how often do you talk to or visit with your immediate neighbors—just about every day, several times a week, several times a month, once a month, several times a year, once a year or less, or never?
Visit the home of a neighbor at least once a month^	How many times in the past twelve months have you been in the home of a neighbor?
Trust the people in your neighborhood*	Think about people in your neighborhood. Generally speaking, would you say that you can trust them a lot, some, only a little, or not at all?
Trust the people who work in the stores where you shop*	Think about people who work in the stores where you shop. Generally speaking, would you say that you can trust them a lot, some, only a little, or not at all?
Trust the people you work with*	Think about people you work with. Generally speaking, would you say that you can trust them a lot, some, only a little, or not at all?
Trust the police in your local community*	Think about the police in your local community. Generally speaking, would you say that you can trust them a lot, some, only a little, or not at all?
Most people can be trusted	Generally speaking, would you say that most people can be trusted or that you can't be too careful in dealing with people?

(continued)

Table 4.1 Continued

Variable	Question wording
Civic attitudes	
Community is an excellent place to live	Overall, how would you rate your community as a place to live—excellent, good, fair, or poor?
People like you can have a big impact on community	Overall, how much impact do you think that people like you can have in making your community a better place to live—no impact at all, a small impact, a moderate impact, or a big impact?
Likely that people would cooperate[#]	Now I'd like to ask you a few questions about the local community where you live. If public officials asked everyone to conserve water or electricity because of some emergency, how likely is it that people in your community would cooperate?
Community leaders care about what happens to me[#]	The people running my community don't really care about what happens to me.
Community will get better in the next twelve months	Do you think your community will get better or worse as a place to live in the next twelve months, or will it stay the same?

The variables utilized in the analysis are dichotomous measures of civic involvement and community engagement. Where the underlying variable is not dichotomous, or the coding to make the underlying measure dichotomous is not straightforward from the question wording, the following symbols identify how the variables were transformed into a binary outcome.

[+] These variables are coded "yes" if respondents reported ever participating in the activity in the previous twelve months.

[^] These variables are coded "yes" if respondents reported this activity at least twelve times in the previous year.

[*] These variables are coded "yes" if respondents reported that they could trust each social group a lot.

[#] These variables are coded "yes" if respondents disagreed with the statement about community leaders, or if they reported that the statement about cooperation was likely or very likely.

Source: From the Social Capital Community Survey

odd-numbered figures) identify the percentage of homeowners and renters who report participating in that activity. When asked whether they voted in the most recent election, for example, the first graph of the pair simply identifies the percentage of homeowners and renters who report that they did. Across each measure of civic involvement in the chapter, the odd-numbered figures show the raw comparisons between homeowners and renters.

However, homeowners and renters differ in meaningful ways that may, apart from their housing choices, impact their civic involvement. For example, homeowners tend to have higher incomes than renters. They are more likely to earn a college degree, and they are, on average, older than renters. Homeowners are more likely to live in suburban communities; renters are more likely to live in the city. These suburban communities may offer fewer opportunities for unplanned neighborly interactions than dense, urban neighborhoods, or they may generate stronger norms of participation, regardless of whether someone owns their own home. To evaluate the specific impact of homeownership on civic involvement, we need to account for these other demographic characteristics in the analysis. If we do not account for them, then the different rates of participation reported in the odd-numbered figures may simply reflect other characteristics that distinguish homeowners from renters. The average homeowner might be more likely to vote in an election, for example, because she is wealthier and has a higher level of education than the average renter, not because she owns her own home.

For each measure of civic involvement, then, the even-numbered figures address the possibility that observed differences between homeowners and renters are the result of other characteristics rather than of their housing choices. These graphs account for demographic differences that are likely to influence whether citizens participate in civic activities. Specifically, these graphs account for the possibility that the observed differences between homeowners and renters in the odd-numbered figures simply reflect different characteristics of owners and renters, or the kinds of communities where they live, rather than identifying the true impact of owning a home on civic involvement.

For ease of interpretation, I plot the odds ratio from the logistic regression analyses described in the appendix. In each even-numbered graph, the bars for homeownership report how much the odds of participation change when someone owns a home. In other words, it tells us the change in the likelihood of a homeowner voting in an election, for example, compared to a comparable renter with similar demographic characteristics (e.g., the same level of education, income, age, etc.).

In each even-numbered figure, I also plot the odds ratio associated with residential stability. These bars tell us how much the odds of participation differ when someone has lived in his or her community for five or more years. In other words, it tells us the difference in the likelihood of a long-term community resident voting in an election, for example, compared to a comparable community member who has lived in the neighborhood for fewer than five years. Separately plotting the odds ratio for homeownership and residential stability in the same graph allows an evaluation of which activities are driven by residential stability and which activities are directly influenced by homeownership.

In each of these even-numbered figures, the size of the bars denotes the magnitude of the odds ratio associated with owning a home or living in a community for more than five years. An odds ratio of 2 would mean that owning a home (or living in a community for more than five years) doubles the likelihood of participation, while an odds ratio of 1 would mean that owning a home (or living in a community for more than five years) has no impact on the likelihood of participation. Negative odds ratios mean that owning a home (or living in a community for more than five years) decreases the likelihood of participation. Where the bars are relatively long, owning a home (or living in a community for more than five years) leads to a substantial increase in the odds of civic engagement. Where they are shorter, the impact is more limited, revealing that homeownership (or living in a community for more than five years) leads to only a marginal change in the likelihood of participation.[13]

Are Homeowners Better Citizens?

In this section, I evaluate whether homeowners engage in a range of community activities at higher rates than renters. For each category of involvement, I begin by briefly reviewing an existing study on the topic before providing a more comprehensive analysis from the Social Capital Community Survey.

Political Participation

When William Fischel introduced the homevoter hypothesis, he laid out a clear set of expectations about why homeowners should be more active in local politics. Homeowners are financially invested in their neighborhoods, he noted, and their concern about the impact of local political decisions on their property values should lead them to become more involved than renters. Because of their financial stake in the future of their communities, Fischel expected homeowners to be more mindful citizens, actively engaged in the politics of their communities.

Despite this hypothesis, Fischel offered little evidence to show how home-owners actually become involved in their neighborhoods. In fact, other than observations from community meetings, he did not identify particular types of activities in which they participated—for example, voting in local elections, supporting political candidates, or contacting their elected officials. Fortunately, the Social Capital Community Survey offers an opportunity to deepen the investigation of the political habits of American homeowners. It includes a handful of measures that identify the ways that citizens engage in the political process—by voting in an election, attending a political rally, or signing a petition, for example.

Homeowners are more likely than renters to report voting in the most recent election (fig. 4.1). Eighty-one percent of homeowners reported voting in the last election, compared to only 51 percent of renters. And while voter participation is the most common form of political involvement, there are many other ways that citizens make their voices heard and influence political decisions in their communities. Looking more broadly at political participation, figure 4.1 reveals that homeowners are more actively engaged in other types of political activities than renters, as well. Nearly 20 percent of homeowners attended a political meeting or rally in the last year, compared to only 13 percent of renters. Thirty-eight percent of homeowners reported signing a petition,

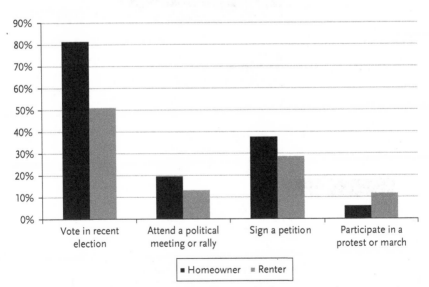

FIGURE 4.1. Participation in political activities, by homeownership status. From the Social Capital Community Survey.

compared to only 29 percent of renters. However, homeowners are slightly less likely than renters to participate in a protest or march.

These data are consistent with several other measures of political participation from the Current Population Survey. Asked whether they vote in local elections, including races for mayor or school board, 41 percent of homeowners report always voting in these elections, compared to only 21 percent of renters. Nineteen percent of homeowners actively supported a political candidate, but just 13 percent of renters did so. Similarly, 32 percent of owners reported regularly discussing politics, but only 20 percent of renters said they did. Finally, twice as many homeowners—15 percent, versus only 8 percent of renters—reported that they contacted a political official in the last year.[14]

Although figure 4.1 shows that homeowners are substantially more likely to vote in elections and engage in other common acts of political participation than renters, the gap between homeowners and renters diminishes substantially when we account for other characteristics. Controlling for demographic differences, the darker bars in figure 4.2 report the odds that homeowners, relative to renters, engage in each of these political activities. Homeownership does increase the odds of voting in an election and attending a political meeting, as reported in figure 4.2. Homeowners are about one and half times

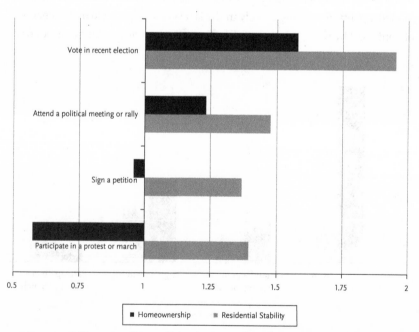

FIGURE 4.2. Odds ratios for participation in political activities. From the Social Capital Community Survey.

as likely to vote in an election, suggesting that electoral participation is a common way for homeowners to participate in politics. However, owning a home appears to decrease the likelihood of signing a petition and participating in a protest.

With the lighter bars, figure 4.2 also reports the odds that a neighborhood resident who has lived in her community for five years or more will engage in each political activity, relative to someone who has lived in her community for less than five years. Notably, for each measure of political participation in figure 4.2, residential stability is associated with an increased likelihood of political participation. Long-term residents are more likely to vote in elections, attend political meetings, and participate in forms of political protest than those who have more recently moved into their communities. This analysis reveals that residential stability uniformly increases political participation, but owning a home has a more targeted impact on only a handful of participation measures.

The analysis from the Current Population Survey corroborates the findings from the Social Capital Community Survey by confirming that owning a home is only a marginally important tool to encourage political engagement. Homeownership substantially increases the likelihood that citizens report voting in a local election, but it has only a slight impact on participation in other political activities, including contacting political officials and discussing politics regularly. Taken together, the analysis of political participation reveals that some of the initial differences between owners and renters are driven by other demographic characteristics, including higher rates of residential stability.

Community Involvement

Of course, political activities are not the only ways citizens get involved in their neighborhoods. When people want to deepen their involvement in their communities, there are lots of other ways to do so. They can go to community meetings, volunteer with local organizations, or work cooperatively with their neighbors on a community project. Each of these activities contributes to building the social connections at the center of robust community life.

Over the last decade, researchers at the Center for Community Capital at the University of North Carolina have been working to understand the way housing choices shape these types of activities. They have been following a group of low-income families through the Community Advantage Program Study, a study that looks at lending to low-income households and asks about the way homeownership impacts their everyday lives. Most of the low-income households in the study were living in neighborhoods with a large share of minority households, putting them at high risk for subprime lending in the years before the housing crisis. But with loans guaranteed through a nonprofit financial institution in Durham, North Carolina, the families in the study were able to purchase their homes with traditional, thirty-year mortgages.[15]

While the researchers at the Center for Community Capital were interested in how homeowners built financial capital, they also wanted to know whether homeownership helped to shape the way low-income households engaged in their communities. They asked whether owning a home had an impact on their community participation, including the types of organizations they joined or the way they interacted with other people in their neighborhoods. Through the study, the researchers could investigate whether homeownership—like other individual traits, including education or income—spurred citizens to become involved in their communities.[16]

When the researchers compared low-income homeowners and renters, they found that homeowners reported higher levels of neighborhood activism. Low-income homeowners reported stronger friendship networks than renters, and they were more likely to become involved in neighborhood groups. While these findings are important, one must take into account that this research focused on low-income homeowners and renters. As a result, it is not clear whether the findings from this research apply to other homeowners across the country, including more traditional homeowners. Despite a growing interest in the way homeownership shapes community engagement, there are only a handful of studies that actually look at the different ways homeowners and renters engage in membership groups and volunteer in their communities.[17]

Again, the Social Capital Community Survey offers a unique opportunity to extend these findings about low-income households to a more representative sample of the population. The survey asks citizens about several types of community involvement and, in doing so, recognizes the multiple ways that citizens get involved in their neighborhoods. If they want to improve their neighborhoods, or voice their opinions, they may decide to volunteer for a local organization, work cooperatively with their neighbors, or join neighborhood groups.

For each measure of community participation, homeowners are more active than renters. Nearly twice as many homeowners—38 versus 22 percent—report working on a community project (fig. 4.3). In the past year,

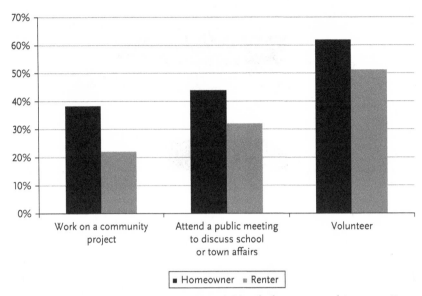

FIGURE 4.3. Participation in community activities, by homeownership status. From the Social Capital Community Survey.

nearly 44 percent of homeowners attended a community meeting to discuss school issues or town affairs, compared to only about 32 percent of renters. Sixty-two percent of homeowners—compared to just 51 percent of renters—report volunteering in their community.

Even when we account for other characteristics of homeowners and renters in the analysis of community engagement, owning a home continues to drive citizens to participate in some of these activities. The darker bars in figure 4.4 confirm that homeownership is associated with a large increase in the odds of working on a community project and attending a public meeting. In fact, homeowners are one and a half times as likely as demographically similar renters to work on a community project, and they are about 1.3 times as likely to attend a community meeting. However, owning a home does not have a big impact on the likelihood of a person volunteering in his or her community.

While figure 4.4 identifies a substantial impact of homeownership on community involvement, it also suggests that residential stability plays an important role in leading people to participate in community activities. Citizens who have lived in their neighborhoods for over five years are more than one and a half times as likely to work on a community project. And although homeownership does not lead people to volunteer, residential stability is an important predictor of participation in volunteer activities. Together, the findings from

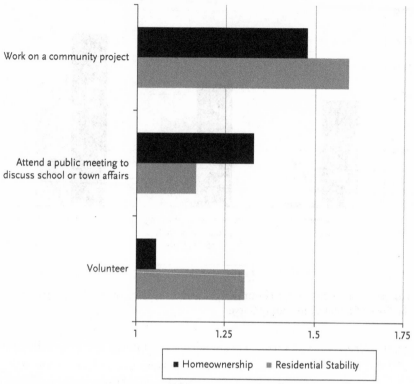

FIGURE 4.4. Odds ratios for participation in community activities. From the Social Capital Community Survey.

figure 4.4 show that both homeownership and residential stability lead citizens to get involved in their communities.

Although people often attend meetings or work cooperatively with their neighbors, these are not the only ways they become active in their neighborhood. Often, when they want to get involved in their community, citizens join membership groups—neighborhood associations, sports leagues, or church groups, for example. The Social Capital Community Survey asks citizens whether they participated in several types of membership groups in the previous year. I select five types of groups (table 4.1) to demonstrate the way homeownership and residential stability influence the types of membership groups that people join.

At first glance, homeowners do appear to be more active than renters in most types of groups (fig. 4.5). Twenty-two percent of homeowners report membership in both neighborhood associations and school groups. Only 16 percent of renters were active in neighborhood associations, and 18 percent of renters were active in school groups. About 15 percent of homeowners

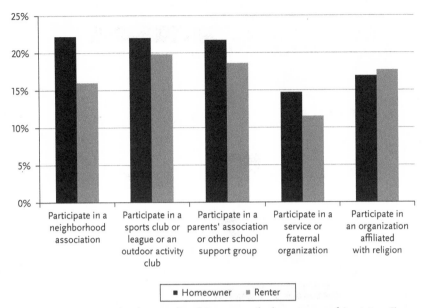

FIGURE 4.5. Participation in membership groups, by homeownership status. From the Social Capital Community Survey.

belonged to a service organization; only 12 percent of renters did. Homeowners were slightly more likely to report membership in sports groups but slightly less likely to report involvement in religious groups. Generally speaking, though, homeowners participated more actively in membership groups than renters.

However, it turns out that the unique impact of homeownership on many of these membership groups was quite limited. After controlling for individual characteristics, the darker bars reveal that owning a home really only increases the odds of participation in neighborhood groups (fig. 4.6). Homeowners may view this participation in neighborhood groups as a way to protect their property investments, unlike participation in other types of groups. However, for the other groups listed in figure 4.6, owning a home does not have a strong or significant impact on participation.

Yet, when we look at residential stability, a slightly different story emerges. The lighter bars in figure 4.6 confirm that living in a community for a long period of time is associated with membership in school groups. While stable households appear less likely to participate in neighborhood associations—a result that is driven largely by other aspects of homeownership—they are more likely to join groups that are involved with local schools. Notably, residential stability does not lead to much higher rates of participation in other types of

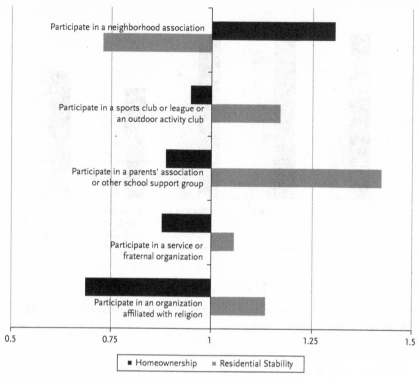

FIGURE 4.6. Odds ratios for participation in membership groups. From the Social Capital Community Survey.

groups. Still, this finding underscores the importance of paying attention to residential stability as a mechanism for enhanced citizenship separately from the financial incentives of owning a home.

Social Capital Resources

While membership groups are one way to build social networks and interact with people in the community, citizens often get to know their neighbors through more informal channels. They talk with them on the sidewalk or swap favors, like babysitting children or lending gardening tools. Although group participation often serves as a vehicle to resolve specific community problems, these informal interactions may actually be the glue that helps to strengthen neighborhood networks and build social bonds.

Several years ago, economist Grace Bucchianeri went to Franklin County, Ohio, to study the ways that women in the community interacted with their neighbors and built social capital. Hoping to understand differences between homeowners and renters, Bucchianeri asked individuals to keep track of their daily events, often tracking events at fifteen- or twenty-minute intervals. As they logged their everyday activities—watching television, socializing with neighbors, or going to the store, for example—they were also asked to describe how they felt about these activities. With this information, Bucchianeri was able to determine whether homeowners reported more frequent contact with their friends and neighbors and whether these interactions brought more positive feelings for owners than for renters.[18]

These impromptu interactions—the unexpected visits by neighbors or the ritual conversations on the street corner—form the building blocks of strong communities. They can help to deepen our attachments to the places where we live and generate feelings of collective efficacy in local neighborhoods. These interactions are often tied to social capital, too. "Social capital" refers to the way interpersonal resources, including social networks, friendships, and other neighborhood relationships, yield material benefits for individuals and households. When searching for a job, or looking for neighbors to help with childcare, people often turn to others they know in their neighborhoods. Knowing the neighbors can lessen concerns about crime in the community and often leads citizens to band together as they strive to improve neighborhood conditions, ultimately helping to reduce fear and mistrust. Although informal patterns of neighborliness may seem mundane, the interpersonal ties created through regular social interaction are often critical to vibrant communities.[19]

While proponents of ownership programs often consider homeownership to be the incubator of neighborly behavior, Bucchianeri found that homeowners and renters socialized in similar ways. The homeowners in her study reported spending about the same amount of time socializing with their friends and neighbors as comparable renters. They also expressed very similar feelings about these interactions, challenging the idea that owning a home is the pathway to creating stronger bonds among neighbors.

Extending these findings beyond Franklin County, the Social Capital Community Survey asks several questions about whether or not citizens socialize regularly with their neighbors. On first glance, homeowners appear to be better neighbors than renters. They are more likely to report working cooperatively with their neighbors and are more likely to socialize regularly with them. Thirty-four percent of homeowners—compared to only 24 percent of renters—report working with neighbors to fix something in their community. Half of homeowners—compared to only 42 percent of renters—socialize regularly with their neighbors, reporting that they talk with their neighbors at least once a week. And homeowners are more likely to report having visited

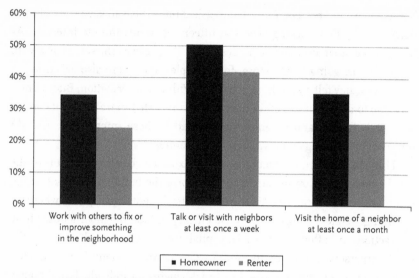

FIGURE 4.7. Participation in neighborly activities, by homeownership status. From the Social Capital Community Survey.

the homes of their neighbors. Thirty-five percent of homeowners have been in the home of a neighbor recently, compared to just 26 percent of renters (fig. 4.7).

However, after accounting for other demographic characteristics of homeowners and renters, the impact of homeownership on these measures of neighborliness largely disappears. Owning a home is associated with only a very small increase in the odds of interacting regularly with neighbors, as shown in the darker bars in figure 4.8. However, the lighter bars reveal that living in a community for five years or more leads to a significant increase in the odds of interacting regularly with neighbors. Residential stability substantially increases the odds of working collectively to improve the neighborhood or visiting neighbors in their homes. These important findings reveal that residential stability, rather than other aspects of homeownership, drives participation in neighborly activities.

While interacting regularly with neighbors is an important way citizens deepen the bonds of social capital, researchers also study trust to understand the strength of social ties in local communities. While broad social networks form the backbone of social capital, citizens need to maintain feelings of trust and reciprocity with their neighbors to meaningfully deploy this capital. These bonds of social trust are critical to organizing successful collective action in communities and yielding the material benefits often associated with social capital.[20]

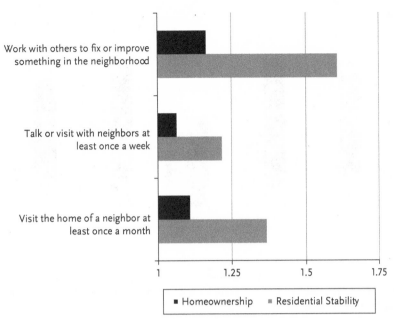

FIGURE 4.8. Odds ratios for participation in neighborly activities. From the Social Capital Community Survey.

There are several ways to measure social trust. One is a generalized measure of trust that asks individuals whether they generally believe that people can be trusted. Another is by asking about trust in specific groups—neighbors, coworkers, shopkeepers, and the police, for example. Together, these items from the Social Capital Community Survey—on generalized trust and particularized trust—help to identify whether homeownership yields greater trust within local communities.

In the simple comparison of homeowners and renters, homeowners are substantially more trusting than renters (fig. 4.9). Notably, 53 percent of homeowners report high levels of trust in their neighbors, compared to only about 23 percent of renters. They report higher levels of particularized trust in all social groups, including coworkers and the police in their community, and are substantially more likely to report that people can generally be trusted. Forty-seven percent of homeowners believe that people can generally be trusted, compared to just 33 percent of renters.

While it appears that homeownership increases feelings of social trust across groups, the analysis in figure 4.10 suggests that it does so only in limited ways. Controlling for other characteristics, the differences between homeowners and renters largely disappear. Homeownership does not substantially

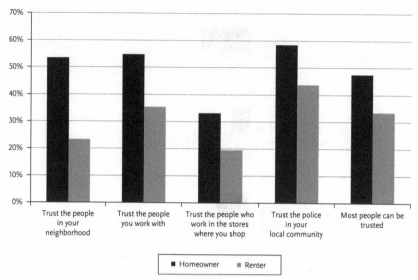

FIGURE 4.9. Indicators of social trust, by homeownership status. From the Social Capital Community Survey.

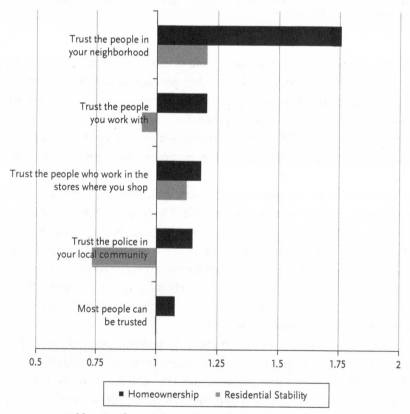

FIGURE 4.10. Odds ratios for social trust. From the Social Capital Community Survey.

increase the odds of reporting higher levels of generalized trust, nor does it lead to a meaningful increase in the odds of trusting shopkeepers, the police, and coworkers, as reported by the darker bars in figure 4.10. However, homeowners are substantially more trusting of the people in their neighborhoods. Owning a home increases the odds that a citizen will report high levels of trust in his or her neighbors, confirming that homeownership helps to build the bonds of social trust between neighbors. On the other hand, the lighter bars in figure 4.10 reveal that residential stability is not a strong predictor of social trust. While stability does lead to a small increase in the odds of trusting neighbors, it is otherwise not an important predictor of social trust for the other measures in figure 4.10.[21]

Civic Attitudes

While homeowners do report higher levels of trust in their neighbors, and long-term residents are more likely to interact regularly with the people in their neighborhood, these measures tell us only about very localized social interactions. In this final empirical section, I investigate broader measures of civic attitudes to understand the ways citizens evaluate their communities. Instead of looking at particular types of political participation or modes of community engagement, these measures identify whether homeowners generally feel more positively about the places they live or feel empowered to make changes in their neighborhoods. The questions from the Social Capital Community Survey investigate whether respondents believe that citizens will cooperate in the event of an emergency and whether they expect their communities to improve. Although they offer a less tangible account of the way homeowners participate in civic life, these indicators do tell us something about the way homeowners and renters feel about the neighborhoods and communities where they live.

Homeowners tend to report more positive feelings about their communities than renters (fig. 4.11). Nearly 45 percent of homeowners report that their community is an excellent place to live, but only 23 percent of renters do. About 37 percent of homeowners believe that they can have a big impact on their communities, compared to only 26 percent of renters. And homeowners are substantially more likely to report that people in their community would cooperate when asked by community leaders, and that the people running their communities care about them. Surprisingly, homeowners are no more likely than renters to believe that their community will improve over the next twelve months.

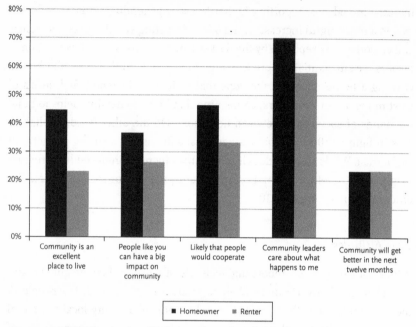

FIGURE 4.11. Civic attitudes, by homeownership status. From the Social Capital Community Survey.

After accounting for other characteristics of homeowners and renters, figure 4.12 shows that owning a home continues to explain some—but not all—of these differences. A homeowner is still more likely to rate his or her community as an excellent place to live and slightly more likely to believe that people can have a big impact on the neighborhoods where they live. Likewise, owning a home leads to a slight increase in the odds that a citizen expects his or her neighbors to cooperate when asked to do so by community leaders. However, homeowners are no more likely than renters to report that community leaders care about them or that their communities will improve. Taken together, figure 4.12 reveals that homeowners do feel positively about their communities but that owning a home is associated with a limited increase in feelings of community attachment.

On the other hand residential stability does not meaningfully increase the odds of reporting positive feelings of community attachment for any of the measures in figure 4.12. In fact, people who have lived in their communities for a long period of time are generally less likely to believe that their community is an excellent place to live and less likely to report that their community is improving.

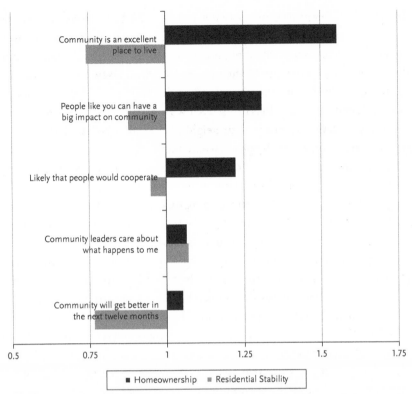

FIGURE 4.12. Odds ratios for civic attitudes. From the Social Capital Community Survey.

Rethinking the Civic Habits of Homeowners

When President Clinton introduced the National Homeownership Strategy, he set out to remind Americans about the enduring civic promise of owning a home. While homeownership had grown central to building wealth in the United States, the president also wanted Americans to consider the power of homeownership to transform citizens into more active, engaged community members. In doing so, he joined a long lineage of his predecessors in touting the civic benefits of homeownership. Owning a home promised to strengthen community life and encourage the formation of good citizenship, he noted as he introduced the National Homeownership Strategy.

But, as it turns out, these claims about homeownership as a tool for investing citizens in their communities are only partially true. While homeownership is often invoked as a panacea for declining social capital, the analysis of civic participation tells a more nuanced story—a story that shows ownership driving involvement in some activities but not in others. Homeowners are more politically active than renters, but they engage in only a narrow range of political activities. They vote more often—especially in local elections—and they are slightly more likely to attend political rallies. Likewise, homeowners are more engaged in neighborhood groups than renters, and they are more likely to attend public meetings to discuss town and school affairs. Homeowners report higher levels of trust in their neighbors, and they believe that they can have a positive impact on the places where they live.

These limited forms of community involvement should give us pause as we reflect on the power of homeownership to transform civic habits. As I will show in the next chapter, these forms of participation are often geared at protecting homeowners' largest investment—their homes. When homeowners attend a community meeting or vote in a local election, they often do so as a way to protect their neighborhoods from changes that they fear will lower property values. These instrumental acts of community engagement emphasize their narrow interests as property owners and corroborate anecdotal accounts about the selective participation of homeowners in civic life.

Beyond this narrow set of activities, homeowners and renters behave quite similarly in their communities. After accounting for education, age, and other characteristics, it turns out that owning a home does not have much of an impact on other measures of community involvement. Homeowners do not join sports groups or religious groups at higher rates than renters. They are more likely to rate their community as an excellent place to live, but they are no more likely than renters to believe that it is improving. On its own, homeownership does not increase the odds of volunteering in a community, nor does it increase the likelihood that one will interact informally with one's neighbors. And although homeowners are more likely to trust their neighbors, they are no more likely to extend that trust to other social groups. Looking broadly across the measures of civic involvement, it turns out that homeowners are not the widely active, deeply engaged citizens we often make them out to be.

Still, the chapter adds another wrinkle to the story about homeownership. By examining the impact of long-term stability on civic involvement, I show that citizens who live in their communities for at least five years often engage more actively in the many of the informal activities central to vibrant community life. For example, residential stability increases the likelihood that a citizen will volunteer in her community. A citizen who lives in his neighborhood for at least five years is more likely to participate in many of the informal acts of neighborliness, including visiting his neighbors' homes and working cooperatively to fix something. Stability is associated with higher levels of participation in school groups and increased participation on community projects. By adding this piece to the story of homeownership, I underscore the importance of investigating the influence of residential stability as a separate tool for building stronger communities—a point I return to in chapter 6.

Even with a detailed analysis of the civic habits of homeowners, this chapter has told only part of the story. It tells us about the way homeowners participate in their communities—the types of groups they join, the types of political activities in which they become involved, and the types of social capital they begin to build—and about the role of residential stability in shaping participation apart from the contours of homeownership. However, the analysis in this chapter doesn't tell us anything about the impact of homeowners' participation on the communities where they live. What are the consequences of their engagement in public life? How does their participation in the routines of civic life shape their neighborhoods? Do homeowners contribute to building stronger, more inclusive communities?

Rescaling the analysis to the level of the community, the next chapter asks about the way homeowners transform the places where they live. Notably, when political leaders talk about higher levels of community involvement, they often suggest that this engagement is inherently good. Participating in community life helps to create shared interests and identities in local communities and teaches us to value different opinions as we interact with people from diverse backgrounds, or so the story goes. However, when homeowners engage in their communities, they often do so with a singular goal in mind— to protect their property values. Their participation in local politics elevates their interests as property owners above other community interests, often trumping other important issues in community politics and civic life. Through a series of case studies, the next chapter asks what happens to communities when homeowners get involved as a way of protecting their largest financial investments. It challenges the idea that expanding homeownership necessarily helps to create stronger, more resilient communities, as proponents of federal homeownership policies often claim.

5

BUILDING COMMUNITY?

HOMEOWNERSHIP AND THE POLITICS OF EXCLUSION

In Winnetka, Illinois, an affluent Chicago suburb on the shores of Lake Michigan, residents spent several years debating a proposal for the construction of affordable housing in their town. Responding to a state law mandating greater parity in affordable housing across municipalities, local Winnetka officials began discussing the creation of a land trust in 2005. The trust would purchase local housing, rehabilitating the units to increase the supply available to low- and middle-income families. When the units were finished, rental housing would be available to families earning about $45,000, and homeownership units would be marketed to families earning $75,000–$105,000.[1]

By all accounts, affordable housing is hard to come by in Winnetka, as it is in many cities and towns across the country. Winnetka is among the most expensive places to live in the Chicago metropolitan area. More than 90 percent of families own their own homes, and the median home value exceeds $900,000. As a result, there are few options for middle-class families and even fewer for those looking to rent their homes. Recognizing the challenges of finding decent, affordable housing, proponents of the land trust hoped that their affordable housing plan would enable teachers, policemen, and shop owners to live in the community where they worked.[2]

Many residents of Winnetka quickly balked at the affordable housing plan, fearful of the types of neighbor that subsidized housing would attract. If the town went forward with the land trust, rental units would be marketed to families making just below the median household income in America—about $53,000, according to the most recent Census estimates. But in Winnetka, the median household income exceeds $200,000—nearly four times the national average. Few families in the town would be eligible for the affordable housing, and the prospect of more renters raised the possibility of inviting "second-class citizens" into the tightly knit community.

Opposition to the affordable housing plan was swift and fierce. Under the banner of the Winnetka Homeowners Association (WHOA), a loosely organized group of residents commenced a campaign against the land trust. Concerned about both the mandate from the state to construct affordable housing and the impact of affordable housing on their suburban community, the group distributed a twenty-five-page publication to village residents, hammering home its opposition to the affordable housing plan. With testimonies from local homeowners, the publication raised the specter of higher crime and lower property values in Winnetka, demonizing renters as pariahs.[3]

Leafing through the publication, you begin to sense the breadth of opposition from many of Winnetka's homeowners to the construction of affordable housing. One contributor called the plan an "un-American, untested and unconstitutional vision of housing utopia," warning about the negative impact of building affordable housing. Drawing on familiar tropes about "affordable" housing in the United States, a handful of residents likened the proposed housing to Cabrini Green, the infamous 3,600-unit public housing development that was recently torn down in Chicago. "Stop that thought," wrote one resident in the WHOA newspaper. "They have cleaned up Cabrini Green, now you want Winnetka Green."[4]

Overlooking the fact that housing units would be available for middle-income households, another contributor described her experience living in mixed-income housing in Chicago, noting that affordable housing would change the social composition of their affluent town. On the basis of her experience, she cautioned against the influx of renters by sounding the alarm about "the friends and relatives of the tenants: the crack head that is the father of one of their six kids…the boyfriend who just got out of jail and needs a place to crash, or his cell mate that got out early and needs a place to stay…the cousin who's on house arrest for a sex crime—living on a common wall with your 5 year old." If the residents of Winnetka allowed affordable housing to be built in their community, they would soon encounter these types of neighbors as they went about their daily lives.

Many contributors to the paper worried that affordable housing would create noticeable changes in the community itself, lowering property values or increasing crime. "I developed and managed affordable housing," wrote one resident in the WHOA newspaper. "Unfortunately, it brings crime, vandalism and loss of property values to the community." Another resident noted that the village "cannot afford another property depreciating hit," highlighting a common concern among homeowners. Without much input into the implementation plan, they worried that affordable housing would drive down property values in their community.[5]

As a matter of principle, many of the citizens in Winnetka did not oppose the construction of affordable housing. Although some objected to the perceived intrusion of the state government into local decisions, the majority focused their opposition on the location of affordable housing in *their* community—a classic strategy of Not in My Back Yard (NIMBY) politics. With some regularity, citizens pointed to other nearby towns as places with a sufficient supply of affordable housing. "Northfield, Glenview and Wilmette all have areas that can accommodate any income bracket," wrote one local resident, referring to inland communities west of Winnetka. "There is plenty of affordable housing on the North Shore," wrote another, buoying his objection by arguing that the current residents of Winnetka didn't need affordable housing. And summing up the position of WHOA, Carry Buck, the president of the group, told a reporter for the *Chicago Tribune*: "There is plenty of affordable housing in neighboring communities."[6]

In communities across the country, people often join groups and launch protests to stop proposed developments in their neighborhoods. Concerned about the negative impact of these developments on their communities, they sign petitions, attend town meetings, and participate in protests or demonstrations to make their voices heard. But as the discussion over affordable housing unfolded in Winnetka, it highlighted the outsized role that homeowners play in local politics. As WHOA emerged as the leading voice of opposition to the plan, the group focused discussions about affordable housing on issues that were centrally important to the community's homeowners, including the possibility that the affordable housing plan would lead to falling property values and attract more renters into their neighborhood. While the discussion about property values highlights a real concern among homeowners, it also provides a coded language for residents to express fears about perceived racial change or economic decline in their communities. Discussions of property values are often a publicly acceptable way for residents to talk more broadly about neighborhood change.

In this chapter, I argue that homeowners in Winnetka engaged in the politics of exclusion as they worked to resist changes that they perceived to be threatening to their town. In the narrowest analysis, "politics of exclusion" refers to the ways that citizens actively work to keep others from living in their community. This could include efforts to prevent certain groups—for example, the homeless or low-income renters—from finding adequate housing in the neighborhood, or efforts to make these groups feel unwelcome in the community.[7]

Drawing on several case studies, I present the politics of exclusion more broadly, arguing that homeowners also engage in the politics of exclusion by subtly demarcating which citizens have a right to participate in public life. When they become involved in their communities, homeowners often elevate the concerns of property owners above other community issues and reinforce stereotypes about renters as unfit for public life. For example, homeowners frequently legitimize their standing in public meetings by referencing their status as taxpayers, reflexively reifying stereotypes about renters as uninterested in community affairs. They reframe public discussions of the common good to narrowly focus on their interests as property owners, thereby reinforcing existing boundaries of segregation between homeowners and renters. By crafting a narrow vision of the community good that privileges property values over other community concerns, I argue that homeowners narrow the opportunity for meaningful political dialogue and exclude renters from engaging as full participants in community affairs.

Critically, these arguments about the politics of exclusion run counter to the way we typically think about community engagement and the public good. We tend to think of participation in the routine acts of civic engagement described in the previous chapter—things like attending public meetings, joining neighborhood groups, or volunteering in one's community—as the currency of active citizenship and tightly knit neighborhoods. Citizens learn to trust one another by participating regularly in their communities, strengthening the social bonds that tie them to their neighbors. As a result, neighborhoods are more resilient, and the practice of democracy is more robust, when citizens are actively engaged in the places where they live.

Yet, as anyone who has attended a town meeting or joined a local political protest knows, civic engagement can be a contentious activity. Participation in public meetings can magnify competing interests, leading a handful of citizens to take an outsized role in local politics. When a small number of voices dominate community affairs, they risk drowning out more diverse ideas that would contribute to a shared vision for the community, creating neighborhoods that are less democratic than they would otherwise be.

Building from the previous chapter, which showed that homeowners are more likely to engage in particular community activities, I rescale the analysis in this chapter to investigate the consequences of their heightened engagement for the neighborhoods where they live. In our rush to celebrate homeowners by lauding their contribution to more active, engaged communities, we have failed to acknowledge that their involvement can lead to communities that are more exclusive. Drawing from a handful of case studies across the country, I analyze homeowners' involvement through the framework of exclusionary politics, investigating what happens when a single class of citizens becomes involved in a specific set of activities to protect a narrow set of interests.

Through this analysis of the politics of exclusion, I advance a theory of NIMBY politics centered on the role of homeowners in community life.[8]

Participation and Public Life

As the citizens of Winnetka debated the proposal for affordable housing, they engaged in the acts of participation typically claimed to be the centerpiece of vibrant public life. They spoke at community meetings and joined local organizations, coming together with their neighbors to voice their opinions about affordable housing in Winnetka. Town meetings drew unexpectedly large crowds into the public debate, and WHOA emerged as the primary group through which local residents expressed their opposition. Through the local newspaper, WHOA created a space for residents who were too busy to attend local meetings to voice their concerns.

We often consider this type of participation in public life—and, specifically, participation through membership groups—to be the backbone of strong communities. In a review of research on membership group participation, political scientist Margaret Kohn notes that political theorists have traditionally treated these voluntary organizations positively, highlighting the ways they strengthen social ties among individuals living in a community. "They strengthen social bonds, build community, foster civic skills, and provide opportunities for collective action," she writes. This classic formulation treats participation as a public good—a way to build communities, to strengthen relationships between neighbors, and to engage citizens in the democratic process.[9]

Contemporary discussions of community engagement and public life often use the publication of *Bowling Alone* by political scientist Robert Putnam as their launching point to describe changing patterns of civic engagement in the United States. Published nearly two decades ago, *Bowling Alone* sounded the alarm that Americans were engaging less and less in community life. Reiterating the classic position on participation and public life, Putnam argued that social capital built through frequent group participation is critical for healthy, democratic, and lively communities. When citizens regularly interact, they are able to resolve collective action dilemmas. They build neighborhood-level social trust and grow increasingly aware of their shared fate when they live in communities with high levels of social capital. As Putnam puts it, "social capital makes us smarter, healthier, safer, richer, and better able to govern a just and stable democracy."[10]

How is social capital built through community engagement, and why is it so important for the creation of healthy communities? How does participation in the routine acts of citizenship—from joining local groups to attending public meetings—help to build social capital and contribute to the creation of strong neighborhoods? One possibility is through the development of civic skills. When citizens participate in the political process or engage with community organizations, they learn the vocabulary of democracy. They begin to understand the structures of government—the way governing institutions function and the relationships between key political actors. Their participation teaches them new strategies for navigating institutional bureaucracies and demanding responses from their political leaders. These civic skills deepen their engagement as citizens, ultimately leading to governments that are more responsive to the needs and demands of local constituencies.[11]

While civic participation teaches citizens how to engage in the governing process, it also helps them to build social relationships in their communities. As they become involved in public life, they develop social networks and deepen the bonds of social trust—both critical ingredients in the development of strong communities. In his work on Chicago neighborhoods, sociologist Robert Sampson identifies these social capital resources as a key component of collective efficacy, or the feeling that neighbors can achieve shared goals in their communities. In tightly knit neighborhoods, citizens watch out for one another. They informally police the social mores of neighborhood children and work together to fix community problems. As Sampson and others have shown, collective efficacy is associated with lower levels of criminal activity and improved public behavior. Broad informal networks built through sustained community engagement create places that are safer, healthier, and more cohesive.[12]

In neighborhoods with well-developed cultures of participation, citizens can strengthen their shared identities by participating in the routine acts of civic engagement. In this normative vision of citizenship, people enter the public sphere as equal political actors to voice their concerns, share their ideas, and discuss the future of their communities. By engaging openly in the democratic process, they reach political consensus and find common ground, developing a shared identity through their sustained public engagement. While these deliberative processes form the foundation for collective action, they also become places for participants to develop shared identities as citizens, discovering common goals and interests as they come together as members of a single community.[13]

Bullish about the promise of community engagement, proponents of deliberative democracy view sustained participation as the solution to Americans' diminishing faith in the democratic process. Today, Americans are increasingly skeptical that democracy functions to serve the interests of the people.

Surveys report declining trust in democratic institutions, reflecting concerns about unresponsive governments, institutional barriers to participation, and the growing concentration of power in the hands of elites relative to regular citizens. But against this crisis of citizenship, in which individuals have lost faith in their government and report lower levels of institutional trust, social capital theorists often tout grassroots participation in the routines of governing as a tool for reinvesting citizens in their communities. Proponents expect that renewed participation will strengthen democracy, counteract the institutional corruption of the political system, and empower citizens to shape the communities where they live. By sharpening residents' civic skills, deepening their social bonds, and identifying their shared interests, this type of engaged participation holds the promise of renewing democracy at the local level.

Focusing on neighborhoods in Chicago, political scientist Archon Fung makes a case for recommitting ourselves to the grassroots practices of democracy to solve local problems. He stresses the participatory angle of citizen involvement, suggesting that empowered participation strengthens place-based attachments in local communities and gives citizens a true voice in local issues, like public education and policing strategies. Along with sociologist Erik Olin Wright, Fung labels this sustained, engaged involvement as "empowered deliberative democracy," using Chicago neighborhoods to illustrate the promise of renewed democracy and self-government that results from sustained forms of community engagement.[14]

Yet these classic accounts of social capital and civic engagement in public life, which paint an overwhelmingly positive account, overlook contrasting ways that engagement can impact communities. These accounts sometimes fail to distinguish between types of social capital or the varying interests that motivate citizens to become involved in their communities. For example, we can distinguish between bonding social capital and bridging social capital. The former describes a process of strengthening relationships between people who already share an identity or a set of attributes. Joining a church group can help to tighten social bonds between members of a religious congregation, and entering into a professional organization—a union or business association, for example—can create resources for workers in a shared profession. Bridging social capital, on the other hand, builds connections across social boundaries. When economically diverse neighbors come together to discuss criminal activity in their community or couples with children interact with childless ones through local service organizations, they are bridging boundaries to deepen their social capital.[15]

Although social capital built through civic participation can lead to stronger communities, it can also reify political divisions and reinforce existing power imbalances. Diverging sharply from the canonical view of civic engagement, a small body of research suggests that social capital built through civic engagement does not always contribute to the formation of more inclusive, democratic communities. When citizens participate in public life, they can do so as a way of putting specific interests ahead of the public good. Their engagement may make it difficult for other actors to engage in the political process, ultimately deepening existing patterns of exclusion and social divisions. In their book *Democratizing Inequalities,* sociologists Caroline Lee, Michael McQuarrie, and Edward Walker bring together a set of essays to probe the way that growing inequalities and political polarization shape patterns of public participation. Instead of simply celebrating the transformative promise of participation, they argue for an agenda that pays attention to the way existing inequalities shape participation and, in turn, the role of participation in reinforcing these entrenched patterns of inequality. This critical perspective acknowledges the possibility that community participation can serve as a tool for maintaining existing structures of social inequality and reinforcing the boundaries of power in local communities.[16]

Confronted with the possibility that civic engagement is not universally good for communities, we are left to consider the dark side of participation. While citizen engagement can contribute to deliberative democracy, it can also heighten extreme voices or reinforce political divisions. When fringe political groups dominate public discourse or community actors with a narrow set of interests set the tone for political deliberations, they limit the opportunities for citizens to productively come together and reach consensus in the public sphere. Pushing beyond the celebratory vision of social capital as the antidote for declining community life, this research accounts for the way public engagement prioritizes specific interests or drowns out particular voices, increasing political inequality or loosening the bonds of social cohesion.[17]

Writing about the dark side of community participation, political scientist Morris Fiorina offers an instructive anecdote regarding a conflict in his hometown, Concord, Massachusetts. Recounting a storyline familiar to almost anyone who has engaged in local politics, Fiorina describes plans by a local private high school, Middlesex, to expand its athletic facilities into a nearby nature conservation area. Although most of the town supported the moderate plans for expansion, including Fiorina himself, he describes how the debate over the expansion plan was overtaken by a small—but vocal—group of citizens who opposed it. He recounts a costly and exhaustive process of winning approval for the expansion plan as a small number of citizens worked tirelessly to stop it.[18]

This story of an otherwise mundane conflict in Concord, Massachusetts is instructive for considering the relationship between homeownership, civic engagement, and community life. Recounting the conflict over the expansion of Middlesex, Fiorina identifies two perspectives on this local struggle. To some observers, the conflict over the growth of Middlesex represents the essence of functioning, grassroots democracy. Citizens were empowered to voice their opinions, and the political process accounted for those voices in the final process. Although the expansion of the school was delayed as citizens voiced their concerns, the process ultimately accounted for the diversity of voices in the Concord community. But for others, the debate in Concord was a classic example of hijacked democracy. A vocal minority, willing to derail the will of the majority of people, pushed their interests above those of the rest of the citizenry. This account identifies the way a small set of voices overwhelmed those of a larger group of citizens in deciding the future of their community. To many observers, the struggles in Concord—and similar struggles in communities across the country—expose the dark side of civic engagement.

Participation and the Politics of Exclusion

Twenty miles south of Winnetka, the Chicago neighborhood of North Kenwood-Oakland has been experiencing a dramatic renaissance. As middle-class African-Americans moved back to the city, North Kenwood-Oakland underwent a gradual process of gentrification. Long-term renters were soon living side by side with recent homebuyers, creating daily struggles as neighbors worked to create a community that fulfilled the needs of both long-term residents and recent homebuyers alike.

In her book *Black on the Block,* sociologist Mary Pattillo meticulously tells the transformative story of this Chicago neighborhood, focusing on the dual role of middle-class African-American homeowners in the community. Valuing the heritage and history of the predominantly African-American community, they used their financial resources and social capital to preserve the integrity of the neighborhood. Yet when they chose to move to North Kenwood-Oakland, they also made a financial investment in that community. As homeowners, they advocated for neighborhood changes with an eye toward protecting the value of their housing investment. As she describes community discussions over the future of public housing and the pressures of economic development, Pattillo identifies the dual role that African-American homeowners play in the North Kenwood-Oakland neighborhood.[19]

To underscore the struggles in the neighborhood, Pattillo describes her own involvement in the community after moving to North Kenwood-Oakland.

Soon after arriving in the neighborhood, she joined the Conservation Community Council, a local organization that evaluates land-use and development decisions. Through her careful ethnographic account of her time on the Council, Pattillo describes the ways that homeowners shaped neighborhood debates about affordable housing, gentrification, and economic development, identifying the outsized role that homeowners played in these discussions. Their voices were considered disproportionately in public meetings and through local community groups. They often justified their position by pointing to their role as taxpayers in the local community. And while they frequently used their social networks and political capital to advocate for longtime neighborhood residents, many of whom lacked the political voice that middle-class homeowners brought to local politics, they were also concerned about the stability and growth of their community. They had invested in North Kenwood-Oakland both as community residents *and* as property owners. Although they believed in the importance of thriving African-American neighborhoods, their pro-development advocacy occasionally pitted them against long-term residents, especially low-income renters in the community.

Offering examples of the types of decisions faced by local homeowners, Pattillo points to the complexities of civic involvement for homeowners who had recently moved into North Kenwood-Oakland. "She might be the head of a community organization that gets a large foundation grant, which requires that her organization implement a vision of community improvement emphasizing home ownership over affordable rental housing," Pattillo writes, identifying the types of challenges that homeowners may encounter as middlemen in a gentrifying neighborhood. "He might be a resident who works to rid the main street of businesses that have not maintained their awnings or signs in favor of newer chain stores that offer premier services at prices that are prohibitive for families on fixed or assisted incomes." Through their involvement in community groups and neighborhood organizations, homeowners are often forced to embrace conflicting roles in the community. They advocate for community changes to advance their interests as property owners while at the same time working to preserve the historical integrity and economic diversity of the neighborhood. However, many of the decisions that raise their property values do not benefit their low-income neighbors—and may in fact make it increasingly difficult for them to stay in North Kenwood-Oakland.[20]

Of course, community conflicts are rarely as straightforward as homeowners gaining at the expense of renters, or newcomers triumphing over long-term residents. In fact, many of the changes in neighborhoods like North Kenwood-Oakland create benefits that are shared by all local residents, regardless of their housing status. Projects to beautify the neighborhood or decrease criminal activity bring changes shared widely by neighborhood residents, and improvements to local schools create opportunities for neighborhood children, regardless of whether they live in homes that their parents own or rent.

Still, the importance of property values for middle-class homeowners in North Kenwood-Oakland marginalized low-income homeowners and long-term renters, threatening the stability of low- and moderate-income families in the neighborhood. "[These families] are targeted by investors who hassle unsuspecting home owners to sell at low prices; they are victimized by subprime lenders who see the potential profits when someone forecloses; and they are subject to the higher property tax levy which is especially onerous for residents with fixed and/or low incomes," Pattillo notes. As they advocate for projects and developments that they expect to improve their property values, homeowners contribute to the worsening of the crisis of housing affordability in American cities. They encourage investments that raise property values, even though soaring property values make neighborhoods less affordable for many low-income households. They may balk at the prospect of public or supportive housing initiatives in their communities, even though affordable housing initiatives frequently benefit long-term neighborhood residents. With an eye toward protecting and defending the value of their homes, homeowners simultaneously narrow the possibilities for creating a more inclusive, democratic community.[21]

While Mary Pattillo provides an unusually nuanced view of the struggles in North Kenwood-Oakland, these types of community development conflicts are common across the country. Several years ago, residents of the Los Angeles community of Santa Monica objected to plans for the construction of a modern housing structure behind one of the neighborhood's historic beachfront bungalows. They worried that the out-of-context development would open the door for other property owners to develop buildings that ignored the architectural integrity of their beachfront community. These non-conforming buildings would threaten property values in the Santa Monica community by changing the historic character of their neighborhood. Like preservation advocates around the country, they sought to maintain the historic character of their neighborhood and minimize construction that might negatively impact housing values in their community. While historic preservation policies typically raise property values, they also make it harder to build additional housing units or to find affordable housing in a historic neighborhood.[22]

And since 2009, neighbors in the wealthy Westchester County suburb of Chappaqua north of New York City have been actively resisting the construction of an affordable housing development. The proposed development was to be built on an overgrown, unused property close to the highway. "In a weed-covered, third-of-an-acre patch...squeezed between Metro-North Railroad tracks, an exit ramp off the Saw Mill Parkway, and a stone bridge over the tracks," wrote one reporter, a local developer planned to construct Chappaqua Station, a modest four-story building. The project would help Westchester County to comply with a desegregation agreement reached with the Department of Housing and Urban Development several years earlier. But in a community made up overwhelmingly of wealthy homeowners, residents grew concerned about the financial consequences of affordable housing. Today, the community remains split on the issue, delaying plans for affordable housing in Chappaqua. This resistance to the construction of affordable housing on the outskirts of major cities contributes to the growing crisis of housing affordability, especially in high-priced cities, like New York and San Francisco.[23]

Often the politics of exclusion are subtler, as homeowners work to label renters as unfit for participation in community politics and civic life. In her book *Behind the White Picket Fence*, sociologist Sarah Mayorga-Gallo illustrates the ways that homeowners in Durham, North Carolina, presented renters as second-class citizens in their own community. As she talked to people in a multiethnic neighborhood of homeowners and renters, Mayorga-Gallo found surprisingly little social integration in a community that, from the outside, appeared to be integrated. Confronting deeply racialized undertones throughout her fieldwork, she points to coded ways that homeowners talked about the renters, portraying them as unfit for participation in the routines of neighborhood life. "White residents described how they labeled renters as disinvested, while Black residents explained how they were ignored by their neighbors because of their skin color and (presumed or real) housing tenure," writes Mayorga-Gallo, explaining how homeowners symbolically exclude renters in their day-to-day activities. She goes on to acknowledge the enduring biases that privilege homeownership in national political discourse, linking these biases to her findings in the Durham neighborhood. "There is a very strong anti-renter bias that prevails in our national conversations on housing, particularly in regard to lower-income renters and renters of color," she writes, arguing that we must work to reframe renting as a dignified housing option.[24]

Homeowners at the Helm of NIMBY Politics

The stories of political conflict in local communities are often classified under the broader banner of NIMBY politics. These stories are typically framed as conflicts between the parochial interests of local citizens and the broader common good. On one hand, proponents of these developments, including policymakers or urban planners, highlight the social good that will result from them. When they make decisions to construct affordable housing in particular neighborhoods or locate undesirable land uses in them, they appeal to the importance of these services beyond the neighborhood itself. Each neighborhood needs to shoulder its share of these developments, as broader constituencies benefit from affordable housing construction or the preservation of historic neighborhoods. Policymakers often highlight the common good, or the broad set of benefits that will result from these planning and land-use decisions.[25]

On the other hand, when citizens engage in local protests to preserve or protect their neighborhoods, they are quick to appeal to their specific interests as neighborhood residents. They object to changes in the historical character of their community, or the construction of affordable housing developments that they expect to lower their property values. And while protecting their housing investments is often the primary reason that citizens engage in these activities, they may also be concerned about other changes in their community.

While the debates over NIMBY politics acknowledge the competing interests that citizens bring to local conflicts, they tend to overlook the outsized role that homeowners play in these struggles. Relying on many of the participation tools that I identified in the previous chapter, homeowners attend local community meetings, vote in local elections, and work together to stop developments that they perceive to be harmful to their communities. These anecdotes about NIMBY politics corroborate a growing body of research identifying the ways that homeowners engage in their communities.[26]

In New York City—a city made up overwhelmingly of renters—homeowners wield disproportionate influence in the local political decisionmaking. Recently, law professor Vicki Been and her colleagues examined decisions to rezone local neighborhoods across the city. Neighborhoods could either be up-zoned, allowing for developers to build taller buildings, or down-zoned, restricting additional development activity. Homeowners typically support efforts to down-zone neighborhoods in order to keep new, out-of-context developments from their communities. Developers, on the other hand, are generally supportive of efforts to up-zone neighborhoods. Guided by Fischel's homevoter hypothesis, Been and her colleagues found that homeowners are powerful actors in urban politics, successfully achieving down-zoning as they work to shape the characteristics of their neighborhoods.[27]

This type of local activism contributes to the politics of exclusion by reinforcing symbolic boundaries between owners and renters. While one approach to understanding exclusionary politics identifies the tactics used to deliberately exclude certain types of people from living in communities, I argue for a framing of the politics of exclusion that highlights ways that citizens work to demarcate the boundaries of inclusionary citizenship. When homeowners assert their right to participate, they often marginalize renters from public debates about the future of their community. This engagement sharpens existing divisions within neighborhoods by reinforcing long-standing political divisions between homeowners and renters. And when they prioritize property values over other community issues, homeowners contribute to the politics of exclusion by narrowing opportunities for robust political discussions, reinforcing symbolic dimensions of segregation in their neighborhoods. In conflicts over affordable housing, like the ones in Winnetka and Chappaqua, examining the role of homeowners in the politics of NIMBYism provides an opportunity for a deeper analysis of how housing choices influence local politics.

While there were not many renters in Winnetka to speak on behalf of the affordable housing proposals, there were plenty of citizens who were supportive of the affordable housing proposals. However, the leaders of WHOA marginalized these voices as they dominated public conversations on the issue. As the group's leaders distributed their newspaper across the community, WHOA quickly emerged as the leading public voice in discussions of affordable housing. Their leaders were quoted frequently in local papers, including the *Chicago Tribune*, and an active Listserv regularly updated Winnetka residents on the progress of their campaign. Soon, residents across the community were inundated with updates from WHOA in their mailboxes, in their inboxes, and in public forums. As they led the opposition to the land trust, WHOA created an important forum for homeowners concerned about the impact of affordable housing developments in Winnetka.

But to many residents in Winnetka, the prominence of WHOA narrowed opportunities for robust political engagement. Although the group implicitly claimed to speak for the town's homeowners, many citizens objected to the tactics and tone the group adopted. In particular, homeowners with opposing viewpoints, including those supportive of the affordable housing plan, often felt unwelcome in the public sphere. Without the resources to build a comparable organizational infrastructure or to respond to the barrage of claims by the leaders of WHOA, they felt overmatched and outmaneuvered in their public engagement. As WHOA emerged as the leading voice of opposition, implicitly claiming to speak for the entire set of homeowners in Winnetka, it narrowed the space for other citizens to weigh in on the plan for affordable housing.

And while the encounters in North Kenwood-Oakland were less contentious than the struggle over affordable housing in Winnetka, they similarly underscore the outsized role homeowners play in setting the public agenda. Mary Pattillo describes how, as she became involved in local community organizations, the interests of homeowners reshaped community relations in her neighborhood, narrowing the possibilities for developing competing voices. "The balance of power in neighborhood decision making favors home owners," she observed. "Their values and norms about appropriate neighborhood decorum are most audibly expressed, and they frequently invoke their status as taxpayers to legiti-mate their demands for action. Home-owning newcomers and their old-timer allies translate their economic power into political voice." Again, through their participation in neighborhood groups, homeowners shape the public discussion to reflect their concerns as property owners. They legitimize their participation by pointing to their status as taxpayers and, in doing so, narrow the set of voices with legitimate claims to participate in the public sphere. Although we rarely think of homeowners' voices as extreme or their demands as unreasonable, these stories suggest that their outsized participation in the public sphere can keep other citizens from making their voices heard.[28]

Of course, homeowners are not exclusively concerned about their property values. When they enter the public arena, they do so with multiple (and often competing) goals for their community. This was clear in North Kenwood-Oakland. Homeowners there purchased homes because they valued living in a historically African-American neighborhood. Like renters, they care about crime rates, proximity to stores, and the availability of parkland because they live in the neighborhood, and their involvement works to improve features of the neighborhood that impact their daily lives. But, as I argued in the previous chapter, homeowners also recognize that these amenities raise the value of their homes. When they become involved in their communities, they also pri-oritize the importance of their homes as financial investments, advocating narrowly for policies expected to raise the values of these investments and resisting changes that would create uncertainty in housing prices. In doing so, homeowners push property values to the forefront of public discussions, creating a narrative in which property values trump other community issues.[29]

Putting property values at the center of public discussions curtails the pos-sibility of citizens engaging more broadly in deliberations about the common good. Classic accounts imagine civic engagement as an opportunity for citizens to come together and deliberate about their shared future, compromising their own narrow interests for the larger good of their community. Alexis de Tocqueville, one of the earliest observers of civic life in the United States, described this tendency toward "self-interest, rightly-understood," as one of the defining features of associational life in the United States. Touring the United States in the early nineteenth century, Tocqueville was struck by the way Americans engaged in voluntary organizations to advance a common good, praising their persistence in pursuing their own interests while simultaneously sacrificing for the benefit of their community.[30]

But with the growing importance of housing values to American homeowners, this issue of property ownership trumps other community issues. In Winnetka, when citizens began attending meetings to protest the plan for affordable housing, their list of grievances was long. They objected to the state legislature interfering in the affairs of their municipality. They expressed concerns about the renters who would live in the proposed affordable housing and about how the land trust would change the social composition of their neighborhood. Many of these concerns circled back to the possibility that affordable housing would lower their property values, replacing broader discussions of the common good with this single issue.

Fearing that low-income renters and middle-income homeowners would irreversibly change the character of the community, opponents of the land trust argued that affordable housing would not bring broader benefits to their community. By defining the community interest narrowly, restricting it to the interests of property owners, WHOA managed to constrict ideas about who constituted a legitimate member of the community. For them, existing homeowners in Winnetka counted as members of the community, and people who would benefit from the construction of affordable housing—whether they lived in Winnetka already or not—were excluded from their imagined community of neighbors. Focusing on property values meant that citizens in Winnetka simply narrowed the set of actors who were considered legitimate participants in the public discussions. Suddenly, middle-income renters were not part of the community for whom public decisions were being made. Through their mobilization around shared interest in maintaining property values, Winnetka homeowners created bonding social capital that reinforced their predominant identity as homeowners and narrowed the possibility for engaging with different perspectives.

This commitment to maintaining property values contributes to growing concerns about inequality in American communities. By emphasizing property values, homeowners reinforce existing physical patterns of exclusion and segregation. Already, American communities are deeply segregated by race and class. Yet efforts to exclude renters from communities contribute to patterns of tenure segregation—the separation of owners and renters in different neighborhoods.[31]

If homeowners and renters were evenly distributed across neighborhoods in the United States, we would expect a ratio of two homeowners for each renter in every neighborhood (because about two-thirds of housing units nationwide are owner-occupied and about one-third are renter-occupied). However, according to the most recent estimates from the Census, in one-quarter of the neighborhoods in the United States, homeowners outnumber renters by a ratio of at least four to one. In 10 percent of neighborhoods, there are at least nine owner-occupied homes for every renter-occupied one. And on the other end of the spectrum, renters make up at least 70 percent of the residents in 10 percent of American neighborhoods. These findings suggest entrenched patterns of tenure segregation, with homeowners living in neighborhoods consisting primarily of homeowners and renters living in communities made up mostly of renters. While I noted in chapter 3 the way housing policies historically contributed to patterns of racial and residential segregation, the stories from this chapter identify the ways that the exclusionary politics of homeowners contribute to patterns of tenure segregation as well.

As homeowners work to protect their property values through sustained engagement in public life, they deepen these patterns of segregation and exclusion. On one hand, they exacerbate patterns of housing segregation when they fight to exclude rental housing from their community. On the other hand, through the politics of exclusion, they reinforce well-documented patterns of racial and economic segregation. High-income, white households are substantially more likely to own their own homes in the United States, and low-income, minority households are more likely to be renters. When they participate in their communities, homeowners often work to keep low-income citizens from living in high-income neighborhoods or to prevent renters from finding housing in neighborhoods composed primarily of homeowners. In Winnetka, homeowners worked to intentionally exclude a particular class of citizens—in this case, moderate-income households—from living in their town. Although framed as an issue of preferences, rights, and property values, the consequence of their participation was the exclusion of non-conforming households.

While the politics of Winnetka were overt in keeping renters and low-income citizens out of their community, policing the boundaries of social exclusion can be a more indirect consequence of heightened civic engagement. One consequence of middle-class residents working to protect their housing investments in North Kenwood-Oakland was an increase in the set of obstacles that low- and moderate-income households experienced living in their neighborhoods. Rising property values forced low-income renters out of the community. It made it difficult for homeowners of moderate means to pay their property taxes and maintain those properties. And as Mary Pattillo noted, those who managed to stay were often subject to predatory investors working to capitalize on the changing neighborhood. Especially in gentrifying neighborhoods, where homeowners see opportunities to build their financial investment through housing, their political engagement contributes to the crisis of affordability, deepening divisions between property owners and renters in American neighborhoods.

Beyond these material patterns of segregation, homeowners reinforce symbolic patterns of exclusion, demonizing renters as unfit for citizenship or arguing that they are unconcerned about the communities where they live. This process constructs symbolic boundaries between homeowners and renters, as Sarah Mayorga-Gallo noted in her study of the Durham neighborhood. It involves innuendo or suggestions about the commitments of renters— questioning whether they are capable of participating in public life, and why they choose not to own their own homes. Often, when homeowners are active in the public sphere, they reinforce the idea that renters are unprepared or unable to fulfill the obligations of civic life, drawing distinctions as to who should have the right to participate and who should not. By privileging the voices of homeowners over the voices of other citizens, these public discussions can reinforce the symbolic boundaries centered on property ownership and the practice of citizenship. This symbolic exclusion deepens long-standing ideas about the role of property ownership in defining membership in the political community and further cements the long-standing belief that homeowners are better citizens—an idea that dates back nearly a century, as I discussed in chapter 2.[32]

Homeownership and Community Life

As they worked to build a nation of homeowners, twentieth-century political leaders argued that expanding homeownership opportunities would contribute to building stronger communities. By tying citizens to the places where they lived and investing them with an interest in civic affairs, the opportunity to own one's home would create more vibrant, resilient places. But extending the analysis from the previous chapter, which showed the selective ways that homeowners engage in their communities, this chapter has argued that their heightened engagement does not always lead to more inclusive places. Although we laud civic engagement as the backbone of strong community life, pointing to the way it creates social bonds or teaches civic skills, the stories from Winnetka, North Kenwood-Oakland, and several other communities suggest that homeowners often engage in the darker side of civic engagement. Driven to protect their property values, their involvement can narrow the opportunity for meaningful political dialogue and prioritize property values over other community interests. Homeowners acting to protect their property values reinforce existing boundaries of segregation and reify long-standing ideas about renters' preparedness for public life. And they may lean on the language of property values—an entirely acceptable topic for public discussion—as coded vernacular to express concerns about other changes in their communities.

Although the contribution of homeowners to the practices of exclusion must be central to any analysis of the politics of homeownership, we also must not ignore the positive role they play in their communities. Research shows that city-sponsored investments in owner-occupied housing can spur positive changes in local communities, especially when these investments attract households with extensive resources into struggling neighborhoods. Specifically, homeowners may get involved in strengthening local schools, and the positive changes they create reverberate for children throughout the neighborhood. Likewise, when we measure collective efficacy—the willingness of neighbors to work together to solve local problems or achieve common goals—communities with high rates of homeownership score strongly. As a result of their greater stability, homeowners emerge as more mindful stewards of their neighborhoods. When people live in their communities for extended periods of time, they are more likely to interact regularly with their neighbors and work collaboratively to solve local problems, as I showed in the previous chapter. And beyond any social connections developed in a community, homeowners may contribute to the upkeep of the neighborhood by maintaining their yards and keeping up their homes more diligently than renters. While this chapter calls attention to the politics of exclusion, it also acknowledges the ways that homeowners work to create better neighborhoods.[33]

Although the evidence in this chapter runs counter to the common accounts of homeowners as citizens engaged in bettering their communities, the analysis is not intended as a simple rebuttal of the positive role that homeowners do play in civic life. Instead, it is meant to complicate the narrative of homeowners as active citizens committed to the common good by highlighting their contribution to exclusionary politics. The case studies I have presented distill some of the key concepts about the darker side of social capital, focusing on the way homeowners narrow political voice, redefine the common good, and reinforce boundaries of exclusion. And while the case studies offer some insight into forms of exclusionary politics and the types of communities where these politics occur, they are not intended as generalizable examples. Like many urban neighborhoods, North Kenwood-Oakland is experiencing a renaissance as middle-class, African-American residents return to the neighborhood, but the process of gentrification is not identical across neighborhoods. The complicated racial dynamics common to gentrifying neighborhoods were not present in the movement of middle-class, African-Americans back to a historically black neighborhood. And while Winnetka, like many American suburbs, is made up primarily of white homeowners, it is wealthier and more homogenous than many suburban communities. While property values are higher in Winnetka than in most suburbs, these high-income households hold a smaller share of their wealth in housing than middle-class ones. Instead of providing generalizable lessons for the study of social exclusion, the cases in this chapter identify patterns of exclusionary politics by drawing attention to the way that building wealth through homeownership influences local communities.

Still, as we ponder the politics of exclusion, we should consider the ways that neighborhood characteristics are likely to influence the emergence of exclusionary politics. One place to look is at the composition of community residents. Homeowners might be more likely to band together, excluding others from their communities, when they live in homogenous communities composed mostly of homeowners, like Winnetka. In these neighborhoods, where residents share a common identity, citizens may perceive threats to their community as more disruptive of existing social relations. But in integrated communities—places with mixed-income residents or mixed-tenure households—the politics of exclusion may be less divisive, since homeowners interact more regularly with households of all stripes. Alternatively, the divisiveness of their politics may simply be subtler, as Sarah Mayorga-Gallo suggests in her research on the multiethnic neighborhood in Durham. Gentrifying neighborhoods present another dimension that might affect the practices of exclusion. When households buy homes in gentrifying communities, they often do so explicitly as a way of building wealth, recognizing that homes in gentrifying neighborhoods are undervalued and their involvement in the community can help to raise local property values. Building wealth through housing may be particularly important to homeowners in gentrifying neighborhoods—perhaps even more so than in other communities.

Returning to Winnetka, the debates over affordable housing offer a valuable case study to explore the politics of exclusion. Although the town is wealthier and more homogenous than most and homes in Winnetka sell for well above the national average, the town's experience offers a glimpse into the ways that communities of homeowners react to changes in their neighborhood. After nearly a decade of debate on the affordable housing plan, WHOA managed to put the issue to a public referendum, allowing the people of Winnetka to weigh in directly on it. About 2,700 citizens turned out to cast a vote on the referendum. Three-quarters of them voted to stop discussions about the expansion of affordable housing, finally putting the issue to rest.[34]

Although citizens expressed a range of emotions about the affordable housing debates, many agreed that the decade-long struggle had left many Winnetka residents exhausted. As one of the town's main proponents of affordable housing recalled, citizens across the political spectrum had simply grown tired of the contentious politics of the issue. "Winnetka residents on all sides are burnt out on the affordable housing issue. . . . The real issue, and the one that needs to be discussed in an open, inclusive setting, is 'What kind of Winnetka do we want to be?'" With the affordable housing issue settled, it was time for the people of Winnetka to engage in a broader conversation about how to build a stronger, more cohesive community.[35]

From this analysis of exclusionary politics, I return to the challenges of building strong communities in the next chapter. For decades, as I have noted throughout the book, political leaders justified their efforts to promote ownership by pointing to the contribution of homeowners to building stronger, more inclusive places. Yet, as I have showed in this chapter, owning a home often leads citizens to engage in exclusionary politics as a way to protect the value of their investments. One of the reasons that housing has become such an important financial investment is because federal tax subsidies, including the mortgage interest deduction, reward homeowners for investing in their homes. In the next chapter, I argue that these subsidies prod homeowners to engage in the politics of exclusion by increasing the investment value of housing. As an alternative to our current subsidies, I propose a series of tax expenditures to reward families who make a long-term commitment to their neighborhood. After all, it is often residential stability, rather than the financial incentives of ownership, that leads to stronger, more cohesive communities.

6

SUBSIDIZING A NATION OF HOMEOWNERS

RETHINKING FEDERAL HOMEOWNERSHIP SUBSIDIES

In 2011, the National Association of Realtors launched the Home Ownership Matters campaign, a nationwide bus tour to promote homeownership. Although the commitment to homeownership had endured through much of the twentieth century, the housing crisis presented a unique challenge to the place of homeownership in American life. As the housing market started to tumble and foreclosures started to climb, many Americans began to doubt whether owning a home would continue to be a great financial investment.

As they launched the tour, the National Association of Realtors realized that they were facing an increasingly skittish American public. By 2008, barely half of Americans believed it was a good time to buy a home—down from over 80 percent only five years earlier. The number of Americans who expected housing prices to continue rising dropped from 70 percent before the crash to barely 20 percent after it. Across the country, citizens were less likely to view homeownership as a safe financial investment and even less likely to report that housing was the best financial investment a family could make.[1]

Although these concerns about the importance of owning a home proved to be short-lived, as homeownership today enjoys the same overwhelming popularity as it did before the housing crisis, this crisis of faith stirred political leaders, trade organizations, and other proponents of homeownership into action. "Over the past several years, home ownership has faced unprecedented challenges," the National Association of Realtors noted in its 2011 annual report. "This has caused some people in Washington and in the media to question whether home ownership is still integral to the dream that has made America so great." Responding to this growing skepticism, the Home Ownership Matters tour set out to remind Americans about the many benefits of owning a home.[2]

FIGURE 6.1. Logo of the National Association of Realtors' Home Ownership Matters campaign of 2011.

Traversing thirty-three states and fifty cities, the tour underscored the sacrosanct idea that homeownership builds tightly knit families and strong neighborhoods. Harkening back to the early twentieth century, the National Association of Realtors rehashed long-standing arguments from the Own Your Own Home campaigns that I described in chapter 2. They reminded Americans that homeownership matters to people, communities, and the country (fig. 6.1).

They leaned heavily on the public benefits of homeownership—the types of benefits at the center of the analysis in this book—to reinforce the importance of owning a home.

While the Home Ownership Matters tour deployed the lofty rhetoric of ownership as the centerpiece of American life, the Association's political lobbying focused narrowly on protecting the tax subsidies enjoyed by American homeowners. Today, American homeowners benefit from a range of tax exemptions and deductions, including an exclusion on capital gains taxes when they sell their homes and a deduction for state and local property taxes. In their campaign, though, the National Association of Realtors focused on the largest—and most beloved—tax expenditure for homeowners: the mortgage interest deduction. Millions of American homeowners deduct the monthly interest payments on their mortgage loans from their federal tax liability through this deduction, which effectively lowers the cost of ownership and encourages citizens to invest more of their wealth in housing.[3]

As they crisscrossed the country, stopping in Minneapolis and Dayton, Orlando and Boise, the National Association of Realtors presented two core arguments in defense of the mortgage interest deduction. First, they argued that federal homeownership subsidies were essential to sustaining high rates of homeownership in the United States. In their campaign materials, they described the mortgage interest deduction as the cornerstone of federal housing policy and noted that millions of American homeowners relied on this tax subsidy to buy a home. Second, they pointed to the broad public benefits that come from expanding ownership opportunities. Communities are stronger and neighborhoods are more cohesive when citizens own their own homes, they argued.

Since the housing crisis, as Americans have questioned the place of homeownership, the mortgage interest deduction has endured substantial criticism. This criticism often takes aim at the first of the two foregoing arguments. Critics argue that the mortgage interest deduction, as currently structured, is regressive and inefficient. It fails to help low- and moderate-income households transition into homeownership and instead rewards high-income households for investing more of their wealth in housing. But in this chapter, I focus on the second argument. Rather than reforming *how* the federal government subsidizes homeownership, I ask *whether* subsidizing homeowners actually makes for good public policy. Do homeownership subsidies, like the mortgage interest deduction, actually create the strong public benefits that the National Association of Realtors (and other groups) commonly claim?

Focusing on the mortgage interest deduction, I apply the analysis from chapters 4 and 5 to evaluate the public benefits of the federal government's efforts to subsidize homeownership. In the previous chapter, I drew on examples from a gentrifying urban neighborhood in Chicago and a wealthy suburb north of the city to demonstrate the ways that homeowners engage in the politics of exclusion to protect their property values. In this chapter, I argue that the constellation of tax policies that reward American homeowners, including the mortgage interest deduction, contribute to the politics of exclusion by increasing the investment value of housing and encouraging homeowners to view their housing as a commodity to be bought and sold for a profit. By increasing the importance of homeownership as a financial investment, these subsidies incentivize homeowners to engage in their communities as a way to protect their property values. In doing so, they cast doubt on the broad public benefits of subsidizing homeownership through the tax code, showing how the civic and social benefits of homeownership have been deeply mischaracterized in our public discourse.

Given the ways that the current subsidies encourage citizens to engage in the politics of exclusion, I use this analysis to argue that the federal government should not subsidize Americans through the tax code to invest in homeownership. Encouraging financial investments in homeownership does not yield the broad public benefits that proponents often claim. As an alternative to these tax expenditures, I argue that the federal government should work to directly subsidize residential stability. Policies designed to encourage residential stability and deepen place-based attachments will contribute to the long-standing goals of deepening civic engagement, strengthening communities, and building better citizens.

The Accidental Deduction: A Short History of Mortgage Interest Deduction

Through the Home Ownership Matters tour, the National Association of Realtors embraced the mortgage interest deduction as the centerpiece of federal homeownership policy, calling it "a remarkably effective tool that facilitates homeownership." Other industry groups, including the National Association of Home Builders, echoed that rhetoric, referring to the deduction as a "cornerstone of American housing policy" and asserting that such subsidies for American homeowners had been around "since the inception of the tax code." Yet a look into the history of this tax expenditure suggests that it was never intended to subsidize American homeowners or to influence the housing choices citizens made. In fact, tracing its origins to the establishment of the original tax code, legal scholar Dennis Ventry calls the mortgage interest deduction an "accidental deduction"—one originally designed to serve another purpose altogether.[4]

The story of the deduction begins in the early twentieth century, a couple of years before the National Association of Realtors launched their original Own Your Own Home campaign. The Sixteenth Amendment, which was ratified in 1913, authorized the federal government to collect an income tax separate from those levied by the states. That year, Congress drafted the original income tax bill—a tax targeted exclusively at wealthy Americans. At a time when the average worker reported an annual income of $600, the federal income tax statute exempted Americans from paying taxes on the first $4,000 they earned. As a result, fewer than 2 percent of all households paid federal income taxes.[5]

The income tax legislation included a series of deductions to offset some of the taxes paid by wealthy Americans, including a deduction for interest paid on all consumer debt. One of the core principles of taxation, according to political scientist Christopher Howard, was the exemption of interest on business debt from taxation. This debt was considered to be income producing and would therefore be taxable under the income tax code. However, in the agricultural states of the American South and West, it was often difficult to distinguish between personal debt and business debt. Landowners borrowed money to purchase their farms, but these were both personal expenses and business expenses, as farmers typically lived on the land where they worked. Opting to simplify the tax code, Congress allowed taxpayers to deduct interest paid on all consumer debt, including mortgage debt used by citizens to buy a home.[6]

Despite the inclusion of mortgage loans in the broad exemption for consumer debt, few taxpayers actually deducted interest payments on the money they borrowed to buy a home. Fewer than half of American households lived in homes they owned in the early twentieth century, and still fewer bought those homes with a substantial mortgage. As a result, American homeowners were not the primary beneficiaries—or the intended recipients—of this broad deduction for consumer debt. Although contemporary rhetoric by the National Association of Realtors paints the mortgage interest deduction as a century-old scheme to reward American homeowners, placing the owner-occupied home at the centerpiece of the American Dream, the original deduction was never intended to influence the housing decisions citizens made or to offer a subsidy to people who owned their own homes. "Deciding how to foster home ownership ... through the tax code was literally the last thing on anyone's mind in the early twentieth century," Christopher Howard argues, dispelling myths about the origins of the mortgage interest deduction. Reaching a similar conclusion, Dennis Ventry notes that "there is no evidence that Congress viewed the deduction as a vehicle for promoting homeownership."[7]

If Congress never intended to subsidize Americans to buy a home, how did the deduction emerge as the centerpiece of federal homeownership policy? The answer weaves together changes in the tax code and the homeownership rate in the postwar period. By 1950, on the back of extensive mortgage subsidy programs for returning veterans, 55 percent of Americans owned their own homes. Ten years later, the American homeownership rate had risen to nearly 62 percent, as I noted in chapter 3. Increasingly, these households started to finance their homes with mortgage loans, paying interest on debt that, in principle, they could deduct from their federal taxes. At the same time, changing tax policies during World War II broadened the tax base to include many middle-income earners. As the marginal tax rate rose, the deduction for consumer debt emerged as an increasingly valuable piece of the tax code for a broader swath of citizens. This combination of events—a larger share of taxpayers, an increasing number of homeowners, and an expansion of households holding mortgage debt—increased the value of the mortgage interest deduction for a growing number of American homeowners.

However, the pivotal moment for the mortgage interest deduction came midway through the presidential administration of Ronald Reagan. In 1986, Congress passed the Tax Reform Act to simplify the increasingly complex American tax code. Among its many provisions, the Act differentiated between forms of consumer debt for the purposes of taxation. It allowed taxpayers to deduct interest paid on some forms of consumer debt but prohibited them from deducting interest paid on other types of debt. Specifically, citizens could continue to deduct interest paid on mortgage debt from their tax liabilities, but they were no longer allowed to deduct interest on credit card debt, automobile loans, or education debt, for example. The Tax Reform Act increased the relative value of the mortgage interest deduction—a provision largely championed by a coalition of builders, realtors, and bankers—and set the stage for the growth of this tax expenditure.[8]

The consequences of this decision for the ways Americans borrowed and spent their money were substantial. As Dean Maki, an economist at Barclays, later noted, the preferential treatment of mortgage loans relative to other forms of consumer debt created an incentive for households to shift their debt toward homeownership. Because Americans could deduct interest paid both on mortgage loans and on home equity loans (i.e., money borrowed against the equity stake in one's home) and could no longer deduct interest on other types of debt, the Tax Reform Act increased the importance of housing as a financial investment. It encouraged households to invest more of their wealth in housing and rewarded them for treating housing equity as a source of cash. As political theorists Richard Avramenko and Richard Boyd would later note, "not only did this [tax reform] increase aggregate consumer debt, but it contributed directly to the mindset of regarding one's house as a financial investment, rather than a home in which one dwells." By increasing the importance of housing as a financial investment, the Act contributed to the growing commodification of housing in the United States.[9]

Today, the mortgage interest deduction remains widely popular, marking it as one of the most sacrosanct public welfare programs. Three-quarters of Americans believe that subsidizing homeowners through the tax code is a reasonable public policy, and nearly two-thirds oppose efforts to reform or eliminate the mortgage interest deduction, according to a recent survey by the National Association of Home Builders. Recognizing the popularity of the deduction, Christopher Howard refers to the mortgage interest deduction, alongside Medicare and Social Security, as the "Holy Trinity of U.S. Social Programs"—a set of public welfare programs largely untouchable because of their broad public support.[10]

Despite this widespread popularity, the benefits of the mortgage interest deduction are not distributed equally among homeowners. The rules of the deduction, as currently structured, disproportionately benefit high-income homeowners at the expense of middle-class ones. Today, homeowners can deduct interest paid on mortgage loans up to $1 million. When they borrow money against the value of their home, they can deduct interest paid on up to $100,000 in home equity loans. And homeowners are permitted to claim the deduction for interest paid on mortgages for both primary and secondary homes.

As a result of these rules, the mortgage interest deduction benefits only a small slice of American homeowners. Since only taxpayers who itemize their deductions are eligible to claim the mortgage interest deduction, barely 30 percent of tax filers are even eligible for it, according to the Tax Policy Center, a joint research group from the Brookings Institution and the Urban Institute. An analysis by the Center on Budget and Policy Priorities found that high-income households—those reporting above $100,000 in income—receive more than three-quarters of the financial benefits of the interest deduction. Likewise, households with an annual income above $200,000—less than 5 percent of American households—reap about 35 percent of the financial benefits. As a result, the deduction is poorly targeted to assist middle-income households to buy homes of their own. Instead, it incentivizes high-income households to invest in larger homes, spending a disproportionate share of their income on housing.[11]

While both broadly popular and deeply regressive, the mortgage interest deduction is also incredibly expensive, ranking among the costliest expenditures in the tax code, according to the Office of Management and Budget. In 2014, the federal government forewent $100 billion in revenue to subsidize homeowners through the mortgage interest deduction. By 2018, the Office of Management and Budget expects the cost of the deduction to rise to more than $150 billion. These annual figures are reported in figure 6.2 alongside the cost of the remaining deductions for homeownership.[12]

The cost of the mortgage interest deduction is particularly striking when compared to other federal programs and tax deductions. For example, the deduction is more than double the entire budget of the Department of Housing and Urban Development—the federal agency tasked with promoting homeownership and affordable rental housing across the country. The deduction also dwarfs the entire budgets of several other cabinet-level departments, including the Department of Education and the Department of Homeland Security. Comparisons to specific programs in the federal budget are equally

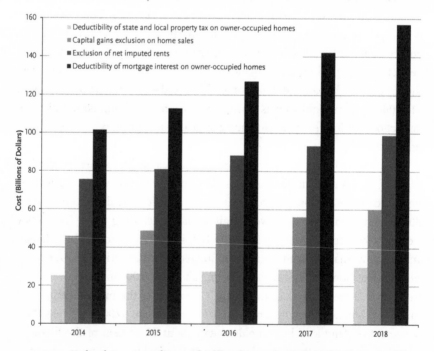

FIGURE 6.2. Federal tax expenditures for homeowners, 2014–2018. Estimates from the Office of Management and Budget, as cited in chapter 6, note 12.

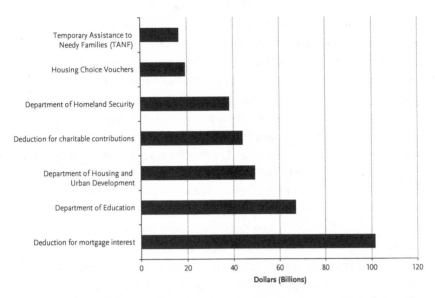

FIGURE 6.3. Comparative cost of federal programs and deductions. Data from publications of the Center on Budget and Policy Priorities, U.S. Department of Housing and Urban Development, U.S. Department of Homeland Security, Office of Management and Budget, and U.S. Department of Education, and from Dina El Boghdady, "White House Budget: HUD to See Bump," *Washington Post,* February 4, 2015, as cited in chapter 6, note 13.

stark. The federal government foregoes more on this subsidy for American homeowners than it spends on rental assistance to the poor through the Housing Choice Voucher program. The entire budget for the Temporary Assistance to Needy Families program—the primary federal program to provide assistance to poor families—is less than one-sixth of the cost of the interest deduction. And the deduction for charitable contributions—another wildly popular tax expenditure—costs the federal government barely one-third of the cost of the interest deduction. Figure 6.3 offers a glimpse of its relative magnitude.[13]

Although the mortgage interest deduction is the costliest subsidy for American homeowners, it is not the only tax expenditure targeted at them. The federal tax code allows taxpayers to deduct their state and local taxes—including local property taxes—from their federal tax liability. While these benefits vary across localities, as property tax rates are set locally, this deduction provides substantial benefits for American homeowners. A recent analysis from the Congressional Joint Committee on Taxation found that 40 million homeowners save an average of $600 annually from the deduction for property taxes. In 2014, according to the Office of Management and Budget, the federal government forewent $25 billion in revenue from this deduction. The cost will rise to nearly $30 billion by 2018 (fig. 6.2).[14]

Homeowners also benefit from a capital gains tax exemption when they sell their homes. Despite the continued insistence on the importance of home-ownership as a financial investment, the federal tax code treats housing differently from other investments. Through the capital gains tax exemption, homeowners are excluded from paying taxes on much of the money they make when they sell their homes, creating financial benefits for investing in housing that do not accrue from other types of investments. Today, married couples can earn up to $500,000 in profit tax-free when they sell their home, and single filers can earn up to $250,000. This favorable treatment of owner-occupied housing encourages families to shift their financial investments toward housing, under-scoring the growing financial importance of homeownership. According to the Office of Management and Budget, the capital gains exclusion costs the fed-eral government $45 billion in revenue in 2014. By 2018, the cost of this capital gains exclusion will rise to $60 billion (fig. 6.2).

Finally, homeowners reap a fourth benefit through the exclusion from tax-ation of imputed rents, or the rental income the owner would report if the owner's monthly payments were considered rent. Many economists believe this benefit is overlooked in discussions about the tax treatment of homeown-ers. When landlords rent out their properties, they report their rental income as taxable income, paying taxes as they would on other income, including their regular salaries. However, homeowners are not required to pay taxes on imputed rental incomes. Estimates from the Office of Management and Budget suggest that the federal government forgoes billions of dollars annu-ally by excluding net imputed rents from taxation. In fact, if the federal gov-ernment had taxed imputed rent in 2014, it would have collected more than $75 billion. By 2018, the expected revenue from imputed rent would reach nearly $100 billion (fig. 6.2).[15]

This constellation of tax expenditures, which saved homeowners nearly $250 billion in 2014, underscores the financial importance of owning a home. These tax expenditures contribute to the commodification of housing by en-couraging citizens to treat their homes as tools to earn a tax-free profit, and they incentivize homeowners to switch their investing toward housing and reap the favorable tax benefits of homeownership. While advocates for these tax policies, including the National Association of Realtors, often justify the cost of these policies by pointing to the public benefits of building a nation of homeowners, I argue that they actually lead to more segregated communities by increasing the investment value of housing. Integrating the evidence from this book, the next section challenges the assumed public benefits from subsidizing homeowners, asking whether communities actually experience the broad social benefits that advocates suggest.

Rethinking the Public Benefits of Homeownership

When the National Association of Realtors launched their Home Ownership Matters campaign, they identified the important public benefits that would come from encouraging Americans to own their own homes. Beyond the expected private benefits from homeownership, including the possibility of better health, improved education, and stronger labor market outcomes for people living in owner-occupied homes, the Association heavily emphasized the public benefits of the mortgage interest deduction to justify their support for it. These included putative benefits to communities and neighborhoods such as lower crime rates and higher levels of civic engagement.[16]

Among their campaign materials, the Association published a brochure, *The Field Guide to the Benefits of Home Ownership*, which highlighted many of the public benefits of subsidizing homeownership. "Home owners tend to stay in their homes longer than renters," the *Field Guide* noted, acknowledging residential stability as one of the underlying mechanisms linking homeownership to broad public benefits. "They also spend more money to improve their home and are more engaged in enhancing their community. Simply put, homeowners care more and take more action. Which leads to nicer neighborhoods, stronger communities and more overall involvement in civic duties."[17]

Identifying a clear set of benefits to communities and neighborhoods offers the most compelling justification for federal tax expenditures like the mortgage interest deduction. As economist Andrew Hanson and his colleagues recently argued in an article for *National Affairs*, proponents must appeal to the public benefits as a justification for continued homeownership subsidies. "The argument in favor of using public funds to encourage ownership is based on the idea that homeowners produce some social benefits outside the benefits they receive themselves," they wrote. The homeownership tour heavily emphasized these spillover benefits into American communities—the way homeownership helps to strengthen neighborhoods, deepen the bonds of social attachment, and create an active, engaged citizenry.[18]

Yet this appeal to the public benefits of owning a home relied on hazy rhetoric and broad generalizations about the transformative power of ownership rather than offering clear evidence to show that owning a home and the subsidies used to encourage it produce community benefits. Against these vague appeals to the institution of homeownership, economists Edward Coulson and Herman Li have similarly argued for the importance of identifying concrete evidence of the spillover effects from subsidizing homeownership. "The justification for the tax treatment of housing, or any subsidization of ownership should not rest on its status as a merit good—that ownership is part of the 'American Dream' and thus 'should' be accessible to any household," they have written. Instead, they argue that there must be a "more compelling justification that ownership creates external benefits; that ownership not only creates private benefits, but also benefits for the neighborhood and broader community."[19]

Although proponents and critics alike agree that the mortgage interest deduction should be justified by appealing to the public benefits of homeownership, public discussions have focused instead on the structure of this deduction rather than an analysis of the public benefits it produces. Today, a growing chorus of critics contends that even if promoting homeownership creates deep social benefits, the current structure of the mortgage interest deduction limits its effectiveness as a tool for expanding homeownership opportunities. They have put forward a number of reforms to create a more efficient subsidy that better targets middle-class households, reorienting the deduction away from high-income households and lowering the costs to the federal government. Some proposals suggest replacing it with a one-time credit for first-time homebuyers, hoping to incentivize younger families and low-income households to buy homes. Others advocate for limiting the deduction to primary residences, rather than second homes, and eliminating the deduction for home equity loans, both of which would decrease the costs to the federal government and redirect the benefits to middle-class households.

Common among these reform efforts are proposals to lower the size of loans eligible for the deduction. The National Commission on Fiscal Responsibility and Reform, a panel appointed by President Barack Obama to identify solutions following the financial crisis, proposed limiting the benefits of the interest deduction to mortgages below $500,000. Others have called for even steeper reductions, gradually lowering the ceiling to mortgage loans of $300,000. Nearly a decade ago, President George W. Bush's Advisory Panel on Federal Tax Reform proposed changing the rules of the deduction to include only interest payments on mortgages below 125 percent of the area median. In a city where the median home was valued at $200,000, for example, homeowners would be able to deduct interest payments for a mortgage up to $250,000. Like the changes for home equity loans and mortgages on second homes, these changes would redistribute the benefits of the deduction away from extremely high-income households and retarget incentives to middle-class Americans.[20]

Still, these efforts to reform the mortgage interest deduction—by capping the allowable limit, eliminating the deduction on second homes, and cutting the benefits for home equity loans—leave unchallenged the central claim put forth by the National Association of Realtors that expanding homeownership opportunities generates broad public benefits. Even reform efforts that acknowledge the limitations of the deduction as a tool for expanding ownership implicitly endorse the idea that subsidizing homeownership is good public policy because it creates benefits that spill over into local communities. While proposals to reform the mortgage interest deduction offer a way forward to improving *how* the federal government should subsidize homeownership, they leave unexplored the more central question of *whether* the federal government should subsidize Americans to own their own homes in the first place.

There are several ways that these subsidies contribute to the politics of exclusion and limit the opportunity to build inclusive communities, challenging claims about the public benefits of subsidizing homeownership. First, the existing subsidies encourage homeowners to treat their homes as financial investments. The mortgage interest deduction and the capital gains exclusion push homeowners to view their housing as a commodity to be bought and sold for a profit rather than simply a place to live. The investment opportunities inherent in homeownership in turn encourage citizens to engage in local politics as a way of protecting their property values, thereby deepening the politics of exclusion.

Beyond this contribution to the exclusionary politics described in the previous chapter, the current constellation of policies rewards citizens for living in segregated residential communities. Today, record numbers of American homeowners live in tenure-segregated communities where homeowners live exclusively with other homeowners. According to recent estimates by the Community Associations Institute, more than 13 million housing units—and over 30 million Americans—live in private communities governed by restrictive homeowners associations. That number has risen by nearly 50 percent from a decade earlier. As a growing number of citizens opt into tenure-segregated communities, these homeowners, living in private, walled-off neighborhoods, are claiming an increasing share of these homeownership subsidies.[21]

This expansion of communities governed by homeowner associations underscores the growing movement to protect property values at all costs. Nearly two decades ago, political scientist Evan McKenzie published a book on the rise of homeowner associations in private, gated communities. Dubbing these planned developments *privatopias,* he argued that their expansion had real consequences for social relations. "Preservation of property values is the highest social goal, to which other aspects of community life are subordinated," McKenzie argued, describing social life in these developments. Across communities, he observed that the enforcement of rules aimed at protecting property values was "rigid, intrusive, and often petty." The growth of these communities underscores the triumph of protecting the financial investment in homeownership at the expense of creating integrated, diverse communities.[22]

Critically, these private communities reinforce patterns of residential segregation and inequality that go beyond the growing separation of homeowners from renters. In a study of gated communities in Florida, a state with a high concentration of such communities, public policy professor Rachel Meltzer reports that their expansion worsens problems of racial segregation. Her research also reveals that properties governed by homeowner associations sell for a premium compared to those outside the private community, confirming that homeowners looking to build wealth often do so by choosing these gated residential communities. These findings suggest that homeowners do more than simply work to exclude people from their communities through normal political channels, as discussed in the previous chapter. By choosing these walled-off communities, they create more systematic barriers that exacerbate patterns of residential segregation and social exclusion.[23]

While these social costs raise doubts about the public benefits from subsidizing homeownership, economist Ed Glaeser also points to the environmental costs of doing so. As Glaeser notes, the decision to rent or own a home is deeply intertwined with the physical structures of housing—whether you live in a single-family home or a multi-unit apartment building. Ninety percent of single-family, detached homes are owner-occupied, and these homes tend to be in sprawling, car-centered suburbs—places where residents rely on automobiles and expend substantial energy heating and cooling their homes. On the other hand, housing units in apartment buildings, which are commonly occupied by renters, are typically concentrated in cities, which decrease environmental burdens by enabling public transportation usage and providing economies of scale for heating and cooling homes. To mitigate the environmental impact of housing, Glaeser argues, we should encourage high-density urban life rather than sprawling suburban communities. However, our current homeownership subsidies do the opposite—they reward citizens who elect to live in low-density suburbs and punish citizens who choose to rent in high-density cities.[24]

Despite rhetoric about the public benefits of homeownership from groups like the National Association of Realtors, the analysis I present in this book suggests that expanding ownership does not create the broad civic and social benefits that we often imagine. Instead, by increasing the investment value of owning a home and reinforcing the commodification of housing, the existing tax expenditures and exemptions contribute to the politics of exclusion and the patterns of residential segregation. Although current tax policies for homeowners do not always strengthen social ties in communities, as proponents often claim, retargeting these subsidies to promote residential stability could, once again, contribute to the century-old goal of building stronger communities. In the next section, I argue that federal policies should reward households who deepen the bonds of social attachment in their communities, regardless of whether they own or rent their homes. Absent convincing empirical evidence about the public benefits that accrue to communities from higher rates of homeownership, the federal government maintains no compelling justification for subsidizing Americans simply because they own their own homes.

Reforming the Tax Code to Strengthen Communities

This section outlines two sets of principles for restructuring federal homeownership subsidies with an eye toward generating broader public benefits, given the limited ones that expanding homeownership through the tax code brings. First, I argue that federal policies should discontinue the preferential tax subsidies that encourage owners to treat their homes as financial instruments. Second, I argue that federal policies should reward households for making a long-term commitment to their neighborhoods, regardless of whether they rent or own their homes. As I showed in chapter 4, many of the community activities that deepen social connections and generate vitality in neighborhoods are driven by residential stability, not homeownership itself. Following these principles can ensure that tax policies around housing will once again engage citizens in their communities.

The first set of principles would be structured around loosening our commitment to housing as a tool for building wealth, acknowledging the ways that doing so leads to more segregated, exclusive communities. This two-pronged principle would involve both curtailing the distorted investment value of housing, especially for high-income households, and creating opportunities to build wealth outside housing markets.

Changes to the federal tax code should begin by treating housing investments like other financial investments, recognizing that the transformation of housing into a financial investment shifts the social relations in communities—the way people engage in their neighborhoods and relate to their neighbors—in ways that lead to exclusion. To start, federal policymakers should consider eliminating the mortgage interest deduction—or at the very least, substantially limiting the financial benefits of claiming it.[25]

While the mortgage interest deduction is the largest tax benefit that incentivizes wealth building through housing investments, other tax policies do so as well. The exemption for capital gains incentivizes homeowners to maximize their housing values as they become involved in their communities. Eliminating it and treating earnings from homeownership like those from other financial investments would help to decrease citizens' reliance on housing as a tool for building wealth.

Although these reforms would treat housing investments on par with other financial investments, weakening citizens' commitment to housing as a financial investment, we should complement these federal policies with local ones that discourage short-term profiteering on homeownership. Accomplishing this goal would involve local regulation of behaviors that treat homeownership exclusively as a vehicle for financial gain. Today, speculative homeownership ignores altogether the idea of deepening place-based attachments, focusing instead on owning homes as a tool for turning a profit. Speculative investors and short-term homeowners often flip houses in high-priced real estate markets, recognizing an opportunity to make a quick profit from minimal investments in the housing stock. As political theorists Richard Avramenko and Richard Boyd remark, "it seems perverse to reward someone for having moved into a home for six months, slapping on a coat of paint, new cabinets, and granite countertops, and to give them a tax-free profit for their contribution to community-building."[26]

Solutions to short-term profiteering need to include a speculator tax on property owners who "flip" properties or a progressive tax to account for rapid price appreciation in short periods of time. Political leaders in several cities, including Seattle, San Francisco, and Washington, DC, have made efforts to discourage speculative housing investments that treat ownership exclusively as a tool for financial gain. For example, several years ago, housing advocates in San Francisco put forth Proposition G, a real estate speculation tax that would have taxed property owners of rental buildings who sold their properties within five years of purchase. Although voters rejected the measure, this real estate speculation tax would have increased affordable housing and limited short-term profiteering on particular types of housing investments.[27]

Efforts to decommodify housing and treat it more fairly as a financial investment must be combined with opportunities for citizens to build wealth through means other than homeownership. As Elliot Schreur, a policy analyst in the Asset Building Program at the New America Foundation, has argued, the tax incentives for homeownership offer limited opportunities for low- and middle-income households. "Wealth building . . . built around tax benefits for homeownership . . . are doing little to help the younger generation to become more financially secure," Schreur notes, pointing to the way that policies designed to help people build wealth through homeownership disadvantage particular types of households. One of his proposed solutions is that governments "modernize tax incentives to help renter families and those in multi-family housing, rather than primarily subsidizing people with big houses." Creating tax incentives that are not focused exclusively on homeownership could create opportunities for other types of families, including renters, low-income households, and young households, to climb the economic ladder.[28]

Efforts to decouple homeownership from wealth building would start to change the way citizens become involved in their communities. Homeowners who are less reliant on their homes as a tool for building wealth are less likely to become involved in the types of political activity that lead to more segregated communities. Moving away from tax policies that solidify the investment value of homeownership, federal policymakers should simultaneously consider an alternative set of tax incentives that encourage households to deepen local social ties in their communities. Instead of rewarding citizens who buy their homes, they should begin to subsidize those who remain in their communities for a long period of time, recognizing that residential stability—more than ownership—is central to vibrant community life.

The principle of rewarding residential stability acknowledges that many of the civic activities lauded by proponents of homeownership, like the National Association of Realtors, are actually driven by the increased stability of homeownership rather than the financial investments homeowners make. When citizens live in their communities for a long period of time, regardless of whether they rent or own their homes, they begin to build the social connections and networks central to strong, vibrant neighborhoods. Taking a closer look at the way homeownership shapes community participation, legal scholar Stephanie Stern points to the ways that most analyses of ownership overlook the importance of increased residential stability. "Stable neighborhoods with higher proportions of long-term residents, both owners and renters, have increased local participation, greater reciprocated exchange of favors, more linkages

between children and adults in the community, and higher levels of neighborhood sociability," she notes.[29]

Looking beyond the instrumental acts of political participation to examine
broader measures of community engagement, I showed in chapter 4 that
long-term, stable households are more likely to interact regularly with their
neighbors, volunteer in their communities, and join school associations, regardless of whether they rent or own their homes. These indicators of informal
social interaction, neighborliness, and participation in social groups are crucial to building neighborhood-level social capital, and rewarding the types of
behaviors that build them will contribute to reversing the trends of decreased
neighborhood socialization. Subsidizing residential stability independently
from homeownership can lead to more positive community outcomes than
the politics of exclusion that results from incentivizing homeownership.[30]

As we begin to think about the ways policies could reward residential
stability, I propose two initial distinctions. On one hand, tax subsidies to
encourage households to "stay put" would reward those who elect to make a
long-term commitment to their neighborhoods. When faced with the opportunity to profit from the sale of their homes, these tax incentives might
encourage households to remain in their communities, maintaining the social
bonds in their neighborhoods. This type of stability tax credit could be pegged
to communities rather than a particular housing unit to enable households to
shift units without disrupting their social ties. By tying the credit to a specific
community—a zip code or metropolitan area, for example—the housing tax
credit would provide flexibility as housing needs change. As parents downsize
when their children leave home, or families seek larger housing units as their
family size grows, the credit would allow households to switch their housing
units without disrupting social ties in their communities. This type of incentive, which would reward stability without encouraging overinvestment in
housing or creating incentives to participate in exclusionary politics, could
replace the mortgage interest deduction as the nation's core housing subsidy.[31]

On the other hand, tax incentives to encourage residential stability could
assist households facing forced mobility as housing costs climb. In many
urban neighborhoods, rising housing prices force households with deep
social ties to leave their communities. Gentrification often pushes rents up,
and long-term, low-income residents are displaced from their communities.
Promoting long-term stability could involve crafting programs to enable families to remain in their communities even as rents rise. These stability programs could be modeled on the Housing Choice Voucher program, a subsidy
to low-income renters to partially cover the cost of housing on the private
market. Voucher recipients pay up to 30 percent of their income for housing

on the private market, and the voucher covers the rest of the fair market rent. Households experiencing displacement as a result of rising rents could be eligible for similarly structured vouchers that would enable them to remain in their communities, reinforcing many of the community benefits derived from long-term residential stability. Unlike Housing Choice Vouchers, which encourage mobility from disadvantaged neighborhoods, these vouchers could enable stability within existing neighborhoods as a vehicle to deepen neighborhood attachment.[32]

These two principles—on one hand, the evenhanded treatment of homeownership as a financial investment and on the other hand, targeted subsidies to reward residential stability—would help to reorient our homeownership policies back toward the long-standing goal of building better communities. In crafting these policies, it is important to remember that early in the twentieth century, as proponents embarked on their plans to extend homeownership opportunities, owning a home was not the financial tool that it is today. Instead, their efforts to promote homeownership were geared to strengthening social ties, rooting people in their communities, and deepening neighborhood attachments. With the emergence of housing as an increasingly important financial investment, owing partly to the tax policies that reward ownership, homeowners have come to see their community involvement as a way to bolster property values. The growing commodification of housing has frayed the link between homeownership and the promise of strengthening communities. Restructuring our homeownership subsidies to create wealth-building opportunities outside housing and encourage residential stability can recommit federal policies to the long-standing goal of engaging citizens in the social life of their communities.

Concluding the Home Ownership Matters Tour

After traveling nearly 12,000 miles, the National Association of Realtors wrapped up their Home Ownership Matters bus tour at their annual conference in Anaheim, California. While the housing crisis had temporarily shaken the American commitment to homeownership, with critics wondering whether renting was the new American Dream, the tour set out to remind citizens of the continued importance of promoting homeownership. Traveling across the country, the Association set their sights on protecting the mortgage interest deduction, one of the core tax expenditures for American homeowners.

Although the realtors concluded their tour in Anaheim, their efforts to promote homeownership and protect the deduction didn't stop there. As nearly 18,000 realtors gathered for the annual convention, the Association urged them to contact their legislators and remind them about the importance of the mortgage interest deduction for buying a home. As the tour had done, the Association wove together a story about the mortgage interest deduction as the cornerstone of the national commitment to homeownership, ignoring some key features of the deduction highlighted in this chapter. They emphasized heavily the century-old rhetoric of homeownership as the foundation of democratic citizenship and neglected to acknowledge that nearly half of homeowners with mortgages—mostly low- and middle-class homeowners—do not benefit from the deduction. In promulgating the myth of a tax expenditure designed to incentivize homeownership, they overlooked the origins of the mortgage deduction as a quirky provision of the tax code. And while they argued that the mortgage interest deduction kept the American homeownership rate high, they ignored comparisons to dozens of other countries—the United Kingdom and Canada, for example—that have similar homeownership rates but provide few tax benefits for owning a home.

Yet, critically for this book's story, the National Association of Realtors invoked the important public benefits of expanding ownership opportunities as they worked to defend the deduction. They argued that promoting homeownership was important for building strong communities. Although this assumption is rarely challenged, especially among advocates of homeownership, I use the analysis in this chapter to argue that rewarding homeowners through the current set of tax subsidies does not yield the public benefits that the National Association of Realtors often claims that it does. Instead, by increasing the investment value of homeownership, these subsidies contribute to the politics of exclusion, as I described in the previous chapter. I argue instead for tax policies that reward residential stability to better fulfill the long-standing goals of strengthening citizenship and building better communities.

In the next and final chapter, I build on this lesson about the separate analysis of residential stability to offer a series of reflections from this book. Touching back on the housing crisis and the way it opened up the key themes of the book, I draw three core lessons for the continued engagement with the study of homeownership. First, I underscore the importance of studying housing as a social phenomenon rather than just an economic one. Next, I advocate for a more serious engagement with the politics of exclusion, including further analyses of the challenges of tenure segregation. And finally, extending from this chapter, I invite an ongoing discussion of ways to promote residential stability outside the contours of homeownership. Drawing on these core reflections from the book, I invite readers to reflect on the broader place of homeownership in American society.

7 CONCLUSION

CITIZENSHIP IN A NATION OF HOMEOWNERS

This book's story leads to a counterintuitive conclusion about the place of homeownership in American life. Although we often laud homeownership as a tool for strengthening citizenship and integrating people into their communities, I have shown that the impact of homeownership on community life is not as clear-cut— and often, not as positive—as proponents claim. Rather than transforming citizens into better neighbors and engaged citizens, owning a home often leads them to participate in the politics of exclusion. Concerned about the value of their homes, they elevate concerns about property values above other issues in their communities. As a result, when they do engage in civic activities or participate in local politics, they often do so as a way of protecting their financial interests. This type of civic involvement can lead to fractured, segregated neighborhoods, with homeowners working to exclude particular practices and people from their communities.

This complicated story of citizen-homeowners cuts against a widely held narrative in the United States that portrays homeowners as more responsible, engaged citizens and neighbors. Legal scholar Mechelle Dickerson refers to this as the Happy Homeowner Narrative—the uncritical belief that homeownership transforms citizens into happier, wealthier, more stable and involved citizens. This narrative is reinforced by a tendency to eulogize homeownership in the public discourse, presenting stories about homeowners as better citizens, neighbors, and even parents, all while stigmatizing renters. But in this book, I have worked to set the record straight. Through a critical analysis of the civic benefits of homeownership, the book has investigated the origins of these claims about citizen-homeowners, explored the reasons why this ideology persists, and considered whether or not these claims to better citizenship and stronger communities are true.[1]

Before identifying this book's three key lessons to guide continued engagement with the ideology of ownership, I review the book's evidence and arguments. Although the chapters can be read independently, weaving them together helps to deepen the analysis by linking the history of homeownership in the United States with contemporary evidence about community life and civic engagement. At the beginning of the book, I laid the foundation of the analysis by identifying two core ideas about homeownership in the United States. First, owning a home is the most important financial investment households will ever make, and Americans hold more wealth in their homes than in any other investment. Second, expanding opportunities for homeownership has long been heralded as the best tool for rooting people in their communities and building stronger neighborhoods. I framed my analysis around these ideas, asking how the importance of building wealth through housing transforms the way citizens engage in their communities, and what the consequences are for civic life.

While the book is not directly about the recent housing crisis, I have used it to highlight the way these two core issues have recently emerged in public discussion about homeownership. Although the importance of owning a home has deep roots in American history, the collapse of the housing market brought to the forefront concerns about whether homeownership would continue to be a good tool for building wealth, and whether expanding ownership opportunities would continue to lead to stronger communities. As homeowners lost their housing wealth in the crash of the market or faced foreclosures as the economy tumbled, they were left to reconsider whether owning a home would continue to stabilize neighborhoods or serve as a strong financial investment.

In chapter 2, I traced the historical origins of the ideology of homeownership, laying the foundation for this book's empirical analysis. Although the rhetoric around ownership as a tool for building communities and strengthening citizenship is commonplace, we rarely consider where this rhetoric came from or why Americans tend to associate owning a home with engaged community life. I argued that these ideas are rooted in a remarkable demographic transition. As Americans moved to cities in the early twentieth century, political leaders embraced homeownership as a tool for rooting people in their communities, encouraging social stability and fighting political radicalism. Notably, although homeownership extended a legacy linking property ownership to political citizenship by generating the shared bonds of civic life, buying a home in the early twentieth century was not the major vehicle for building wealth that it is today.

Through an analysis of several early twentieth-century campaigns that encouraged Americans to buy their own homes, I dug into the roots of this homeownership ideology. Campaign leaders engaged ideas about patriotism and citizenship in their promotional materials, laying out many of the same arguments about homeownership, citizenship, and community life that we still hear today. As they leaned heavily on the rhetoric linking property ownership and citizenship, they suggested that housing choices—the decision to rent or buy—gave citizens the right to participate in public life and the political process. As owning a home came to demarcate the boundaries of citizenship, these campaigns reframed personal decisions about buying a home as choices imbued with deep social and political meaning. This important ideology would endure unscathed through much of the twentieth century.

Despite the rhetoric of homeownership as a marker of citizenship, most Americans in the early twentieth century were unable to buy their own homes. In fact, in the 1930s, when President Hoover convened his conference on homebuilding and homeownership, fewer than half of Americans lived in homes they owned. Owning a home often required a substantial down payment, and mortgage credit was scarce. These obstacles kept millions of Americans from buying a home and joining the ranks of upstanding citizen-homeowners.

Over the course of the twentieth century, the federal government was deeply committed to the project of building a nation of homeowners. It took an active role in expanding ownership opportunities by ensuring the availability of mortgage credit, facilitating the construction of owner-occupied housing in the suburbs, and tackling discrimination in housing and mortgage markets. On the back of this federal intervention, especially in the postwar period, the number of Americans who owned their own homes grew by leaps and bounds. By the 1960s, more than 60 percent of Americans lived in homes they owned.

Still, the remarkable expansion of ownership opportunities masked deep disparities in the homeownership rate. Although millions of Americans bought their own homes in the decades after World War II, federal housing policies also reinforced patterns of social exclusion. By the end of the twentieth century, white Americans were almost twice as likely to own a home than African-Americans or Latinos. Most wealthy Americans lived in homes of their own, but most poor Americans did not. In chapter 3, I showed the critical role of the federal government in guiding the expansion of ownership in the twentieth century while also calling attention to the exclusionary nature of homeownership. This analysis highlighted the sharp contrast between the inclusionary rhetoric of ownership and the exclusionary practices that have kept more Americans from owning their homes. In this portion of the book, I introduced the concept of tenure segregation to highlight patterns of residential segregation between owners and renters.

Despite enduring patterns of social exclusion, political leaders continued to lean heavily on the rhetoric of citizenship as they worked to expand owner-ship opportunities, identifying the broad civic benefits that would come from more and more Americans buying their homes. When President Clinton in-troduced the National Homeownership Strategy—a plan to create ownership opportunities for 8 million first-time homebuyers—he quickly pointed to the benefits of improved citizenship and stronger communities. Yet only a handful of studies explore whether or not homeowners engage more actively in their communities than renters or whether they are more likely to fulfill the obligations of citizenship. In chapter 4, I have offered a careful analysis of the Social Capital Community Survey to craft a more nuanced, evenhanded account of the way American homeowners participate in public life.

The story that emerged casts doubt on the claims to citizenship that are central to ongoing efforts to expand ownership opportunities. Homeowners are more involved in some political activities than renters, including voting in elections and attending political rallies, but they are not much more likely to engage in other types of political activities. Similarly, they are more likely to join neighborhood associations but are no more active in other types of mem-bership groups than renters. And while homeowners are more likely to attend community meetings and work cooperatively on neighborhood problems, they do not report much stronger informal social interaction with their neigh-bors. This analysis offers a much more balanced account of the civic habits of homeowners—an account that suggests homeowners are not always the com-munity-minded, civically engaged citizens we often make them out to be.

To deepen this analysis, I also identify the importance of residential sta-bility in leading citizens to become involved in their communities. Separate from the impact of homeownership, I show that residential stability is associ-ated with higher levels of participation in several noninstrumental types of community engagement. Citizens who have lived in their communities for more than five years are more likely to interact informally with their neigh-bors, become active in school groups, and volunteer with an organization in their communities. This analysis of residential stability provides the backdrop for the policies that I later recommend.

While detailing the civic habits of American homeowners, the analysis in chapter 4 tells only part of the story. It suggests that homeowners are often motivated by their financial investments in housing when they become in-volved in community activities, but it doesn't tell us anything about the way their participation shapes the communities where they live. In chapter 5, I have told the stories of several communities, including a wealthy suburb of Chicago and a gentrifying neighborhood in the city, to argue that homeowners' financial investments in housing often lead them to participate in exclusionary ways. Concerned about the value of their largest investment, they engage in local politics to keep particular types of people from living in their communities or to restrict particular types of land-use decisions. In doing so, homeowners often elevate the voices of property owners over other community members, and they marginalize renters as unfit for civic participation. The framework of exclusionary politics casts doubt on the idea that homeowners work to build more integrated, inclusive communities. Instead, this framework suggests that homeowners often exacerbate NIMBY politics as they work to protect their property values.

Notably, by pushing back against the notion of any kind of civic engagement as an inherently positive social good, I have linked the exclusionary politics of homeownership to the growing importance of building wealth through housing—a connection that has rarely been acknowledged in research on housing and the current expansion of private asset–based systems of welfare. The investment value of housing often leads homeowners to become property value warriors, seeing the worth of their communities predominantly through the lens of their financial investments. This approach to political participation and community engagement reinforces patterns of segregation and social exclusion, challenging the often-touted benefits of homeownership for strengthening community life.

In chapter 6, I have shown that the current constellation of federal homeownership subsidies contributes to the politics of exclusion by increasing the investment value of owning a home and encouraging households to treat their homes as financial investments. While critics of the mortgage interest deduction often note that it favors wealthy Americans and does little to achieve the stated goal of boosting the number of people who own their own homes, they have rarely asked whether subsidizing homeownership makes for good public policy in the first place. Through the framework of exclusionary politics, I argue that the mortgage interest deduction contributes to patterns of segregation by encouraging citizens to view their homes primarily as financial investments.

As an alternative to the mortgage interest deduction, I argue that federal policies can achieve many of the stated goals of building stronger communities and crafting better citizens by directly investing in residential stability. After all, I have shown that it is often this stability, rather than the financial incentives associated with homeownership, that leads citizens to participate in community life. Regular neighborly interactions help to build community social capital, and participation in the noninstrumental acts of civic engagement, including volunteering with community organizations, is an important tool for creating stronger neighborhoods. Accordingly, I have offered a series of recommendations for ways to subsidize residential stability rather than directly subsidizing homeownership.

Critical Lessons for the Future of Homeownership

Building from this book's story, I use this section to outline three important lessons to guide continued engagement with the study of homeownership in American society. First, I argue for the importance of studying homeownership as a social phenomenon rather than simply an economic one. While buying a home is an important vehicle for economic mobility, the study of ownership as a social phenomenon points to the way that owning a home shapes social relations, including the ways people interact in their communities. This approach to homeownership demands that we engage with the broader social and political forces that influence citizens' homeownership decisions, including the changing politics of the welfare state.

Second, I highlight the contradictions of social inclusion and exclusion that this book reveals. While the inclusionary rhetoric of homeownership portrays it as an institution widely available to integrate people into the contours of upstanding citizenship, the exclusionary politics associated with owning a home demonstrates how citizens are marginalized and excluded from doing so. The consequences of this exclusionary politics are significant, as it limits opportunities for economic and social mobility. I argue for a more sustained analysis of tenure segregation—the residential separation of homeowners and renters—to complement existing research on patterns of racial and economic segregation.

Finally, in an effort to evaluate the social and political outcomes associated with housing decisions, I argue that researchers should clarify the mechanisms linking homeownership to these outcomes. In this book, I have shown that owning a home influences some types of civic behavior because it roots homeowners in their communities but influences other types of behaviors because it incentivizes them to protect their financial investments in their homes. Understanding why ownership matters is critical as researchers continue to study the effect of owning a home on educational attainment, labor market outcomes, and health measures.

Studying Homeownership as a Social Problem

This book's first lesson concerns the way citizens approach the decision to buy a house. I have argued throughout that the approach to homeownership as an economic decision often eclipses approaches to it as a social phenomenon. When Americans talk about buying a home, they largely do so through a framework that centers on the importance of housing as a tool for building wealth or climbing the economic ladder. Political leaders describe homeownership as an engine of economic growth, and Americans frequently point to the financial benefits of buying a home. Although these are important ways to think about homeownership, this approach cannot come at the expense of analyzing ownership as a social phenomenon.[2]

Especially since the housing crisis, the economic approach to the study of homeownership has gained momentum. The enormous amount of household wealth lost as housing values plummeted was one of the most important storylines from the housing crisis, and political leaders responded to the crisis by renewing their commitment to building wealth through homeownership. Trade groups, like the National Association of Realtors, doubled down on their commitment to promoting homeownership, tacitly acknowledging their own economic interests in sustaining a robust market for homeownership. As they lobbied to protect the tax subsidies for American homeowners, the Association emerged as one of the top political lobbies in the country. In 2014, according to the Center for Responsive Politics, the group spent more than $55 million lobbying political leaders, making it the second-largest political lobby, behind only the U.S. Chamber of Commerce.[3]

While the crisis exposed the array of actors who have a financial interest in the future of homeownership, it also underscored the transformation of homeownership into a global financial commodity. As banks repackaged individual mortgages into mortgage-backed securities and sold them to investors around the globe, they cemented homeownership as a broad investment strategy encompassing the financial goals of both individual homeowners and international investors. While buying a home was a wealth-building tool for individual households, the trade in mortgage-backed securities pointed to the transformation of ownership into a financial vehicle for global investors.

While the housing crisis brought the dominant economic approach to studying homeownership to the forefront of public discussions, it served as a stark reminder about the importance of engaging with ownership as a social phenomenon, as well. In this book, I argue for an approach to housing studies that emphasizes the social relationships inherent in homeownership. Owning a home transforms the way citizens engage with their neighbors and communities, as I showed in chapter 4. It deepens certain types of community engagement and spurs participation in particular political activities. Homeownership is a marker of status attainment for millions of Americans, and the ability to buy a home determines the types of neighborhoods where families can live. These are important *social aspects* of homeownership, and they need to be considered alongside efforts to identify the investment value of ownership.

Throughout the book, I have linked the economic approach to homeownership to the study of housing as a social phenomenon by showing how the concentration of wealth in housing shifts the material interests that drive citizens to engage in public life. Owning a home transforms the way citizens interact with their neighbors, civic leaders, and elected officials, often leading them to prioritize their interests as property owners. But beyond these measures of civic engagement, homeownership may also shape public opinion on social policies or deepen political ideologies. Recently, political scientist Ben Ansell showed that homeowners are less supportive of social spending programs when housing prices are rising—a finding that suggests that the private accumulation of wealth through homeownership can directly impact public policies.[4]

This finding pushes scholars to engage more deeply with the politics of the welfare state and the way it shapes housing choices. Homeowners now rely on their housing wealth to save for retirement and send their children to college—a phenomenon that grew alongside the retrenchment of the welfare state. Yet the extent to which the private accumulation of wealth through homeownership represents a *trade-off* with a more generous welfare state remains an important empirical puzzle. Although there is some research on homeownership and welfare state politics in western Europe, research on the changing role of the state and social policy is largely silent on the place of homeownership, especially in the United States.[5]

Inclusionary Rhetoric and Exclusionary Politics

Studying homeownership as a social phenomenon leads into this book's second important lesson, which concerns the gulf between what we expect homeownership to do and what it actually does. Throughout the twentieth century, as political leaders worked to expand opportunities to own a home, they leaned heavily on the importance of homeownership as a marker of social inclusion. I have shown that political leaders often deployed this rhetoric of ownership as an inclusionary marker of citizenship, especially as they worked to resolve the crisis of citizenship in the early twentieth century. Citizens who owned their own homes were deemed to be good citizens, upstanding patriots, and better Americans, while those who rented were viewed as less capable of participating in the political process. These norms linking property ownership to the promise of upstanding citizenship endured throughout the twentieth century, and owning a home was often invoked as a tool to deepen claims to citizenship.

Yet enduring patterns of social exclusion have marred this inclusionary story of homeownership. Historically, ownership opportunities have been more limited for African-Americans, and those with poor credit histories have had a harder time qualifying for the mortgage credit necessary to buy a home. The persistent racial disparities in ownership opportunities reinforce core dimensions of social stratification in the United States, with African-Americans having fewer opportunities to build wealth or move into better neighborhoods as they are excluded from buying homes. These discriminatory practices have contributed to enduring patterns of racial segregation, with the persistence of predominately white, owner-occupied suburbs juxtaposed with largely African-American, renter-occupied neighborhoods in central cities.[6]

The series of case studies I presented wove together the themes of inclusion and exclusion to highlight the exclusionary politics of homeownership, identifying some of the ways homeowners exclude and marginalize renters from public life. They rely on their status as taxpaying property owners to bolster their claims to citizenship, reinforce symbolic boundaries between owners and renters, and demarcate the types of citizens allowed a legitimate voice for participation in public life. Owners often resist the entrance into their communities of particular groups of people or types of developments they expect will lower their property values. In doing so, they exclude certain types of citizens from living in high-status neighborhoods. As they work to build wealth through their homes, they often actively restrict the opportunity for others to do so.

These acts of political exclusion challenge the inclusionary rhetoric of homeownership by recasting it as a tool to marginalize nonowners from public life. Much of the history of suburbanization identifies the exclusionary real estate practices and racially divisive patterns of mortgage lending that excluded millions of minority households from owning their own homes. These practices created the patterns of racial segregation that persist in metropolitan areas today. But in this book, I have argued that the exclusionary politics of homeowners reinforces many of these historic patterns of discrimination through more informal modes of exclusion. While low-income renters and

African-American citizens were historically excluded from neighborhoods by racial covenants or redlining, they are now kept from high-opportunity neighborhoods by patterns of exclusionary politics. As homeowners become involved in their communities to protect their household wealth, they create barriers to others living in their neighborhoods. This participation is not value-neutral and instead, prizes homeowners' own interests as property owners above the interests of other members of their communities.

Pushing beyond standard analyses of residential segregation, I argue that we should pay more attention to patterns of tenure segregation—the separation of homeowners and renters. Today, research on residential segregation centers largely on racial segregation in metropolitan areas and deepening patterns of economic inequality across communities. But given the importance of homeownership to economic mobility and the prospects of moving to better neighborhoods, researchers need to analyze patterns of residential segregation between homeowners and renters as a distinct form of segregation. Patterns of tenure segregation are consequential beyond their close relationship to patterns of social and economic segregation.

These concerns about tenure-segregated communities gained public attention in the aftermath of the housing crisis, as renters started moving into neighborhoods that were made up mostly of homeowners. In 2013 the *New York Times* reported a story about the neighborhood of Hillshire on the outskirts of Memphis, Tennessee. During the housing crisis, several long-standing homeowners had lost their homes to foreclosure and been forced to move from their neighborhood. Investors bought their properties and began renting them to other Memphis families. Many homeowners in Hillshire doubted the capacity of renters to participate as equal partners in their community and worried that renters would be unable to build social connections in the neighborhood. Although these renters shared some of the same community concerns as their homeowners next door, they were immediately viewed with skepticism as they moved into a neighborhood occupied predominantly by homeowners. Like many stories of renters moving into neighborhoods made up largely of homeowners, the story of Hillshire exposed the challenges of integrating tenure-segregated communities.[7]

Residential Stability and the Social Benefits of Ownership

Finally, throughout this book I have argued for careful consideration of the reasons that homeownership has been linked to the claims of enhanced citizenship. I have offered two pathways to explain the reasons that homeownership matters. On one hand, owning their homes leads people to become more active in particular types of community activities because it roots them in their communities. Homeowners are more likely to interact socially with their neighbors and volunteer with community organizations because owning a home increases their stability in neighborhoods. They deepen their social bonds and community networks when they live in their neighborhoods for a long period of time.[8]

On the other hand, owning a home deepens other forms of engagement in communities because homeowners reap a set of financial rewards from their participation in public life. They are more likely to attend political meetings or vote in local elections because these types of participation serve as strategies to protect their financial investments in homeownership. However, participation driven by the financial incentives of homeownership often results in the exclusionary politics at the core of this book.

Accepting the simple characterization of homeowners as better citizens ignores the nuanced—and often competing—ways that homeownership shapes participation decisions. It is important to be assertive in distinguishing between these two mechanisms: the residential stability associated with ownership on one hand and the financial incentives derived from it on the other. The vague appeal to homeownership as an axiomatic social good often fails to characterize why homeownership leads to enhanced citizenship, or how federal legislators could craft better policies to incentivize positive civic outcomes.

Engaging with the rhetoric of political and civic leaders throughout this book, I have shown that there is widespread disregard for the mechanisms linking homeownership to enhanced citizenship. Political leaders rarely distinguish the power of ownership to stabilize households in their communities from the way homeownership helps to build household wealth. Instead, these mechanisms are simply wrapped into a vague appeal for homeownership as a tool for enhanced citizenship, neglecting the fact that promoting stability incentivizes different behaviors and outcomes from those that encourage Americans to build wealth through housing.

By clarifying when the stability of ownership matters versus when buying a home matters because of the financial stakes, policymakers can better target housing policies to produce the intended social or political outcomes. For example, policies that stabilize households in their communities would strengthen the bonds of neighborliness in ways that policies designed to increase the investment value of housing will not. Subsidies targeted specifically at promoting residential stability would better fulfill many of the normative goals currently associated with the push to build a nation of homeowners.

These policies could replace contemporary subsidies that incentivize financial investments in housing and deepen exclusionary politics.

Beyond the expected civic benefits of homeownership, distinguishing between the mechanisms linking it to social outcomes should be broadly applicable to other social benefits commonly associated with homeownership. For example, proponents often link homeownership to educational attainment and greater success in finding a job. Distinguishing between competing mechanisms can help to craft policies directed at these specific goals. Ultimately, the vague appeal to homeownership as the foundation of civic life, or a pathway to improved educational attainment, neglects the critical question of *why* we think homeownership matters so much.

Citizenship and Community in a Nation of Homeowners

In the early 1980s, sociologist Jim Kemeny published a critical analysis of housing systems in Western Europe. Critiquing the efforts to push homeownership as the preferred form of residential tenure, Kemeny offered a series of reflections on the state of housing studies that would prove prescient nearly three decades later. Researchers seemed to endlessly celebrate homeownership, he wrote, but they rarely scrutinized it as a critical social problem. "I found that homeownership was often eulogized, sometimes simply taken for granted, but rarely studied as a social phenomenon," Kemeny noted.[9]

Decades later, as I embarked on my own investigation into the enhanced citizenship claims of homeownership, these remarks continued to resonate. On the heels of the housing crisis, as millions of Americans lost their homes and millions more watched the wealth they had built through housing evaporate almost overnight, I was surprised by the limited critical reflection on the place of homeownership in public life. In fact, since the crisis, political leaders have continued to reflexively push homeownership as the best housing option for all Americans, and public opinion on homeownership has rebounded to the same levels as before the housing crisis. Today, 90 percent of Americans believe that homeownership is central to the American Dream; nearly three-quarters of renters aspire to own their own homes. Despite the disruptions to homeownership over the last decade, more than half of Americans continue to believe that buying a home is the best financial investment they can make. The ideology of ownership is powerful enough that it has endured largely uninterrupted in the years since the housing crisis. The American people continue to turn to their homes as tools for economic mobility, and political leaders continue to lean on homeownership as a vehicle for strengthening citizenship.[10]

This book offers a contribution to critical studies of homeownership, turning a lens on the enhanced citizenship claims of homeownership. By framing the analysis within the politics of exclusion, I offer a way for rethinking the power of homeownership to reshape social relations in American communities. While Americans typically frame the decision to buy a home as an individual choice, I have argued that our individual housing decisions have broad consequences for patterns of residential segregation. In working to protect their property values, citizens create and reinforce boundaries of social exclusion. By limiting the residential choices available to other citizens, they limit their opportunities to access neighborhood resources, including better schools and social networks.[11]

The implications of this analysis are substantial. On one hand, by calling into question one of the core justifications for expanding ownership opportunities, I invite a broader reflection on the types of housing policy that contribute to our efforts to encourage more and more Americans to own their own homes. Casting doubt on one of the primary justifications used by homeownership advocates, I have challenged scholars and policymakers to consider other ways that we can encourage the deepening of social relations and better citizenship. Specifically, I believe that the current constellation of housing policies and tax expenditures, which privilege ownership over other housing options, fails to adequately account for the needs of diverse households. Owning a home may not be the best housing choice for every household, and singularly rewarding homeownership is inadequate for meeting the housing needs of an increasingly diverse country.

I have also asked readers to understand homeownership as a meaningful social choice rather than simply an individual decision. While the decision to buy a home is typically framed as a deeply personal one, I have argued that ownership decisions are influenced by government policies and have enduring social consequences. Historically, buying a home was not the great wealth-building vehicle that it is today. At a certain point, the expansion of homeownership seemed to offer a way to solve a litany of social problems, including urban unrest and the limitations of democracy. But homeownership also contributes to exclusionary politics. We need to acknowledge not only the types of problems that homeownership solves but also the types of challenges the expansion of ownership as a tool for building wealth has created.

All told, perhaps this book's most critical reflection is identifying the need to reconsider the contours of citizenship in a nation of homeowners. When proponents launched the Own Your Own Home and the Better Homes in America campaigns in the early twentieth century, they argued that homeowners were more engaged in the norms of citizenship, contributing to the formation of strong community life. But now, recognizing their engagement in exclusionary politics, these claims to citizenship seem largely anachronistic. Although the rhetoric of citizenship has endured, this book's analysis has exposed the frayed link between ownership and the norms of citizenship. As Americans increasingly turn to their homes as a means of building wealth, we need to ask ourselves whether owning a home continues to be a useful tool for deepening claims to citizenship and whether pushing homeownership continues to be the best way to build stronger communities.

APPENDIX

In this methodological note, I provide additional information on the empirical analysis in chapter 4. It includes information on both of the surveys that I used to track the civic habits of homeowners, as well as the specifications of the regression models used to identify the impact of homeownership and residential stability.

The main analyses in chapter 4 draw on the Social Capital Community Survey, which investigates the ways American citizens build and sustain social capital resources. The survey was first fielded in 2000, and a follow-up survey, which I use in this analysis, was fielded in 2006. The Saguro Seminar at Harvard University's Kennedy School of Government commissioned the survey to measure the civic and social habits of Americans. The survey includes a nationally representative sample of approximately 3,000 American adults, with a dozen community surveys to supplement the nationally representative survey. The analysis in chapter 4 includes only the nationally representative sample of survey respondents.

One of the main benefits of the Social Capital Community Survey is the breadth of indicators available to measure social capital, community engagement, and political participation. While I report about two dozen measures in chapter 4, the survey includes dozens of additional indicators to evaluate how citizens engage in their communities, build social capital, and become involved in politics. In fact, the Social Capital Community Survey offers the widest range of survey measures that is available to understand the ways citizens engage in their communities, making it the ideal source for studying homeowners' civic habits. It also includes a unique measure of residential stability that asks respondents how long they have lived in their communities.

At several points throughout chapter 4, I supplement the analysis of the Social Capital Community Survey with analyses of the Current Population Survey, a monthly survey conducted by the U.S. Bureau of Labor Statistics. Where possible, I separately validate the findings from the Social Capital Community Survey with a parallel analysis of the Current Population Survey, as many of the measures from the latter are drawn directly from the former.

The primary purpose of the Current Population Survey is to measure employment trends across the country. However, several times each year, the survey asks respondents about their participation in community activities, political affairs, and civic life. These variables are measured in three supplements of the Current Population Survey: the Volunteer Workers, the Civic Engagement, and the Voting and Registration supplements. These supplements are measured either biennially or annually. For the supplemental analyses, I draw on the most recent supplement available at the time of the analysis (i.e., the November 2012 Voting and Registration supplement, the November 2013 Civic Engagement supplement, and the September 2014 Volunteer Workers supplement).

While the Current Population Survey includes a substantially larger number of respondents than the Social Capital Community Survey, there are two drawbacks that limit the utility of the Current Population Survey as the main source of data for chapter 4. First, the number of indicators available in this survey is limited, meaning that most of the measures analyzed in this chapter are not available in it. Second, it does not include a unique indicator of residential stability, and it is therefore impossible to separate the impact of residential stability from the effect of homeownership.

For the regression analysis behind the even-numbered figures in chapter 4 (e.g., fig. 4.2, fig. 4.4, etc.), I estimate a logistic regression from the Social Capital Community Survey to identify the change in the odds associated with the measures of homeownership and residential stability. The regressions are weighted using the respondent weights in the survey data. For homeownership, I utilize a dichotomous measure indicating whether or not the respondent reported owning his or her home. For residential stability, I utilize a dichotomous measure identifying whether or not the respondent reported living in his or her community for at least five years. The regression models also include several other standard demographic variables, including race, ethnicity, education level, marital status, gender, age, employment status, income, the presence of children in the household, and metropolitan status (e.g., rural, suburban, urban).

For each pair of graphs (e.g., fig. 4.1 and fig. 4.2), I first report the raw comparison between homeowners and renters in the odd-numbered graphs (e.g., fig. 4.1). These graphs simply compare the percentage of homeowners who report participation in each activity to the percentage of renters who report participation without controlling for other respondent characteristics. Then, the second graph adjusts those comparisons by accounting for various social and demographic characteristics, as reported above. This analysis acknowledges that homeowners and renters differ from each other in meaningful ways, and these differences may account for the increased likelihood of homeowners participating in their communities.

From the logistic regression analyses, the even-numbered graphs (e.g., fig. 4.2) present the exponentiated coefficients to understand the way that homeownership and residential stability shape civic involvement. These odds ratios identify how homeownership and residential stability influence the likelihood of civic participation, controlling for other characteristics in the models.

NOTES

CHAPTER 1

1. Raphael W. Bostic, and Brian J. Surette, "Have the Doors Opened Wider? Trends in Homeownership Rates by Race and Income," *Journal of Real Estate Finance and Economics* 23 (3) (2001): 411–34. U.S. Census Bureau, "Residential Vacancies and Homeownership in the Fourth Quarter 2014," January 29, 2015, accessed July 20, 2015, http://www.census.gov/housing/hvs/files/currenthvspress.pdf.

2. James Surowiecki, "Home Economics," *New Yorker*, March 10, 2008. Carolina Reid, "To Buy or Not to Buy? Understanding Tenure Preferences and the Decisionmaking Processes of Lower-Income Households," in *Homeownership Built to Last*, edited by Eric S. Belsky, Christopher E. Herbert, and Jennifer H. Molinsky, 143–71 (Washington, DC: Brookings Institution Press, 2014). Allstate-National Journal Poll, "New Poll: Americans Still Believe Deeply in Homeownership as an Integral Part of the American Dream," March 8, 2011, accessed July 20, 2015, https://www.allstate.com/resources/Allstate/attachments/heartland-monitor/Heartland_VIII_Data.pdf.

3. Claudia, Vargas, "After Three Years, Some Success from Camden Housing Plan," *Philadelphia Inquirer*, June 4, 2008. Julia Terruso, "New Homeowners in Camden Predominantly Women," *Philadelphia Inquirer*, June 16, 2013.

4. Michael S. Carliner, "Development of Federal Homeownership 'Policy,'" *Housing Policy Debate* 9 (2) (1998): 299–321.

5. Alexander Keyssar, *The Right to Vote: The Contested History of Democracy in the United States* (New York: Basic Books, 2009). Donald A. Krueckeberg, "The Grapes of Rent: A History of Renting in a Country of Owners," *Housing Policy Debate* 10 (1) (1999): 9–30.

6. Keyssar, *The Right to Vote*.

7. George W. Bush, "National Homeownership Month, 2002: A Proclamation by the President of the United States," June 4, 2002, accessed July 20, 2015, http://georgewbush-whitehouse.archives.gov/news/releases/2002/06/20020604-23.html.

George W. Bush, "National Homeownership Month, 2005: A Proclamation by the President of the United States," May 25, 2005, accessed July 20, 2015, http:// georgewbush-whitehouse.archives.gov/news/releases/2005/05/20050525-14 .html.

8. U.S. Congress, Senate Committee on Banking, Housing and Urban Affairs, *Increasing Minority Homeownership, and Expanding Homeownership to All Who Wish to Attain It*, 108th Congress, 2003, S. Hrg. 108–573.

9. U.S. Department of Housing and Urban Development, "Homeownership Success Story," n.d., accessed July 20, 2015, http://portal.hud.gov/hudportal/HUD?src=/ program_offices/public_indian_housing/ih/codetalk/onap/nwonap/siletz.

10. In fig. 1.1, I include respondents who identified each statement as either a major or a minor reason to buy a home. These statements about the financial reasons for owning a home are drawn from a longer list of statements in the National Housing Survey. The survey also reports that Americans believe that owning your own home confers substantial lifestyle benefits. Families feel safer and enjoy greater control over their living environment when they own their own homes. Many homeowners report that homeownership creates a good environment for raising children, and a family can make design or renovation decisions without consulting their landlord. Rachel Bogardus Drew and Christopher E. Herbert, "Post-recession Drivers of Preferences for Homeownership," *Housing Policy Debate* 23 (4) (2013): 666–87.

11. In a poll conducted by the *National Journal*, respondents were asked to identify the best reason to become a homeowner. Half of the respondents pointed to one of the financial reasons offered, noting that homeownership enables households to build equity, make a long-term investment or receive a tax benefit. Allstate-National Journal Poll, "New Poll: Americans Still Believe Deeply in Homeownership as an Integral Part of the American Dream," March 8, 2011, accessed July 20, 2015, https://www.allstate.com/resources/Allstate/attachments/heartland-monitor/Heartland_VIII_Data.pdf.

12. The data from fig. 1.2 report housing wealth from the 2007 Survey of Consumer Finances in Christopher E. Herbert, Daniel T. McCue, and Rocio Sanchez-Moyano, "Is Homeownership Still an Effective Means of Building Wealth for Low-Income and Minority Households?," in *Homeownership Built to Last*, edited by Eric S. Belsky, Christopher E. Herbert, and Jennifer H. Molinsky, 50–98 (Washington, DC: Brookings Institution Press, 2013), table 1. During the Great Recession, as housing values fell, housing equity as a proportion of household wealth fell, especially for low-income and minority homeowners. However, as housing values rebounded, housing wealth as a share of total wealth started to grow. Christopher E. Herbert, Daniel T. McCue, and Rocio Sanchez-Moyano, "Is Homeownership Still an Effective Means of Building Wealth for Low-Income and Minority Households?," working paper no. HBTL-06 (Cambridge, MA: Joint Center for Housing Studies, Harvard University, 2013). Edward N. Wolff, "Recent Trends

in the Size Distribution of Household Wealth," *Journal of Economic Perspectives* 12 (3) (1998): 131–50, and "Recent Trends in Household Wealth in the United States: Rising Debt and the Middle-Class Squeeze," working paper no. 589 (Annandale-on-Hudson, NY: Levy Economic Institute, Bard College, 2007).

13. Raphael W. Bostic and Kwan Ok Lee, "Mortgages, Risk, and Homeownership among Low- and Moderate-Income Families," *American Economic Review* 98 (2) (2008): 310–14. Jesse Bricker, Arthur B. Kennickell, Kevin B. Moore, and John Sabelhaus, "Changes in U.S. Family Finances from 2007 to 2010: Evidence from the Survey of Consumer Finances," *Federal Reserve Bulletin* 98 (2) (2012).

14. Zhu Xiao Di, Eric Belsky, and Xiaodong Liu. "Do Homeowners Achieve More Household Wealth in the Long Run?," *Journal of Housing Economics* 16 (3–4) (2007): 274–90. Tracy M. Turner and Heather Luea, "Homeownership, Wealth Accumulation and Income Status," *Journal of Housing Economics* 18 (2) (2009): 104–14. Thomas Shapiro, Tatjana Meschede, and Sam Osoro, "The Roots of the Widening Racial Wealth Gap: Explaining the Black-White Economic Divide" (Waltham, MA: Institute on Assets and Social Policy, Brandeis University, 2013). Christopher E. Hebert, Daniel T. McCue, and Rocio Sanchez-Moyano, "Is Homeownership Still an Effective Means of Building Wealth for Low-Income and Minority Households?," in Belsky et al., *Homeownership Built to Last*, 50–98. Donald R. Haurin, Patric H. Hendershott, and Susan M. Wachter, "Expected Home Ownership and Real Wealth Accumulation of Youth," working paper no. 5629 (Cambridge, MA: National Bureau of Economic Research, 1996). Thomas P. Boehm and Alan Schlottmann, "Wealth Accumulation and Homeownership: Evidence for Low-Income Households," *Cityscape* 10 (2) (2008): 225–56. Michal Grinstein-Weiss, Clinton Key, Shenyang Guo, Yeong Hun Yeo, and Krista Holub, "Homeownership and Wealth among Low- and Moderate-Income Households," *Housing Policy Debate* 23 (2) (2013): 259–79.

15. Tamara Keith, "Walking Away from the Housing She Can Afford," *All Things Considered*, National Public Radio, December 25, 2009, accessed July 20, 2015, http://www.npr.org/templates/story/story.php?storyId=121907594.

16. These types of struggles would lead to a broader discussion in the public sphere about the end of homeownership, and whether Americans would turn to renting. Thomas J. Sugrue, "The New American Dream: Renting," *Wall Street Journal*, August 14, 2009; Barbara Kiviat, "The Case against Homeownership," *Time*, September 11, 2010; Derek Thompson, "The End of Ownership: Why Aren't Young People Buying More Houses?," *Atlantic*, February 29, 2012; Derek Thompson, "'We Wish Like Hell We Had Never Bought': Voices from the Housing Crisis," *Atlantic*, March 2, 2012; Richard Florida, "Renting the American Dream," *Atlantic*, April 23, 2013. There is also a growing body of research on the decision-making process of underwater homeowners. Brett White, "Underwater and Not Walking Away: Shame, Fear and the Social Management of the Housing Crisis," *Wake Forest Law Review* 45 (2010): 971–1024.

17. Jennifer H. Molinsky, Eric S. Belsky, and Christopher E. Herbert, "Introduction: Balancing Access, Affordability, and Risk after the Housing Crisis," in Belsky et al., *Homeownership Built to Last* (Washington, DC: Brookings Institution Press, 2014), 17.

18. There is a substantial literature on the causes and consequences of the housing crisis and the recession. Charles V. Bagli, *Other People's Money: Inside the Housing Crisis and the Demise of the Greatest Real Estate Deal Ever Made* (New York: Dutton, 2013). Belsky et al., *Homeownership Built to Last*. Atif Milan and Amir Sufi, *House of Debt: How They (and You) Caused the Great Recession, and How We Can Prevent It from Happening Again* (Chicago: University of Chicago Press, 2015). Viral V. Acharya, Matthew Richardson, Stijn van Nieuwerburgh, and Lawrence J. White, *Guaranteed to Fail: Fannie Mae, Freddie Mac, and the Debacle of Mortgage Finance* (Princeton, NJ: Princeton University Press, 2011). Timothy Howard, *The Mortgage Wars: Inside Fannie Mae, Big-Money Politics, and the Collapse of the American Dream* (New York: McGraw-Hill, 2013). Nicolas P. Retsinas and Eric S. Belsky, *Low-Income Homeownership: Examining the Unexamined Goal* (Washington, DC: Brookings Institution Press, 2002). Michael Lewis, *The Big Short: Inside the Doomsday Machine* (New York: Norton, 2011). Alyssa Katz, *Our Lot: How Real Estate Came to Own Us* (New York: Bloomsbury, 2009). Jennifer Taub, *Other People's Houses: How Decades of Bailouts, Captive Regulators and Toxic Bankers Made Home Mortgages a Thrilling Business* (New Haven: Yale University Press, 2014). Herman Schwartz, *Subprime Nation: American Power, Global Capital, and the Housing Bubble* (Ithaca, NY: Cornell University Press, 2009).

19. These statistics come from an analysis of subprime lending from the Joint Center for Housing Studies at Harvard University, "The State of the Nation's Housing, 2008" (Cambridge, MA: Joint Center for Housing Studies, Harvard University, 2008), figure 4.

20. There is a substantial body of research on the subprime lending industry, including the performance of subprime loans and their contribution to the recession. Christopher L. Foote, Kristopher Gerardi, Lorenz Goette, and Paul S. Willen, "Just the Facts: An Initial Analysis of Subprime's Role in the Housing Crisis," *Journal of Housing Economics* 17 (4) (2008): 291–305. Anthony Sanders, "The Subprime Crisis and Its Role in the Financial Crisis," *Journal of Housing Economics* 17 (4) (2008): 254–61.

21. Jeff Kearns, "Fed Says U.S. Wealth Fell 38.8% in 2007–2010 on Housing," *Bloomberg News*, June 12, 2012; Yian Q. Mui, "Americans Saw Wealth Plummet 40 Percent from 2007 to 2010, Federal Reserve Says," *Washington Post*, June 11, 2012.

22. Anne B. Shlay, "Low-Income Homeownership: American Dream or Delusion?," *Urban Studies* 43 (3) (2006): 511–31. William M. Rohe and Harry L. Watson, *Chasing the American Dream: New Perspectives on Affordable Homeownership* (Ithaca, NY: Cornell University Press, 2007).

23. In her recent book, Mechele Dickerson refers this ideology of ownership as the Happy Homeowners Narrative—the uncritical belief that homeownership transforms citizens into happier, wealthier, more stable and involved citizens. Dickerson, *Homeownership and America's Financial Underclass: Flawed Premises, Broken Promises, New Prescriptions* (New York: Cambridge University Press, 2014). Rachel Bogardus Drew, "Constructing Homeownership Policy: Social Constructions and the Design of the Low-Income Homeownership Policy Objective," *Housing Studies* 28 (4) (2013): 616–31. Shlay, "Low-Income Homeownership," 511–31. Richard Ronald, *The Ideology of Home Ownership: Homeowner Societies and the Role of Housing* (New York: Palgrave Macmillan, 2008). Kristen David Adams, "Homeownership: American Dream or Illusion of Empowerment," *South Carolina Law Review* 60 (2008): 574–615.

24. This approach to the study of housing and homeownership invites sociologists back into the subdiscipline. Recently, sociologist Mary Pattillo noted that few sociologists are studying housing as a social institution: "The study of housing, per se, is somewhat secondary to what many sociologists focus on because homes and apartments are first and foremost physical entities, not social relations or institutions." Pattillo, "Housing: Commodity versus Right," *Annual Review of Sociology* 39 (1) (2013): 510–11. With this critique, Pattillo joins a group of scholars concerned about the place of sociologists in the study of homeownership. Jim Kemeny, "Home Ownership and Privatization," *International Journal of Urban and Regional Research* 4 (3) (1980): 372–88, and *Myth of Home Ownership: Private Versus Public Choices in Housing Tenure* (New York: Routledge, Kegan and Paul, 1982). Peter Saunders, "Domestic Property and Social Class," *International Journal of Urban and Regional Research* 2 (1–4) (1978): 233–51, and *A Nation of Home Owners* (London: Unwin Hyman,1990). Donald L. Foley, "The Sociology of Housing," *Annual Review of Sociology* 6 (1980): 457–78.

CHAPTER 2

1. According to the National Housing Agency, residential construction was in sharp decline during World War I. In 1909, there were 573,000 nonfarm housing starts, but that figure had dropped 30 percent by 1914. It continued to fall sharply as the war began. In 1918, only 174,000 residential units were constructed. The federal government ordered a restriction on other construction projects to dedicate building materials to the war efforts, and this further contributed to the sharp decline in housing construction. National Housing Agency, "Housing after World War I: Will History Repeat Itself?," National Housing Bulletin no. 4 (Washington, DC: National Housing Agency, 1945).

2. Herbert Hoover, "Statement Announcing the White House Conference on Home Building and Home Ownership," September 15, 1931, accessed July 21, 2015, http://www.presidency.ucsb.edu/ws/?pid=22804.

3. In his memoir, Hoover writes about the importance of expanding home-ownership and sound housing opportunities as the secretary of commerce. "When I came to the Department [of Commerce] I was convinced that a great contribution to reconstruction and a large expansion in employment could be achieved by supplying the greatest social need of the country—more and better housing. Adequate housing for people of lesser incomes had fallen behind because of restrictions on construction during the war; but even without this setback fully 30 per cent of our housing was below American ideals of decent family life. The cost of construction was excessive, the designs were wretched, and the sentiment, 'Own your own home,' was losing force," he wrote. *The Memoirs of Herbert Hoover* (New York: Macmillan, 1952), 92.

4. David M. Kennedy, *Freedom from Fear: The American People in Depression and War, 1929–1945* (New York: Oxford University Press, 2001).

5. Herbert Hoover, "Address of President Hoover at the Opening Meeting of the President's Conference on Home Building and Home Ownership," 1931, Better Homes—White House Conference on Home Building File, Printed Material, 1931, Dec. 2–3, box 74A, Presidential Papers—Subject File, Herbert Hoover Presidential Library, West Branch, Iowa.

6. Herbert Hoover, "Address of President Hoover at the Opening Meeting of the President's Conference on Home Building and Home Ownership," 1931, Better Homes—White House Conference on Home Building File, Printed Material, 1931, Dec. 2–3, box 74A, Presidential Papers—Subject File, Herbert Hoover Presidential Library.

7. William Cronon, *Nature's Metropolis: Chicago and the Great West* (New York: Norton, 1991).

8. Campbell Gibson, "Population of the 100 Largest Cities and Other Urban Places in the United States: 1790–1990," working paper no. 27, Population Division, U.S. Bureau of the Census, June 1998, accessed July 20, 2015, http://www.census.gov/population/www/documentation/twps0027/twps0027.html.

9. Robert H. Wiebe, *The Search for Order, 1877–1920* (New York: Hill and Wang, 1967).

10. Building and Housing File, 1925, box 64, folder 01221, Commerce Papers, Herbert Hoover Presidential Library.

11. Margaret Garb, *City of American Dreams: A History of Home Ownership and Housing Reform in Chicago, 1871–1919* (Chicago: University of Chicago Press, 2011). John Modell and Tamara K. Hareven, "Urbanization and the Malleable Household: An Examination of Boarding and Lodging in American Families," *Journal of Marriage and Family* 35 (3) (1973): 467–79. Michael B. Katz, Michael J. Doucet, and Mark J. Stern, *The Social Organization of Early Industrial Capitalism* (Cambridge, MA: Harvard University Press, 1982). Olivier Zunz, *The Changing Face of Inequality: Urbanization, Industrial Development, and Immigrants in Detroit, 1880–1920* (Chicago: University of Chicago Press, 1983). Richard Harris,

"Working-Class Home Ownership in the American Metropolis," *Journal of Urban History* 17 (1) (1990): 46–69, and "The End Justified the Means: Boarding and Rooming in a City of Homes, 1890–1951," *Journal of Social History* 26 (2) (1992): 331–58.

12. Paul S. Boyer, *Urban Masses and Moral Order in America, 1820–1920* (Cambridge, MA: Harvard University Press, 1992).

13. While many of these reform efforts were rooted in Progressive politics, the Progressive movement fell quickly on hard times as the war ended and a growing conservative movement began to rethink the role of the government. Conservatives, like Herbert Hoover, imagined a greater role for the federal government in orchestrating business interests and guiding private organizations to fulfill national goals, including the promotion of homeownership. This vision relied increasingly on voluntary organizations to promote community life and the practices of citizenship. Michael E. McGerr, *The Decline of Popular Politics: The American North, 1865–1928* (New York: Oxford University Press, 1986). Lewis L. Gould, *America in the Progressive Era, 1890–1914* (New York: Longman, 2001). Christopher Capozzola, *Uncle Sam Wants You: World War I and the Making of the Modern American Citizen* (New York: Oxford University Press, 2008).

14. Constance Perin, *Everything in Its Place: Social Order and Land Use in America* (Princeton, NJ: Princeton University Press, 1977). Dolores Hayden, *Redesigning the American Dream: The Future of Housing, Work, and Family Life* (New York: Norton, 1986).

15. LeeAnn Lands, "Be a Patriot, Buy a Home: Re-imagining Home Owners and Home Ownership in Early 20th Century Atlanta," *Journal of Social History* 41 (4) (2008): 943–65, and *The Culture of Property: Race, Class, and Housing Landscapes in Atlanta, 1880–1950* (Athens: University of Georgia Press, 2009). Lawrence J. Vale, "The Ideological Origins of Affordable Homeownership Efforts," in *Chasing the American Dream: New Perspectives on Affordable Homeownership*, edited by William M. Rohe and Harry L. Watson, 15–40 (Ithaca, NY: Cornell University Press, 2007).

16. Carl M. Hames, *Hill Ferguson, His Life and Works* (Birmingham: University of Alabama Press, 1978).

17. Lynn Dumenil, *The Modern Temper: American Culture and Society in the 1920s* (New York: Hill and Wang, 1995). Jeffrey M. Hornstein, *A Nation of Realtors: A Cultural History of the Twentieth-Century American Middle Class*. Durham, NC: Duke University Press, 2005), 34.

18. "Planning an Own Your Own Home Campaign: Suggestions Taken from Cities Where Campaigns Have Been Successfully Held," *National Real Estate Journal*, December 1918, 153–56.

19. "Many 'Own Your Home' Campaigns Being Planned for 1918," *National Real Estate Journal*, February 1918, 71–72.

20. "McAdoo Deprecates Home Building," *New York Times*, February 5, 1918.

21. Even when commercial groups worked to promote homeownership, they often pointed to the civic benefits of expanding homeownership opportunities, ignoring their own commercial interests in their publicity materials. For example, the National Lumber Manufacturers Association published a booklet, *Housing and Industry*, that underscored the core place of the owner-occupied home in the growth of the nation. "The backbone of a community, as well as that of a nation, is its home-loving citizens," wrote R. S. Whiting, the publication's author. "Therefore, the very life and existence of this great country of ours depends largely upon the number of individual homes owned, as well as the nature of their surroundings"; Whiting, *Housing and Industry* (Chicago: National Lumber Manufacturers Association).

22. Building and Housing File, 1928, box 64, folder 01225, Commerce Papers, Herbert Hoover Presidential Library. The list of sponsoring civic organizations also included the American Civic Association, American Construction Council, American Home Economics Association, Chamber of Commerce, Garden Club of America, General Federation of Women's Clubs, National Conference of Parents and Teachers, and National Federation of Music Clubs.

23. Elizabeth Carlisle, "Why and How to Teach Civic Effectiveness as Illustrated by School Participation in the Community Better Homes Campaign," publication no. 2 (Washington, DC: Better Homes in America, 1930), Building and Housing, Better Homes in America, Printed Matter, 1923–1927 and undated, box 66, folder 01242, Herbert Hoover Presidential Library.

24. Better Homes in America—White House Conference on Home Building and Ownership File, 1933 and undated, box 74, Presidential Papers—Subject Files, Herbert Hoover Presidential Library. Karen E. Altman, "Consuming Ideology: The Better Homes in America Campaign," *Critical Studies in Mass Communication* 7 (3) (1990): 286–307. Janet Hutchison, "The Cure for Domestic Neglect: Better Homes in America, 1922–1935," *Perspectives in Vernacular Architecture* 2 (1986): 168–78, "Better Homes and Gullah," *Agricultural History* 67 (2) (1993): 102–18, and "Building for Babbitt: The State and the Suburban Home Ideal," *Journal of Policy History* 9 (2) (1997): 184–210. Paul C. Luken and Suzanne Vaughan, "'... Be a Genuine Homemaker in Your Own Home': Gender and Familial Relations in State Housing Practices, 1917–1922," *Social Forces* 83 (4) (2005): 1603–25, and "Standardizing Childrearing through Housing," *Social Problems* 53 (3) (2006): 299–331.

25. Building and Housing File, 1923, box 64, folder 01219, Commerce Papers, Herbert Hoover Presidential Library.

26. Building and Housing File, 1925, box 64, folder 01221, Commerce Papers, Herbert Hoover Presidential Library.

27. Building and Housing File—Better Homes in America, Printed Matter, 1923–1927 and undated, box 66, folder 01242, Commerce Papers, Herbert Hoover Presidential Library.

28. "Are You Sittin' Pretty?," *Buffalo Courier*, April 14, 1924.

29. "Build Homes to Make Good Citizens," *Chicago Commerce*, August 2, 1919. In the 1870s, Friedrich Engels addressed the issue of homeownership in creating docile factor workers by tying them to the existing system of industrial production. Encouraging workers to own their own homes would validate the oppressive system of class relations under capitalism, creating a new obstacle for the revolutionary spirit of the working class, according to Engels. Friedrich Engels, *Housing Question* (New York: Firebird, 1979).

30. Fred Reed, "Rushing the 'Buy a Home' Campaign," *National Real Estate Journal*, May 1917, 70–71.

31. Better Homes in America, Plan Book for Demonstration Week, June 4–10, 1923, Building and Housing File—Better Homes in America, Printed Matter, 1923–1927 and undated, box 66, folder 01242, Commerce Papers, Herbert Hoover Presidential Library.

32. Dell Upton, "Pattern Books and Professionalism: Aspects of the Transformation of Domestic Architecture in America, 1800–1860," *Winterthur Portfolio* 19 (2–3) (1984): 107–50. Clifford Edward Clark, *American Family Home, 1800–1960* (Chapel Hill: University of North Carolina Press, 1986). Andrew Jackson Downing, *The Architecture of Country Houses: Including Designs for Cottages, and Farmhouses, and Villas, with Remarks on Interiors, Furniture, and the Best Modes of Warming and Ventilating* (New York: Dover, 1969). Andrew Jackson Downing and Robert Twombly, *Andrew Jackson Downing: Essential Texts* (New York: Norton, 2012).

33. Building and Housing File—Better Homes in America, Printed Matter, 1923–1927 and undated, box 66, folder 01242, Herbert Hoover Presidential Library.

34. "Real Estate Columns of the Want Ad Section of the Sunpapers, Buy Now," *Baltimore Sun*, Monday, November 3, 1924. These types of editorializing were common in newspapers throughout the country. In 1925, the *Los Angeles Times* wrote: "Home-ownership, stability and good citizenship have almost become synonymous phrases. Rarely is one disassociated from the other two. Agitators are generally found among the floating population, composed of renters. This is the general rule"; "Fact and Comment," *Los Angeles Times*, November 1, 1925. In 1919, the *Chicago Daily Tribune* took to celebrate homeownership and the campaigns to promote it. "The idea has been tried with astounding success in many cities. The advantage to the city as a whole, from the standpoint of better citizenship alone, is so great as to more than justify all the efforts that may be expended"; "'Own Your Own Home' Campaign by Realty Men," *Chicago Daily Tribune*, February 2, 1919.

35. Building and Housing File, Own Your Own Home, 1925–1928 and undated, box 68, folder 01270, Commerce Papers, Herbert Hoover Presidential Library.

36. "The 'Own Your Home' Campaigns," *National Real Estate Journal*, June-July 1918. John P. Dean, *Homeownership: Is It Sound?* (New York: Harper, 1945), 41.

37. "The 'Own Your Home' Movement' the Crying Need of the Nation," *National Real Estate Journal*, June–July 1918.
38. "Many 'Own Your Home' Campaigns Being Planned for 1918," *National Real Estate Journal*, February 1918, 71–72.
39. Herbert Hoover, "Address of President Hoover at the Opening Meeting of the President's Conference on Home Building and Home Ownership," 1931, Better Homes—White House Conference on Home Building File, Printed Material, 1931, Dec. 2–3, box 74A, Presidential Papers—Subject File, Herbert Hoover Presidential Library.
40. Wilbur was a close confidant of President Hoover and would serve as secretary of the interior for the duration of Hoover's time as president. After leaving office, Wilbur would become a fierce critic of the New Deal policies of Hoover's successor, Franklin D. Roosevelt.

CHAPTER 3

1. John P. Dean, *Home Ownership: Is It Sound?* (New York: Harper, 1945), 2.
2. Proponents of thrifts argued that these institutions helped to ward off the evils of communism and socialism lurking in the country's urban centers by uniting citizens with a shared commitment to homeownership. Advertisements for these building and loan associations suggested that thrifts turned the average worker into a good capitalist, committed to promoting democratic capitalism rather than overthrowing it. David Mason, *From Buildings and Loans to Bail-outs: A History of the Savings and Loan Industry, 1831–1989* (New York: Cambridge University Press, 2004). Michael J. Lea, "Innovation and the Cost of Mortgage Credit: A Historical Perspective," *Housing Policy Debate* 7 (1) (1996): 147–74.
3. Michael S. Carliner, "Development of Federal Homeownership 'Policy,'" *Housing Policy Debate* 9 (2) (1998): 299–321. J. Paul Mitchell, *Federal Housing Policy and Programs: Past and Present* (New Brunswick, NJ: Center for Urban Policy Research, 1985). Joseph E. Morton, *Urban Mortgage Lending: Comparative Markets and Experience* (Princeton, NJ: Princeton University Press, 1956). Frederick J. Eggers, "Homeownership: A Housing Success Story," *Cityscape* 5 (2) (2001): 43–56. Gail Radford, *Modern Housing for America: Policy Struggles in the New Deal Era* (Chicago: University of Chicago Press, 1997).
4. While this chapter is concerned with federal housing policies, many city governments and local community groups work to promote homeownership as well. Victoria Basolo, "Explaining the Support for Homeownership Policy in US Cities: A Political Economy Perspective," *Housing Studies* 22 (1) (2007): 99–119. Alexander von Hoffman, *House by House, Block by Block: The Rebirth of America's Urban Neighborhoods* (New York: Oxford University Press, 2004).
5. Douglas S. Massey and Nancy A. Denton, *American Apartheid: Segregation and the Making of the Underclass* (Cambridge, MA: Harvard University Press, 1993).

Christopher Bonastia, *Knocking on the Door: The Federal Government's Attempt to Desegregate the Suburbs* (Princeton, NJ: Princeton University Press, 2010). Richard R. W. Brooks and Carol M. Rose, *Saving the Neighborhood: Racially Restrictive Covenants, Law, and Social Norms* (Cambridge, MA: Harvard University Press, 2013). Camille Zubrinksy Charles, *Won't You Be My Neighbor? Race, Class, and Residence in Los Angeles* (New York: Russell Sage Foundation, 2009).

6. Kevin Fox Gotham, "Racialization and the State: The Housing Act of 1934 and the Creation of the Federal Housing Administration," *Sociological Perspectives* 43 (2) (2000): 291–317. Gotham shows that the number of foreclosures climbed from 78,000 in 1926 to over 230,000 in 1932. Annual residential permits for new housing units dropped from 490,000 units to fewer than 26,000 units.

7. J. Paul Mitchell, "Historic Overview of Federal Policy: Encouraging Home-ownership," in Mitchell, *Federal Housing Policy and Programs*, 39–46. Kent W. Colton, *Housing in the Twenty-First Century: Achieving Common Ground* (Cambridge, MA: Harvard University Press, 2003). Daniel Immergluck, *Credit to the Community: Community Reinvestment and Fair Lending Policy in the United States* (New York: M. E. Sharpe, 2004), 36–37. Milton P. Semer, Julian H. Zimmerman, Ashley Foard, and John M. Frantz, "Evolution of Federal Legislative Policy in Housing: Housing Credits," in Mitchell, *Federal Housing Policy and Programs*, 69–106.

8. Alex F. Schwartz, *Housing Policy in the United States* (New York: Routledge, 2010). Kenneth T. Jackson, *Crabgrass Frontier: The Suburbanization of the United States* (New York: Oxford University Press, 1987). Kent W. Colton, *Housing in the Twenty-First Century: Achieving Common Ground* (Cambridge, MA: Harvard University Press, 2003).

9. Amy E. Hillier, "Redlining and the Home Owners' Loan Corporation," *Journal of Urban History* 29 (4) (2003): 394–420. Kenneth T. Jackson, "Race, Ethnicity, and Real Estate Appraisal: The Home Owners Loan Corporation and the Federal Housing Administration," *Journal of Urban History* 6 (1980): 419–52. Kristen B. Crossney and David W. Bartelt, "The Legacy of the Home Owners' Loan Corporation," *Housing Policy Debate* 16 (3–4) (2005): 547–74, and "Residential Security, Risk, and Race: The Home Owners' Loan Corporation and Mortgage Access in Two Cities," *Urban Geography* 26 (8) (2005): 707–36.

10. Jackson, *Crabgrass Frontier*, 203.

11. Schwartz, *Housing Policy in the United States*. Patric H. Hendershott and Kevin E. Villani, "Direct Intervention in the Mortgage Market," in Mitchell, *Federal Housing Policy and Programs*, 123–41.

12. Gertrude Sipperly Fish, *The Story of Housing* (New York: Macmillan, 1979), 200.

13. Schwartz, *Housing Policy in the United States*. Jackson, *Crabgrass Frontier*. Colton, *Housing in the Twenty-First Century*. David M. French, "The Contest for a National System of Home-Mortgage Finance," *American Political Science Review* 35 (1) (1941): 53–69. Carliner, "Development of Federal Homeownership 'Policy,'"

299–321. Robert E. Lloyd, "Government-Induced Market Failure: A Note on the Origins of FHA Mortgage Insurance," *Critical Review* 8 (1) (1994): 61–71.

14. Jackson, *Crabgrass Frontier*, 205. Rosalyn Baxandall and Elizabeth Ewen, *Picture Windows: How the Suburbs Happened* (New York: Basic Books, 2000). Robert A. Beauregard, *When America Became Suburban* (Minneapolis: University of Minnesota Press, 2006). According to the Census, the number of households living in homes they owned in the United States rose from 44 million in 1950 to 53 million in 1960.

15. Herbert J. Gans, *The Levittowners* (New York: Columbia University Press, 1982). Dianne Harris, *Second Suburb: Levittown, Pennsylvania* (Pittsburgh: University of Pittsburgh Press, 2013). Barbara M. Kelly, *Expanding the American Dream* (Albany: State University of New York Press, 1993). David Kushner, *Levittown* (New York: Walker Books, 2009).

16. Suzanne Mettler, *Soldiers to Citizens: The G.I. Bill and the Making of the Greatest Generation* (New York: Oxford University Press, 2005). Melissa Murray, "When War Is Work: The G.I. Bill, Citizenship, and the Civic Generation," *California Law Review* 96 (4) (2008): 967–98.

17. Michael J. Bennett, *When Dreams Came True: The GI Bill and the Making of Modern America* (Lincoln, NE: Potomac Books, 1996). Edward Humes, *Over Here: How the G.I. Bill Transformed the American Dream* (New York: Harcourt, 2006). Takashi Yamashita, "The Effect of the GI Bill on Homeownership of World War II Veterans," 2008, unpublished working paper, Department of Economics, Reed College.

18. Jackson, *Crabgrass Frontier*, 241.

19. Gwendolyn Wright, *Building the Dream: A Social History of Housing in America* (Cambridge, MA: MIT Press, 1983). Richard M. Flanagan, "The Housing Act of 1954: The Sea Change in National Urban Policy," *Urban Affairs Review* 33 (2) (1997): 265–86. Alexander Von Hoffman, "A Study in Contradictions: The Origins and Legacy of the Housing Act of 1949," *Housing Policy Debate* 11 (2) (2000): 299–326. Jon C. Teaford, "Urban Renewal and Its Aftermath," *Housing Policy Debate* 11 (2) (2000): 443–65. United States Housing and Home Finance Agency, *Handbook of Information on Provisions of the Housing Act of 1949 and Operations Under the Various Programs* (Washington, DC: Housing and Home Finance Agency, Office of the Administrator, 1950).

20. Sylvia C. Martinez, "The Housing Act of 1949: Its Place in the Realization of the American Dream of Homeownership," *Housing Policy Debate* 11 (2) (2000): 467–87. Robert E. Lang and Rebecca R. Sohmer, "Legacy of the Housing Act of 1949: The Past, Present, and Future of Federal Housing and Urban Policy," *Housing Policy Debate* 11 (2) (2000): 291–98.

21. While the American population grew by 50 percent between 1920 and 1950, the number of registered automobiles tripled. In 1925, 17 million cars were registered in the United States; by 1955, the number of registered automobiles had grown

to 52 million. Thomas W. Hanchett, "Financing Suburbia: Prudential Insurance and the Post–World War II Transformation of the American City," *Journal of Urban History* 26 (3) (2000): 312–28. John F. Bauman, Roger Biles, and Kristin M. Szylvian, *From Tenements to the Taylor Homes: In Search of an Urban Housing Policy in Twentieth-Century America* (University Park: Pennsylvania State University Press, 2000). Beauregard, *When America Became Suburban*. Andres Duany, Elizabeth Plater-Zyberk, and Jeff Speck, *Suburban Nation: The Rise of Sprawl and the Decline of the American Dream* (New York: Macmillan, 2001). Jackson, *Crabgrass Frontier*.

22. Adam Gordon, "The Creation of Homeownership: How New Deal Changes in Banking Regulation Simultaneously Made Homeownership Accessible to Whites and Out of Reach for Blacks," *Yale Law Journal* 115 (1) (2005): 186–226. Thomas M. Shapiro, "Race, Homeownership and Wealth," *Washington University Journal of Law and Policy* 20 (2006): 53–74.

23. Thomas J. Sugrue, *The Origins of the Urban Crisis: Race and Inequality in Postwar Detroit* (Princeton, NJ: Princeton University Press, 2005).

24. United States National Advisory Commission on Civil Disorders, *Report of the National Advisory Commission on Civil Disorders* (Washington, DC: U.S. Government Printing Office, 1968), 261.

25. Although the Section 235 program was short-lived, it helped more than 400,000 low-income households to buy a home. John McClaughry, "The Troubled Dream: The Life and Times of Section 235 of the National Housing Act," *Loyola University of Chicago Law Journal* 6 (1975): 1–35. Schwartz, *Housing Policy in the United States*. Martinez, "The Housing Act of 1949: Its Place in the Realization of the American Dream of Homeownership," 467–87. Kevin Fox Gotham, "Separate and Unequal: The Housing Act of 1968 and the Section 235 Program," *Sociological Forum* 15 (1) (2000): 13–37.

26. Manuel B. Aalbers, *Place, Exclusion and Mortgage Markets* (New York: Wiley, 2011). Christian A. L. Hilber and Yingchun Liu, "Explaining the Black–White Home-ownership Gap: The Role of Own Wealth, Parental Externalities and Locational Preferences," *Journal of Housing Economics* 17 (2) (2008): 152–74. Antero Pietila, *Not in My Neighborhood: How Bigotry Shaped a Great American City* (Chicago: Rowman and Littlefield, 2010). Calvin Bradford, "Financing Home Ownership: The Federal Role in Neighborhood Decline," *Urban Affairs Review* 14 (3) (1979): 313–35.

27. Douglas S. Massey and Nancy A. Denton, *American Apartheid: Segregation and the Making of the Underclass* (Cambridge, MA: Harvard University Press, 1993). Christopher Bonastia, *Knocking on the Door: The Federal Government's Attempt to Desegregate the Suburbs* (Princeton, NJ: Princeton University Press, 2010). Nancy A. Denton, "Half Empty or Half Full: Segregation and Segregated Neighborhoods 30 Years after the Fair Housing Act," *Cityscape* 4 (3) (1999): 107–22. John Yinger, "Sustaining the Fair Housing Act," *Cityscape* 4 (3) (1999): 93–106.

28. One study, conducted in the early 1980s in Boston, found that blacks were invited to inspect one-third fewer units than comparable whites in their housing searches, pointing to persistent discrimination even under the Fair Housing Act. John Yinger, "Measuring Racial Discrimination with Fair Housing Audits: Caught in the Act," *The American Economic Review* 76 (5) (1986): 881–93, and *Closed Doors, Opportunities Lost: The Continuing Costs of Housing Discrimination* (New York: Russell Sage Foundation, 1997).

29. Richard D. Marsico, "Fighting Poverty through Community Empowerment and Economic Development: The Role of the Community Reinvestment and Home Mortgage Disclosure Acts," *New York Law School Journal of Human Rights* 12 (1994): 281–309. Douglas S. Massey, "Racial Discrimination in Housing: A Moving Target," *Social Problems* 52 (2) (2005): 148–51. Schwartz, *Housing Policy in the United States.*

30. John Taylor and Josh Silver, "The Community Reinvestment Act at 30: Looking Back and Looking to the Future," *New York Law School Law Review* 53 (2008): 203–25. Ren Essene and William Apgar, "The 30th Anniversary of the CRA: Restructuring the CRA to Address the Mortgage Finance Revolution," in *Revisiting the CRA: Perspectives on the Future of the Community Reinvestment Act*, edited by Prabal Chakrabarti, David Erickson, Ren S. Essene, Ian Galloway, and John Olson, 12–29 (San Francisco: Federal Reserve Bank of San Francisco, 2009). Allen J. Fishbein, "The Community Reinvestment Act after Fifteen Years: It Works, but Strengthened Federal Enforcement Is Needed," *Fordham Urban Law Journal* 20 (1992): 293–310. William C. Apgar and Mark Duda. "The Twenty-Fifth Anniversary of the Community Reinvestment Act: Past Accomplishments and Future Regulatory Challenges," *Economic Policy Review* 9 (2) (2003): 169–91.

31. Dean, *Home Ownership: Is It Sound?*, 120. Margaret Garb, *City of American Dreams: A History of Home Ownership and Housing Reform in Chicago, 1871–1919* (Chicago: University of Chicago Press, 2011).

32. Garb, *City of American Dreams*. Becky M. Nicolaides, *My Blue Heaven: Life and Politics in the Working-Class Suburbs of Los Angeles, 1920–1965* (Chicago: University of Chicago Press, 2002). Gans, *The Levittowners*, table 2.

33. Paul Pierson, "The New Politics of the Welfare State," *World Politics* 48 (2) (1996): 143–79, and *Dismantling the Welfare State? Reagan, Thatcher and the Politics of Retrenchment* (New York: Cambridge University Press, 1994). Monica Prasad, *The Land of Too Much: American Abundance and the Paradox of Poverty* (Cambridge, MA: Harvard University Press, 2012). Richard Clayton and Jonas Pontusson, "Welfare-State Retrenchment Revisited: Entitlement Cuts, Public Sector Restructuring, and Inegalitarian Trends in Advanced Capitalist Societies," *World Politics* 51 (1) (1998): 67–98.

34. Jacob S. Hacker, *The Great Risk Shift: The New Economic Insecurity and the Decline of the American Dream* (New York: Oxford University Press, 2004), 243–44. While there is a small literature on the politics of housing and the changing welfare

state, as I note in the conclusion, there is remarkably little research on the relationship in the American context. Some theorists have characterized homeownership as a substitute for the provisions of a generous welfare state. This represents a trade-off inherent in the politics of risk, as ownership emerges as a substitute for public management of social risk. However, others argue that the prevalence of homeowners may, in fact, be a political justification for retrenchment programs and policies. When citizens own their own homes, political leaders may see an opportunity to cut back on the provision of welfare services, including public programs of health insurance, retirement benefits, or unemployment insurance. Dalton Conley and Brian Gifford, "Home Ownership, Social Insurance, and the Welfare State," *Sociological Forum* 21 (1) (2006): 55–82. Ben Ansell, "The Political Economy of Ownership: Housing Markets and the Welfare State," *American Political Science Review* 108 (2) (2014): 383–402. Ulf Torgersen, "Housing: The Wobbly Pillar under the Welfare State," *Scandinavian Housing and Planning Research* 41987: 116–26. Jim Kemeny, "Home Ownership and Privatization," *International Journal of Urban and Regional Research* 4 (3) (1980): 372–88, "Comparative Housing and Welfare: Theorising the Relationship," *Journal of Housing and the Built Environment* 16 (1) (2001): 53–70, and "'The Really Big Trade-Off' between Home Ownership and Welfare: Castles' Evaluation of the 1980 Thesis, and a Reformulation 25 Years On," *Housing, Theory and Society* 22 (2) (2005): 59–75. Janneke Toussaint and Marja Elsinga, "Exploring 'Housing Asset–Based Welfare': Can the UK Be Held Up as an Example for Europe?," *Housing Studies* 24 (5) (2009): 669–92. John Doling and Nick Horsewood, "Home Ownership and Pensions: Causality and the Really Big Trade -off," *Housing, Theory and Society* 28 (2) (2010): 166–82. John Doling and Richard Ronald, "Home Ownership and Asset-Based Welfare," *Journal of Housing and the Built Environment* 25 (2) (2010): 165–73.

35. Schwartz argues that changes in nonhousing welfare provisions have led to a greater reliance on housing values. "I briefly show how the erosion of nonhousing welfare state provision in the United States, and particularly defined benefit pensions, led to a greater reliance on home equity as a substitute for traditional forms of social protection—the micro-erosions"; Herman Schwartz, "Housing, the Welfare State, and the Global Financial Crisis: What Is the Connection?," *Politics and Society* 40 (1) (2012): 48.

36. These figures are from the Case-Shiller Price Index used by Shiller. The prices are indexed to housing values in 1890 and show the relative steadiness of prices throughout the twentieth century. Robert J. Shiller, *Irrational Exuberance* (Princeton, NJ: Princeton University Press, 2015).

37. Bethany McLean, "A House Is Not a Credit Card," *New York Times*, November 13, 2014. Sheldon Garon, *Beyond Our Means: Why America Spends While the World Saves* (Princeton, NJ: Princeton University Press, 2011). Louis Hyman, *Debtor Nation: The History of America in Red Ink* (Princeton, NJ: Princeton University Press, 2013).

38. Many critics argue that the federal government lacks a valid rationale for favoring one tenure choice over another—a set of claims I take up in chapter 6. James Poterba and Todd Sinai, "Tax Expenditures for Owner-Occupied Housing: Deductions for Property Taxes and Mortgage Interest and the Exclusion of Imputed Rental Income," *American Economic Review* 98 (2) (2008): 84–89. Edward L. Glaeser and Jesse M. Shapiro, "The Benefits of the Home Mortgage Interest Deduction," working paper no. 9284 (Cambridge, MA: National Bureau of Economic Research, 2002). Edward L. Glaeser, "Rethinking the Federal Bias toward Homeownership," *Cityscape* 13 (2) (2011): 5–37. James R. Follain, David C. Ling, and Gary A. McGill, "The Preferential Income Tax Treatment of Owner-Occupied Housing: Who Really Benefits?," *Housing Policy Debate* 4 (1) (1993): 1–24.

39. U.S. Census Bureau, "Housing Characteristics: 2010," October 2011, table 5, accessed July 20, 2015, http://www.census.gov/prod/cen2010/briefs/c2010br-07. pdf. Stuart A. Gabriel and Stuart S. Rosenthal, "Homeownership Boom and Bust 2000 to 2009: Where Will the Homeownership Rate Go from Here?," working paper no. 11-03 (Washington, DC: Research Institute for Housing America, 2011). Edward L. Glaeser, "Housing Policy in the Wake of the Crash," *Daedalus* 139 (4) (2010): 95–106.

CHAPTER 4

1. U.S. Census Bureau, "Historical Census of Housing Tables—Ownership Rates," October 31, 2011, accessed July 22, 2015, http://www.census.gov/hhes/www/housing/census/historic/ownrate.html.

2. Sanjaya DeSilva and Yuval Elmelech, "Housing Inequality in the United States: Explaining the White-Minority Disparities in Homeownership," *Housing Studies* 27 (1) (2012): 1–26. Stuart A. Gabriel and Stuart S. Rosenthal, "Homeownership in the 1980s and 1990s: Aggregate Trends and Racial Gaps," *Journal of Urban Economics* 57 (1) (2005): 101–27. Meghan Kuebler and Jacob S. Rugh, "New Evidence on Racial and Ethnic Disparities in Homeownership in the United States from 2001 to 2010," *Social Science Research* 42 (5) (2013): 1357–74. James E. Long and Steven B. Caudill, "Racial Differences in Homeownership and Housing Wealth, 1970–1986," *Economic Inquiry* 30 (1) (1992): 83–100. Raphael W. Bostic and Brian J. Surette, "Have the Doors Opened Wider? Trends in Homeownership Rates by Race and Income," *Journal of Real Estate Finance and Economics* 23 (3) (2001): 411–34.

3. William J. Clinton, "Remarks on the National Homeownership Strategy," June 5, 1995, accessed July 22, 2015, http://www.presidency.ucsb.edu/ws/?pid=51448.

4. U.S. Department of Housing and Urban Development, "Urban Policy Brief, Number 2, Homeownership and Its Benefits," August 1995, accessed July 22, 2015, http://www.huduser.org/publications/txt/hdbrf2.txt.

5. The findings in this chapter contribute to a growing body of research on the civic and political habits of American homeowners. While this chapter draws on a nationally representative sample of American adults, many previous studies rely on samples of low-income respondents, or respondents from specific geographic communities. Kevin R. Cox, "Housing Tenure and Neighborhood Activism," *Urban Affairs Review* 18 (1) (1982): 107–29. Terry C. Blum and Paul William Kingston, "Homeownership and Social Attachment," *Sociological Perspectives* 27 (2) (1984): 159–80. Paul William Kingston, John L. P. Thompson, and Douglas M. Eichar, "The Politics of Homeownership," *American Politics Research* 12 (2) (1984): 131–50. William M. Rohe and Michael A. Stegman, "The Impact of Home Ownership on the Social and Political Involvement of Low-Income People," *Urban Affairs Review* 30 (1) (1994): 152–72. John I. Gilderbloom and John P. Markham, "The Impact of Homeownership on Political Beliefs," *Social Forces* 73 (4) (1995): 1589–1607. David A. Reingold, "Public Housing, Home Ownership, and Community Participation in Chicago's Inner City," *Housing Studies* 10 (4) (1995): 445–69. Peter H. Rossi and Eleanor Weber, "The Social Benefits of Homeownership: Empirical Evidence from National Surveys," *Housing Policy Debate* 7 (1) (1996): 1–35. Denise DiPasquale and Edward L. Glaeser, "Incentives and Social Capital: Are Homeowners Better Citizens?," *Journal of Urban Economics* 45 (2) (1999): 354–84. Norine Verberg, "Homeownership and Politics: Testing the Political Incorporation Thesis," *Canadian Journal of Sociology* 25 (2) (2000): 169–95. Mark Purcell, "Neighborhood Activism among Homeowners as a Politics of Space," *Professional Geographer* 53 (2) (2001): 178–94. Carolyn A. Dehring, Craig A. Depken II, and Michael R. Ward, "A Direct Test of the Homevoter Hypothesis," *Journal of Urban Economics* 64 (1) (2008): 155–70. Kim Manturuk, Mark Lindblad, and Roberto G. Quercia, "Homeownership and Local Voting in Disadvantaged Urban Neighborhoods," *Cityscape* 11 (3) (2009): 213–30. Thomas Rotolo, John Wilson, and Mary Elizabeth Hughes, "Homeownership and Volunteering: An Alternative Approach to Studying Social Inequality and Civic Engagement," *Sociological Forum* 25 (3) (2010): 570–87. Gina Peek, "Better Citizens? The Relationship between Home Ownership and Religious and Political Volunteerism in the United States," *International Journal of Home Economics* 4 (1) (2011): 39–54. Kim Manturuk, Mark Lindblad, and Roberto G. Quercia, "Homeownership and Civic Engagement in Low-Income Urban Neighborhoods: A Longitudinal Analysis," *Urban Affairs Review* 48 (5) (2012): 731–60. Michal Grinstein-Weiss, Yeong Hun Yeo, Kim R. Manturuk, Mathieu R. Despard, Krista A. Holub, Johanna K. P. Greeson, and Roberto G. Quercia, "Friends and Neighbors: Social Capital and Homeownership in Low- to Moderate-Income Neighborhoods," *Social Work Research* 37 (1) (2013): 37–53.

6. Edward N. Wolff, "Recent Trends in the Size Distribution of Household Wealth," *Journal of Economic Perspectives* 12 (3) (1998): 131–50. Jesse Bricker, Arthur B. Kennickell, Kevin B. Moore, and John Sabelhaus, "Changes in U.S. Family Finances from 2007 to 2010: Evidence from the Survey of Consumer Finances," *Federal Reserve Bulletin* 98 (2): 2012.

7. Local community characteristics influence property values, and a long research tradition documents the types of characteristics (e.g., school quality, historic preservation, local zoning, subsidized housing, etc.) capitalized in home values. Wallace E. Oates, "The Effects of Property Taxes and Local Public Spending on Property Values: An Empirical Study of Tax Capitalization and the Tiebout Hypothesis," *Journal of Political Economy* 77 (6) (1969): 957–71. Ioan Voicu and Vicki Been, "The Effect of Community Gardens on Neighboring Property Values," *Real Estate Economics* 36 (2) (2008): 241–83. John M. Clapp, Anupam Nanda, and Stephen L. Ross, "Which School Attributes Matter? The Influence of School District Performance and Demographic Composition on Property Values," *Journal of Urban Economics* 63 (2) (2008): 451–66. Mai Thi Nguyen, "Does Affordable Housing Detrimentally Affect Property Values? A Review of the Literature," *Journal of Planning Literature* 20 (1) (2005): 15–26. Eric Brunner and Jon Sonstelie, "Homeowners, Property Values, and the Political Economy of the School Voucher," *Journal of Urban Economics* 54 (2) (2003): 239–57.

8. William A. Fischel, *The Homevoter Hypothesis: How Home Values Influence Local Government Taxation, School Finance, and Land-Use Policies* (Cambridge, MA: Harvard University Press, 2001).

9. Fischel argues that we would expect homeowners to be more invested in local politics than politics at the national or state level because the decentralized nature of local government decisions means that they are often more consequential for property values. Fischel, *The Homevoter Hypothesis*, 4.

10. Kamhon Kan, "Residential Mobility and Social Capital," *Journal of Urban Economics* 61 (3) (2007): 436–57.

11. Claude S. Fischer, "Ever-More Rooted Americans," *City and Community* 1 (2) (2002): 177–98.

12. Andrew Oswald, "The Housing Market and Europe's Unemployment: A Non-technical Paper," in *Homeownership and the Labour Market in Europe*, edited by Casper van Ewijk and Michiel van Leuvensteijm, 43–52 (New York: Oxford University Press, 2009), and "A Conjecture on the Explanation for High Unemployment in the Industrialized Nations: Part 1," working paper no. 475 (Coventry: University of Warwick 1996). Richard K. Green and Patric H. Hendershott, "Home-ownership and Unemployment in the US," *Urban Studies* 38 (9) (2001): 1509–20.

13. While the analyses in this chapter highlight the association between home-ownership and civic involvement, they cannot fully account for the possibility that the coefficients on homeownership are driven by other unmeasured variables associated with both ownership and community participation. In more technical papers, researchers have addressed these concerns about selection effects—namely, the idea that citizens who select into ownership are also more likely to participate in their communities for reasons unrelated to their status as homeowners—through a series of methodological tools, including exploiting

randomized experiments, instrumental variable analysis, propensity score matching, and placebo strategies. Brian J. McCabe, "Are Homeowners Better Citizens? Homeownership and Community Participation in the United States," *Social Forces* 91 (3) (2013): 929–54. Gary V. Engelhardt, Michael D. Eriksen, William G. Gale, and Gregory B. Mills, "What Are the Social Benefits of Homeownership? Experimental Evidence for Low Income Households," *Journal of Urban Economics* 67 (3) (2010): 249–58. Denise DiPasquale and Edward L. Glaeser, "Incentives and Social Capital: Are Homeowners Better Citizens?," *Journal of Urban Economics* 45 (2) (1999): 354–84. Manturuk et al., "Homeownership and Civic Engagement in Low-Income Urban Neighborhoods." *Urban Affairs Review* 48 (5) (2012): 731–60.

14. These political participation measures from the Current Population Survey are drawn from several waves of the Civic Engagement supplement, as I detail in the appendix.

15. Sarah F. Riley, HongYu Ru, and Roberto G. Quercia. "The Community Advantage Program Database: Overview and Comparison with the Current Population Survey," *Cityscape* 11 (3) (2009): 247–56.

16. This research on homeowners and community participation builds on a long research tradition exploring the reasons that people become involved in their communities. Several decades ago, Verba, Schlozman, and Brady made one of the key contributions to the study of civic engagement with the resource model of participation. They argued that the availability of resources—and particularly the presence of strong social networks, greater financial resources, or a preponderance of time—motivates citizens to participate in civic affairs. Sidney Verba, Kay Lehman Schlozman, and Henry E. Brady, *Voice and Equality: Civic Voluntarism in American Politics* (Cambridge, MA: Harvard University Press, 1995). Henry E. Brady, Sidney Verba, and Kay Lehman Schlozman, "Beyond SES: A Resource Model of Political Participation," *American Political Science Review* 89 (2) (1995): 271–94. Kevin Milligan, Enrico Moretti, and Philip Oreopoulos, "Does Education Improve Citizenship? Evidence from the United States and the United Kingdom," *Journal of Public Economics* 88 (9–10) (2004): 1667–95. James A. Kitts, "Not in Our Backyard: Solidarity, Social Networks, and the Ecology of Environmental Mobilization," *Sociological Inquiry* 69 (4) (1999): 551–74. Chaeyoon Lim, "Social Networks and Political Participation: How Do Networks Matter?," *Social Forces* 87 (2) (2008): 961–82. Doug McAdam and Ronnelle Paulsen, "Specifying the Relationship between Social Ties and Activism," *American Journal of Sociology* 99 (3) (1993): 640–67. Florence Passy and Marco Giugni, "Social Networks and Individual Perceptions: Explaining Differential Participation in Social Movements," *Sociological Forum* 16 (1) (2001): 123–53. David Horton Smith, "Determinants of Voluntary Association Participation and Volunteering: A Literature Review," *Nonprofit and Voluntary Sector Quarterly* 23 (3) (1994): 243–63.

17. From the Community Advantage Program Study, researchers at the Center for Community Capital have reported several studies on the civic habits of low-income

homeowners. Kim Manturuk, Mark Lindblad, and Roberto Quercia, "Friends and Neighbors: Homeownership and Social Capital among Low- to Moderate-Income Families," *Journal of Urban Affairs* 32 (4) (2010): 471–88. Manturuk et al., "Homeownership and Civic Engagement in Low-Income Urban Neighborhoods." Manturuk et al., "Homeownership and Local Voting in Disadvantaged Urban Neighborhoods." Mark Lindblad, Kim Manturuk, and Roberto Quercia, "Sense of Community and Informal Social Control among Lower Income Households: The Role of Homeownership and Collective Efficacy in Reducing Subjective Neighborhood Crime and Disorder," *American Journal of Community Psychology* 51 (1–2) (2013): 123–39.

18. Grace Wong Bucchianeri, "The American Dream or the American Delusion? The Private and External Benefits of Homeownership for Women," 2011, unpublished manuscript, Wharton School of Business, University of Pennsylvania.

19. The study of social capital has generated a remarkable body of research in the social sciences, much of it concerned about the formation of social capital in local neighborhoods and communities. This research shows that people living in communities with dense social ties report better health outcomes and lower rates of mortality. Especially in emergency conditions—heat waves or powerful storms, for example—these interpersonal networks ensure that residents keep a watchful eye on one another. Ray Forrest and Ade Kearns, "Social Cohesion, Social Capital and the Neighbourhood," *Urban Studies* 38 (12) (2001): 2125–43. Avery M. Guest and Susan K. Wierzbicki, "Social Ties at the Neighborhood Level: Two Decades of GSS Evidence," *Urban Affairs Review* 35 (1) (1999): 92–111. Catherine E. Ross and Sung Joon Jang, "Neighborhood Disorder, Fear, and Mistrust: The Buffering Role of Social Ties with Neighbors," *American Journal of Community Psychology* 28 (4) (2000): 401–20. Eric Klinenberg, *Heat Wave: A Social Autopsy of Disaster in Chicago* (Chicago: University of Chicago Press, 2003). Kimberly A. Lochner, Ichiro Kawachi, Robert T. Brennan, and Stephen L. Buka, "Social Capital and Neighborhood Mortality Rates in Chicago," *Social Science and Medicine* 56 (8) (2003): 1797–1805. Kenneth Temkin and William M. Rohe, "Social Capital and Neighborhood Stability: An Empirical Investigation," *Housing Policy Debate* 9 (1) (1998): 61–88.

20. Like the research on social capital, there is a robust research tradition identifying the determinants of social trust and the way that trust matters for other social outcomes. Kenneth Newton, "Trust, Social Capital, Civil Society, and Democracy," *International Political Science Review* 22 (2) (2001): 201–14. Edward L. Glaeser, David I. Laibson, José A. Scheinkman, and Christine L. Soutter, "Measuring Trust," *Quarterly Journal of Economics* 115 (3) (2000): 811–46. Alberto Alesina and Eliana La Ferrara, "Who Trusts Others?," *Journal of Public Economics* 85 (2) (2002): 207–34. S. V. Subramanian, Daniel J. Kim, and Ichiro Kawachi, "Social Trust and Self-Rated Health in US Communities: A Multilevel Analysis," *Journal of Urban Health* 79 (1) (2002): S21–S34. Dietlind Stolle, "Bowling Together, Bowling

Alone: The Development of Generalized Trust in Voluntary Associations," *Political Psychology* 19 (3) (1998): 497–525. Dietlind Stolle, Stuart Soroka, and Richard Johnston, "When Does Diversity Erode Trust? Neighborhood Diversity, Interpersonal Trust and the Mediating Effect of Social Interactions," *Political Studies* 56 (1) (2008): 57–75. Eric M. Uslaner and Richard S. Conley, "Civic Engagement and Particularized Trust: The Ties That Bind People to Their Ethnic Communities," *American Politics Research* 31 (4) (2003): 331–60.

21. In a previous study, I have also shown that homeowners are more likely than renters to trust their neighbors to return a lost wallet but no more likely to expect a stranger to do so. Brian J. McCabe, "Homeownership and Social Trust in Neighbors," *City and Community* 11 (4) (2012): 389–408.

CHAPTER 5

1. Brian J. McCabe, "When Property Values Rule," *Contexts* 13 (1) (2014): 38–43. Lisa, Black, "Winnetka's Affordable Housing Plan Divides Village," *Chicago Tribune*, March 30, 2011.

2. These estimates for population and housing characteristics in Winnetka come from the five-year estimates of the 2008–2012 American Community Survey.

3. Unlike formal homeowners associations, many of which regulate the activities of homeowners in residential communities, the Winnetka Homeowners Association was not empowered to enforce regulations. Instead, WHOA was a voluntary membership organization run by a group of local homeowners.

4. These quotes are from the twenty-five-page newspaper published by the Winnetka Homeowners Association, April 2011. For the history of Cabrini Green, see Brian J. Miller, "The Struggle over Redevelopment at Cabrini-Green, 1989–2004," *Journal of Urban History* 34 (6) (2008): 944–60; D. Bradford Hunt, *Blueprint for Disaster: The Unraveling of Chicago Public Housing* (Chicago: University of Chicago Press, 2009); Sudhir Venkatesh, *American Project: The Rise and Fall of a Modern Ghetto* (Cambridge, MA: Harvard University Press, 2002).

5. Although opponents of subsidized housing often claim that the construction of these units lowers property values, the findings from a growing body of research suggest that the construction of subsidized units does not lead to the declines that critics often fear, especially when these units are well designed and managed. Len Albright, Elizabeth S. Derickson, and Douglas S. Massey, "Do Affordable Housing Projects Harm Suburban Communities? Crime, Property Values, and Taxes in Mount Laurel, NJ," *City and Community* 12 (2) (2013): 89–112. Douglas S. Massey, Len Albright, Rebecca Casciano, Elizabeth Derickson, and David N. Kinsey, *Climbing Mount Laurel: The Struggle for Affordable Housing and Social Mobility in an American Suburb* (Princeton, NJ: Princeton University Press, 2013). Amy Ellen Schwartz, Ingrid Gould Ellen, Ioan Voicu, and Michael H. Schill, "The External Effects of Place-Based Subsidized Housing," *Regional Science*

and Urban Economics 36 (6) (2006): 679–707. Mai Thi Nguyen, "Does Affordable Housing Detrimentally Affect Property Values? A Review of the Literature," *Journal of Planning Literature* 20 (1) (2005): 15–26.

6. Black, "Winnetka's Affordable Housing Plan Divides Village."

7. There is a broad literature on the process of "othering" minority and out-groups through the politics of exclusion. In research on housing and cities, the politics of exclusion historically focused on racial integration in the suburbs. Michael N. Danielson, "The Politics of Exclusionary Zoning in Suburbia," *Political Science Quarterly* 91 (1) (1976): 1–18, and *The Politics of Exclusion* (New York: Columbia University Press, 1976).

8. Building a theory of exclusionary politics from the rights of property owners extends work by Edward G. Goetz and Mara Sidney, who identify conflicts over affordable housing in Minneapolis/St. Paul as a struggle over the "ideology of property"; Goetz and Sidney, "Revenge of the Property Owners: Community Development and the Politics of Property," *Journal of Urban Affairs* 16 (4) (1994): 319–34. Donald A. Krueckeberg, "The Grapes of Rent: A History of Renting in a Country of Owners," *Housing Policy Debate* 10 (1) (1999): 9–30.

9. Margaret Kohn, "Review: Panacea or Privilege? New Approaches to Democracy and Association," *Political Theory* 30 (2) (2002): 289. Susan E. Clarke, "Community and Problematic Citizenship," *Political Geography* 27 (1) (2008): 22–28. Miranda Joseph, *Against the Romance of Community* (Minneapolis: University of Minnesota Press, 2002). Lynn A. Staeheli, "Citizenship and the Problem of Community," *Political Geography* 27 (1) (2008): 5–21.

10. Robert D. Putnam, *Bowling Alone: The Collapse and Revival of American Community* (New York: Simon and Schuster, 2001), 290.

11. Sidney Verba, Kay Lehman Schlozman, and Henry Brady, *Voice and Equality: Civic Voluntarism in American Politics* (Cambridge, MA: Harvard University Press, 1995), and *The Unheavenly Chorus: Unequal Political Voice and the Broken Promise of American Democracy* (Princeton, NJ: Princeton University Press, 2012).

12. Robert J. Sampson, Stephen W. Raudenbush, and Felton Earls, "Neighborhoods and Violent Crime: A Multilevel Study of Collective Efficacy," *Science* 277 (1997): 918–24. Jeffrey D. Morenoff, Robert J. Sampson, and Stephen W. Raudenbush, "Neighborhood Inequality, Collective Efficacy, and the Spatial Dynamics of Urban Violence," *Criminology* 39 (3) (2001): 517–58. Robert J. Sampson, Jeffrey D. Morenoff, and Thomas Gannon-Rowley, "Assessing 'Neighborhood Effects': Social Processes and New Directions in Research," *Annual Review of Sociology* 28 (2002): 443–78.

13. Marian Barnes, Janet Newman, Andrew Knops, and Helen Sullivan, "Constituting 'the Public' in Public Participation," *Public Administration* 81 (2) (2003): 379–99. Francesca Polletta and James M. Jasper, "Collective Identity and Social Movements," *Annual Review of Sociology* 27 (2001): 283–305. James Bohman and William Rehg, *Deliberative Democracy: Essays on Reason and Politics* (Cambridge, MA: MIT Press, 1997). Jürgen Habermas, *The Structural Transformation of the Public*

Sphere: An Inquiry into a Category of Bourgeois Society (Cambridge, MA: MIT Press, 1991).

14. Archon Fung, *Empowered Participation: Reinventing Urban Democracy* (Princeton, NJ: Princeton University Press, 2006). Archon Fung and Eric Olin Wright, "Deepening Democracy: Innovations in Empowered Participatory Governance," *Politics and Society* 29 (1) (2001): 5–41, and *Deepening Democracy: Institutional Innovations in Empowered Participatory Governance* (London: Verso, 2003).

15. Xavier de Souza Briggs, "Brown Kids in White Suburbs: Housing Mobility and the Many Faces of Social Capital," *Housing Policy Debate* 9 (1) (1998): 177–221. Dora L. Costa and Matthew E. Kahn, "Civic Engagement and Community Heterogeneity: An Economist's Perspective," *Perspectives on Politics* 1 (1) (2003): 103–11. Elizabeth Theiss-Morse and John R. Hibbing, "Citizenship and Civic Engagement," *Annual Review of Political Science* 8 (1) (2005): 227–49. Pamela Paxton, "Is Social Capital Declining in the United States? A Multiple Indicator Assessment," *American Journal of Sociology* 105 (1) (1999): 88–127. Larissa Larsen, Sharon L. Harlan, Bob Bolin, Edward J. Hackett, Diane Hope, Andrew Kirby, Amy Nelson, Tom R. Rex, and Shaphard Wolf, "Bonding and Bridging: Understanding the Relationship between Social Capital and Civic Action," *Journal of Planning Education and Research* 24 (1) (2004): 64–77.

16. Caroline W. Lee, Michael McQuarrie, and Edward T. Walker, *Democratizing Inequalities: Dilemmas of the New Public Participation* (New York: New York University Press, 2015).

17. Jan W. van Deth and Sonja Zmerli, "Introduction: Civicness, Equality, and Democracy—A 'Dark Side' of Social Capital?," *American Behavioral Scientist* 53 (5) (2010): 631–39. Christopher R. Browning, "Illuminating the Downside of Social Capital: Negotiated Coexistence, Property Crime, and Disorder in Urban Neighborhoods," *American Behavioral Scientist* 52 (11) (2009): 1556–78. James DeFilippis, "The Myth of Social Capital in Community Development," *Housing Policy Debate* 12 (4) (2001): 781–806. Alejandro Portes and Patricia Landolt, "The Downside of Social Capital," *American Prospect*, May 1, 1996. Sonja Zmerli, "Social Capital and Norms of Citizenship: An Ambiguous Relationship?," *American Behavioral Scientist* 53 (5) (2010): 657–76.

18. Morris Fiorina, "Extreme Voices: A Dark Side of Civic Engagement," in *Civic Engagement in American Democracy*, edited by Theda Skocpol and Morris Fiorina, 395–425 (New York: Russell Sage Foundation, 1999).

19. Mary Pattillo, *Black on the Block: The Politics of Race and Class in the City* (Chicago: University of Chicago Press, 2007).

20. While part of the story in *Black on the Block* highlights these differences between renters and owners, Mary Pattillo notes that the homeowner-renter divide is not the only source of stratification in North Kenwood-Oakland. She also details the intricacies of social class, the challenges of aging, and the various ways that citizens use their neighborhoods as sources of social conflict. Pattillo, *Black on the Block*, 119.

21. Pattillo, *Black on the Block*, 138.
22. Anita Varghese, "Modern Home Approved in Historic District," *LookOut News*, December 13, 2007. Martha Groves, "A Battle Rages on the Home Front," *Los Angeles Times*, July 21, 2002.
23. Joseph Berger, "An Affordable Housing Project Faces Opposition in Wealthy Chappaqua," *New York Times*, February 17, 2014. Henry Grabar, "The Biggest Problem with San Francisco's Rent Crisis: The Suburbs," *Slate.com*, June 22, 2015.
24. Sarah Mayorga-Gallo, *Behind the White Picket Fence: Power and Privilege in a Multiethnic Neighborhood* (Durham, NC: University of North Carolina Press, 2014), 150.
25. Although the classic narrative of NIMBY activism pits the self-interest of local activists against the common good, defined by the powerful state, recent efforts to retheorize NIMBY politics challenges that framework. Specifically, these theorists object to the idea that planners are the arbiters of the common good. For example, the choice to build a homeless shelter reflects the broad social, economic, and political decisions made by state leaders, and simply looking at the placement decisions neglects these broader structural forces. Robert W. Lake, "Planners' Alchemy Transforming NIMBY to YIMBY: Rethinking NIMBY," *Journal of the American Planning Association* 59 (1) (1993): 87–93. Robert W. Lake, "Volunteers, NIMBYs, and Environmental Justice: Dilemmas of Democratic Practice," *Antipode* 28 (2) (1996): 160–74. Timothy A. Gibson, "NIMBY and the Civic Good," *City and Community* 4 (4) (2005): 381–401. Michael Dear, "Understanding and Overcoming the NIMBY Syndrome," *Journal of the American Planning Association* 58 (3) (1992): 288–300. Katie McClymont and Paul O'Hare, "'We're Not NIMBYs!' Contrasting Local Protest Groups with Idealised Conceptions of Sustainable Communities," *Local Environment* 13 (4) (2008): 321–35. Carissa Schively, "Understanding the NIMBY and LULU Phenomena: Reassessing Our Knowledge Base and Informing Future Research," *Journal of Planning Literature* 21 (3) (2007): 255–66. Mark N. Wexler, "A Sociological Framing of the NIMBY (Not-in-My-Backyard) Syndrome," *International Review of Modern Sociology* 26 (1) (1996): 91–110.
26. Gabriel M. Ahlfeldt and Wolfgang Maennig, "Homeownership and NIMBYism: A Spatial Analysis of Airport Effects," working paper no. 0085 (London: Spatial Economics Research Centre, London School of Economics, 2011). Matt A. Barreto, Mara A. Marks, and Nathan D. Woods, "Homeownership: Southern California's New Political Fault Line?," *Urban Affairs Review* 42 (3) (2007): 315–41. Joanna Duke, "Exploring Homeowner Opposition to Public Housing Developments," *Journal of Sociology and Social Welfare* 37 (1) (2010): 49–74. Corianne Payton Scally, "The Nuances of NIMBY Context and Perceptions of Affordable Rental Housing Development," *Urban Affairs Review* 49 (5) (2013): 718–47. William A. Fischel, "Why Are There NIMBYs?," *Land Economics* 77 (1) (2001): 144–52.

27. Vicki Been, Josiah Madar, and Simon Thomas McDonnell, "Urban Land-Use Regulation: Are Homevoters Overtaking the Growth Machine?," *Journal of Empirical Legal Studies* 11 (2) (2014): 227–65.

28. Pattillo, *Black on the Block*, 15.

29. John R. Logan and Harvey L. Molotch, *Urban Fortunes: The Political Economy of Place* (Berkeley: University of California Press, 1988).

30. Alexis de Tocqueville, *Democracy in America* (1835) (London: Penguin Classics, 2003).

31. Karla Hoff and Arijit Sen, "Homeownership, Community Interactions, and Segregation," *American Economic Review* 95 (4) (2005): 1167–89.

32. When homeowners justify their involvement by pointing to their status as taxpayers, they not only reinforce ideas about the exclusion of nonowners from participating in public life but also neglect the ways that renters do pay property taxes indirectly through their monthly rental payments.

33. Edward Scanion, "Low-Income Homeownership Policy as a Community Development Strategy," *Journal of Community Practice* 5 (1–2) (1998): 137–54. William M. Rohe and Leslie S. Stewart, "Homeownership and Neighborhood Stability," *Housing Policy Debate* 7 (1) (1996): 37–81. George C. Galster, "Empirical Evidence on Cross-tenure Differences in Home Maintenance and Conditions," *Land Economics* 59 (1) (1983): 107–13, and *Homeowners and Neighborhood Reinvestment* (Durham, NC: Duke University Press, 1987). Colin C. Chellman, Ingrid Gould Ellen, Brian J. McCabe, Amy Ellen Schwartz, and Leanna Stiefel, "Does City-Subsidized Owner-Occupied Housing Improve School Quality?," *Journal of the American Planning Association* 77 (2) (2011): 127–41. Donald R. Haurin, Robert D. Dietz, and Bruce A. Weinberg, "The Impact of Neighborhood Homeownership Rates: A Review of the Theoretical and Empirical Literature," *Journal of Housing Research* 13 (2) (2003): 119–52.

34. Gregory Trotter, "Different Approaches to Affordable Housing in Winnetka, Wilmette," *Chicago Tribune*, May 14, 2013.

35. Black, "Winnetka's Affordable Housing Plan Divides Village." Gregory Trotter, "Carry Buck May Retire from the Winnetka Home Owners Association," *Chicago Tribune*, April 17, 2013.

CHAPTER 6

1. Pew Research Center, Social and Demographic Trends, "Home Sweet Home. Still. Five Years after the Bubble," April 12, 2011, accessed July 23, 2015, http://www.pewsocialtrends.org/files/2011/04/Housing-Economy.pdf. Dennis Jacobe, "In U.S., Majority Still Say Now Is a Good Time to Buy a Home," April 22, 2011, accessed July 24, 2015, http://www.gallup.com/poll/147248/Majority-Say-Good-Time-Buy-Home.aspx. Carroll J. Glynn, Carole A. Lunney, and Michael E. Huge, "Public Perceptions of the U.S. Residential Housing Market before, during, and after the Housing Bubble (1990–2009)," *Public Opinion Quarterly* 73 (4) (2009): 807–32.

2. National Association of Realtors, "Seize the Day: 2011 Annual Report," July 18, 2012, accessed July 24, 2015, http://www.realtor.org/sites/default/files/annual-report-2011-seize-the-day-2012-07-18.pdf.

3. Throughout this chapter, I refer to the tax expenditures for homeowners as subsidies. According to the Center on Budget and Policy Priorities, "'Tax expenditures' are substitutes delivered through the tax code as deductions, exclusions and other tax preferences. Tax expenditures reduce the amount of tax that households or corporations owe"; Center on Budget and Policy Priorities, "Policy Basics: Federal Tax Expenditures," March 11, 2015, accessed July 24, 2015, http://www.cbpp.org/research/policy-basics-federal-tax-expenditures.

4. National Association of Home Builders, "Mortgage Interest Deduction," accessed July 24, 2015, http://www.nahb.org/en/research/nahb-priorities/mortgage-interest-deduction.aspx. National Association of Realtors, "Mortgage Interest Deduction Home," accessed July 24, 2015, http://www.realtor.org/topics/mortgage-interest-deduction/videos.

5. Christopher Howard, *The Hidden Welfare State* (Princeton, NJ: Princeton University Press, 1997), 52. Dennis J. Ventry, "The Accidental Deduction: A History and Critique of the Tax Subsidy for Mortgage Interest," *Law and Contemporary Problems* 73 (2010): 233–84. Monica Prasad, *The Land of Too Much: American Abundance and the Paradox of Poverty* (Cambridge, MA: Harvard University Press, 2012).

6. Howard, *The Hidden Welfare State*. Richard K. Green and Susan M. Wachter, "The American Mortgage in Historical and International Context," *Journal of Economic Perspectives* 19 (4) (2005): 93–114.

7. Ventry, "The Accidental Deduction," 241. Howard, *The Hidden Welfare State*, 48.

8. Dean M. Maki, "Household Debt and the Tax Reform Act of 1986," *American Economic Review* 91 (1) (2001): 305–19.

9. Maki, "Household Debt and the Tax Reform Act of 1986." Richard Avramenko and Richard Boyd, "Subprime Virtues: The Moral Dimensions of American Housing and Mortgage Policy," *Perspectives on Politics* 11 (1) (2013): 121.

10. National Association of Home Builders, "NAHB National Survey," January 2–5, 2012. Howard, *The Hidden Welfare State*.

11. Benjamin H. Harris and Daniel Baneman, "Who Itemizes Deductions?," *Tax Notes*, January 17, 2011, accessed July 24, 2015, http://www.urban.org/research/publication/who-itemizes-deductions/view/full_report. Will Fischer and Chye-Ching Huang, "Mortgage Interest Deduction Is Ripe for Reform," Center on Budget and Policy Priorities, June 25, 2013, accessed July 23, 2015, http://www.cbpp.org/research/mortgage-interest-deduction-is-ripe-for-reform.

12. Throughout the chapter, I draw on revenue projections from the Office of Management and Budget to describe the costs of federal tax expenditures. Office of Management and Budget, "Fiscal Year 2014 Budget of the U.S. Government,

Federal Receipts," n.d., accessed July 24, 2015, https://www.whitehouse.gov/sites/default/files/omb/budget/fy2014/assets/receipts.pdf.

13. The comparative costs of various federal programs and departments are drawn from various sources in the federal government. Temporary Assistance to Needy Families: Center on Budget and Policy Priorities, "Policy Basics: An Introduction to TANF," June 14, 2015, accessed July 24, 2015, http://www.cbpp.org/research/policy-basics-an-introduction-to-tanf. Housing choice vouchers: U.S. Department of Housing and Urban Development, "Public and Indian Housing, Tenant-Based Rental Assistance, Budget Requests," n.d., accessed July 24, 2015, http://portal.hud.gov/hudportal/documents/huddoc?id=9-fy16cj-tenant-basedra.pdf. Department of Homeland Security: U.S. Department of Homeland Security, "FY 2015 Budget-in-Brief," n.d., accessed July 24, 2015, http://www.dhs.gov/publication/fy-2015-budget-brief. Deduction for Charitable Contributions: Office of Management and Budget, "Fiscal Year 2014 Budget of the U.S. Government, Federal Receipts," n.d., accessed July 24, 2015, https://www.whitehouse.gov/sites/default/files/omb/budget/fy2014/assets/receipts.pdf. U.S. Department of Housing and Urban Development: Dina El Boghdady, "White House Budget: HUD to See Bump," *Washington Post,* February 4, 2015. Department of Education: Department of Education, "Budget Office—U.S. Department of Education," n.d., accessed July 24, 2015, http://www2.ed.gov/about/overview/budget/index.html.

14. Tax Policy Center, "Home Ownership: What Are the Tax Benefits?," December 31, 2007, accessed July 25, 2015, http://www.taxpolicycenter.org/briefing-book/key-elements/homeownership/encourage.cfm.

15. Bruce Bartlett, "Taxing Homeowners As If They Were Landlords," *New York Times,* September 3, 2013.

16. Beyond the research, widely cited throughout the book, on the expected public benefits of homeownership, there is also an extensive literature on the private benefits of ownership, including the relationship between owning a home and educational attainment, health outcomes, and labor market outcomes. Ryan Finnigan, "Racial and Ethnic Stratification in the Relationship between Home-ownership and Self-Rated Health," *Social Science and Medicine* 115 (2014): 72–81. Joseph Harkness and Sandra Newman, "Differential Effects of Homeownership on Children from Higher- and Lower-Income Families," *Journal of Housing Research* 14 (1) (2003): 1–19. Joseph Harkness and Sandra Newman, "Effects of Homeowner-ship on Children: The Role of Neighborhood Characteristics and Family Income," *Economic Policy Review* 9 (2) (2003): 87–107. Robert D. Dietz and Donald R. Haurin, "The Social and Private Micro-level Consequences of Homeownership," *Journal of Urban Economics* 54 (3) (2003): 401–50. William M. Rohe and Victoria Basolo, "Long-Term Effects of Homeownership on the Self-Perceptions and Social Interaction of Low-Income Persons," *Environment and Behavior* 29 (6) (1997): 793–819. William M. Rohe and Michael A. Stegman, "The Effects of Homeownership:

On the Self-Esteem, Perceived Control and Life Satisfaction of Low-Income People," *Journal of the American Planning Association* 60 (2) (1994): 173–84.

17. National Association of Realtors, "Field Guide to the Social Benefits of Home Ownership," March 2015, accessed July 24, 2015, http://www.realtor.org/field-guides/field-guide-to-social-benefits-of-home-ownership.

18. Andrew Hanson, Ike Brannon, and Zackary Hawley, "Rethinking Tax Benefits for Home Owners," *National Affairs* 19 (2014): 53. In his analysis of federal homeownership, economist Ed Glaeser argues that the external benefits of enhanced citizenship are the most important justification for homeownership subsidies: "The post-crash case for subsidizing ownership comes down to the connection between homeownership and citizenship"; Glaeser, "Rethinking the Federal Bias toward Homeownership," *Cityscape* 13 (2) (2011): 6.

19. N. Edward Coulson and Herman Li, "Measuring the External Benefits of Homeownership," *Journal of Urban Economics* 77 (2013): 57. Lily L. Batchelder, Fred T. Goldberg, Jr., and Peter R. Orszag, "Efficiency and Tax Incentives: The Case for Refundable Tax Credits," *Stanford Law Review* 59 (1) (2006): 23–76.

20. Will Fischer and Chye-Ching Huang, "Mortgage Interest Deduction Is Ripe for Reform," Center of Budget and Policy Priorities, June 25, 2013, accessed July 23, 2015, http://www.cbpp.org/research/mortgage-interest-deduction-is-ripe-for-reform. Glaeser, "Rethinking the Federal Bias toward Homeownership." John D. Landis and Kirk McClure, "Rethinking Federal Housing Policy," *Journal of the American Planning Association* 76 (3) (2010): 319–48.

21. In 2013, the Community Associations Institutes estimated that 26.3 million housing units and 65.7 million residents lived in association-governed communities. The Institute estimates that homeowners associations and other planned communities account for half of these units, while condominiums and cooperatives account for the other half. Community Associations Institute, "National and State Statistical Review for 2013," accessed July 24, 2015, http://www.cairf.org/research/factbook/2013_statistical_review.pdf.

22. Evan McKenzie, *Privatopia: Homeowner Associations and the Rise of Residential Private Government* (New Haven: Yale University Press, 1996), and "Planning through Residential Clubs: Homeowners' Associations," *Economic Affairs* 25 (4) (2005): 28–31. Tony Manzi and Bill Smith-Bowers, "Gated Communities as Club Goods: Segregation or Social Cohesion?," *Housing Studies* 20 (2) (2005): 345–59.

23. Rachel Meltzer, "Do Homeowners Associations Affect Citywide Segregation? Evidence from Florida Municipalities," *Housing Policy Debate* 23 (4) (2013): 688–713. Rachel Meltzer and Ron Cheung, "How Are Homeowners Associations Capitalized into Property Values?," *Regional Science and Urban Economics* 462014: 93–102. Elena Vesselinov, "Members Only: Gated Communities and Residential Segregation in the Metropolitan United States," *Sociological Forum* 23 (3) (2008): 536–55.

24. Glaeser, "Rethinking the Federal Bias toward Homeownership." Research also acknowledges the impact of suburbanization and living in suburban communities on the norms of democratic participation. Thad Williamson, *Sprawl, Justice, and Citizenship: The Civic Costs of the American Way of Life* (New York: Oxford University Press, 2011). J. Eric Oliver, *Democracy in Suburbia* (Princeton, NJ: Princeton University Press, 2001). J. Eric Oliver, Shang E. Ha, and Zachary Callen, *Local Elections and the Politics of Small-Scale Democracy* (Princeton, NJ: Princeton University Press, 2012). Juliet Gainsborough, *Fenced Off: The Suburbanization of American Politics* (Washington, DC: Georgetown University Press, 2001).

25. Avramenko and Boyd, "Subprime Virtues."

26. Avramenko and Boyd, "Subprime Virtues," 122.

27. Katie J. Wells, "A Housing Crisis, a Failed Law, and a Property Conflict: The US Urban Speculation Tax," *Antipode* 47 (4) (2015): 1043–1061. Marisa Lagos, "Tax to Break S.F. Real Estate Speculation Headed to Voters," *San Francisco Chronicle*, June 18, 2014. J. K. Dineen, "Tenants, Homeowners at Odds over Prop G," *San Francisco Chronicle*, October 3, 2014.

28. Elliot Schreur, "America's Homeownership Subsidies Are a Terrible Way to Help Young People Build Wealth," New America Foundation, October 28, 2014, accessed July 24, 2015, https://www.newamerica.org/asset-building/americas-homeownership-subsidies-are-a-terrible-way-to-help-young-people-build-wealth.

29. Stephanie M. Stern, "Residential Protectionism and the Legal Mythology of Home," *Michigan Law Review* 107 (7) (2009): 1125, and "Reassessing the Citizenship Virtues of Homeownership," *Columbia Law Review* 11 (4) (2011): 890–938.

30. Avery M. Guest and Susan K. Wierzbicki, "Social Ties at the Neighborhood Level: Two Decades of GSS Evidence," *Urban Affairs Review* 35 (1) (1999): 92–111.

31. While Avramenko and Boyd recommend a "staying put" tax credit to replace the deductibility of moving expenses, I propose a more expansive effort to replace the mortgage interest deduction with a deduction for residential stability. Avramenko and Boyd, "Subprime Virtues."

32. Notably, there are many reasons that families are forced to move from their homes, including eviction and foreclosure, and research suggests that forced mobility often has negative consequences for families and children. Vicki Been, Ingrid Gould Ellen, Amy Ellen Schwartz, Leanna Stiefel, and Meryle Weinstein, "Does Losing Your Home Mean Losing Your School? Effects of Foreclosures on the School Mobility of Children," *Regional Science and Urban Economics* 41 (4) (2011): 407–14. Kathryn L. Pettit and Jennifer Comey, "The Foreclosure Crisis and Children: A Three-City Study," Urban Institute, March 1, 2012, accessed July 24, 2015, http://www.urban.org/research/publication/foreclosure-crisis-and-children-three-city-study. Matt Desmond, "Eviction and the Reproduction of Urban Poverty," *American Journal of Sociology* 118 (1) (2012): 88–133.

CHAPTER 7

1. Mechele Dickerson, *Homeownership and America's Financial Underclass: Flawed Premises, Broken Promises, New Prescriptions* (New York: Cambridge University Press, 2014), 37. Richard Ronald, *The Ideology of Home Ownership: Homeowner Societies and the Role of Housing* (New York: Palgrave Macmillan, 2008), 2. Edward G. Goetz and Mara Sidney, "Revenge of the Property Owners: Community Development and the Politics of Property," *Journal of Urban Affairs* 16 (4) (1994): 319–34. Donald A. Krueckeberg, "The Grapes of Rent: A History of Renting in a Country of Owners," *Housing Policy Debate* 10 (1) (1999): 9–30.
2. Reviewing sociological research on housing as a commodity and a right, Mary Pattillo argues: "It is difficult to identify what precisely constitutes a sociology of housing ... because much research has shifted to the study of neighborhoods, racial conflict, families, social movements, urban politics, or financial institutions and is often now published in interdisciplinary journals. Where sociologists have exited, economists, architects, planners, geographers, policy researchers, historians, and cultural studies scholars have entered"; Pattillo, "Housing: Commodity versus Right," *Annual Review of Sociology* 39 (2013): 511.
3. Center for Responsive Politics, "Lobbying Database," n.d., accessed July 25, 2015, https://www.opensecrets.org/lobby.
4. Ben Ansell, "The Political Economy of Ownership: Housing Markets and the Welfare State," *American Political Science Review* 108 (2) (2014): 383–402.
5. Neda Delfani, Johan De Deken, and Caroline Dewilde, "Home-Ownership and Pensions: Negative Correlation, but No Trade-Off," *Housing Studies* 29 (5) (2014): 657–76. Richard Ronald and John Doling, "Testing Home Ownership as the Cornerstone of Welfare: Lessons from East Asia for the West," *Housing Studies* 27 (7) (2012): 940–61. Ulf Torgersen, "Housing: The Wobbly Pillar under the Welfare State," *Scandinavian Housing and Planning Research* 4 (1987): 116–26. Dalton Conley and Brian Gifford, "Home Ownership, Social Insurance, and the Welfare State," *Sociological Forum* 21 (1) (2006): 55–82. Richard Roland and Marja Elsigna, *Beyond Home Ownership: Housing, Welfare and Society* (New York: Routledge, 2011). Herman Schwartz and Leonard Seabrooke, "Varieties of Residential Capitalism in the International Political Economy: Old Welfare States and the New Politics of Housing," *Comparative European Politics* 6 (3) (2008): 237–61.
6. Dalton Conley, *Being Black, Living in the Red: Race, Wealth, and Social Policy in America* (Berkeley: University of California Press, 1999). Melvin L. Oliver and Thomas M. Shapiro, *Black Wealth/White Wealth: A New Perspective on Racial Inequality* (New York: Routledge, 1997).
7. Shaila Dewan, "As Renters Move In, Some Homeowners Fret," *New York Times*, August 29, 2013.
8. Mark R. Lindblad and Roberto G. Quercia, "Why Is Homeownership Associated with Nonfinancial Benefits? A Path Analysis of Competing Mechanisms," *Housing Policy Debate* 25 (2) (2015): 263–88. Eiji Yamamura, "How Do Neighbors Influence Investment in Social Capital? Homeownership and Length of

Residence," *International Advances in Economic Research* 17 (4) (2011): 451–64. William M. Rohe, Shannon Van Zandt, and George McCarthy, "Home Ownership and Access to Opportunity," *Housing Studies* 17 (1) (2002): 51–61.

9. Jim Kemeny, *Myth of Home Ownership: Private versus Public Choices in Housing Tenure* (New York: Routledge, Kegan and Paul, 1982), xii. Ian Winter, *Radical Home Owner: Housing Tenure and Social Change* (Basel: Gordon and Breach Science Publishers, 1995). Jim Kemeny, *Housing and Social Theory* (New York: Routledge, 1992). Susan Saegert, Desiree Fields, and Kimberly Libman, "Deflating the Dream: Radical Risk and the Neoliberalization of Homeownership," *Journal of Urban Affairs* 31(3) (2009): 297–317. Raquel Rolnik, "Late Neoliberalism: The Financialization of Homeownership and Housing Rights," *International Journal of Urban and Regional Research* 37 (3) (2013): 1058–66.

10. David Streitfeld and Megan Thee-Brenan, "Despite Fears, Owning Home Retains Allure, Poll Shows," *New York Times*, June 29, 2011. Carol Morello, Peyton M. Craighill, and Scott Clemens, "More People Express Uncertainty in Chance to Achieve the American Dream," *Washington Post*, September 28, 2013. American Enterprise Institute for Public Policy Research, "AEI Political Report: A Monthly Poll Compilation," May 2013, accessed July 25, 2015, http://www.aei.org/wp-content/uploads/2013/05/-aei-political-report-may-2013-pdf_08440695891.pdf. Rasmussen Reports, "Americans Still View Home Ownership as a Strong Investment," December 18, 2014, accessed July 25, 2015, http://www.rasmussenreports.com/public_content/business/housing/december_2014/americans_still_view_home_ownership_as_strong_investment.

11. Among the most important challenges of limited access to neighborhoods is schooling. Recent research highlights the interconnectedness between schools and housing choices. Annette Lareau, "Schools, Housing and the Reproduction of Inequality," in *Choosing Homes, Choosing Schools*, edited by Annette Lareau and Kimberly A. Goyette, 169–206 (New York: Russell Sage Foundation, 2014). Lareau and Goyette, *Choosing Homes, Choosing Schools*. Heather Beth Johnson, *The American Dream and the Power of Wealth: Choosing Schools and Inheriting Inequality in the Land of Opportunity* (New York: Routledge, 2014). Owning a home is also associated with assessments of neighborhood quality and residential satisfaction. Meredith Greif, "The Intersection of Homeownership, Race and Neighbourhood Context: Implications for Neighbourhood Satisfaction," *Urban Studies* 52 (1) (2014): 50–70. Michal Grinstein-Weiss, Yeong Yeo, Katrin Anacker, Shannon Van Zandt, Elizabeth B. Freeze, and Roberto G. Quercia, "Home-ownership and Neighborhood Satisfaction among Low- and Moderate-Income Households," *Journal of Urban Affairs* 33 (3) (2011): 247–65.

WORKS CITED

Aalbers, Manuel B. 2011. *Place, Exclusion and Mortgage Markets*. New York: Wiley.

Acharya, Viral V., Matthew Richardson, Stijn van Nieuwerburgh, and Lawrence J. White. 2011. *Guaranteed to Fail: Fannie Mae, Freddie Mac, and the Debacle of Mortgage Finance*. Princeton, NJ: Princeton University Press.

Adams, Kristen David. 2008. "Homeownership: American Dream or Illusion of Empowerment." *South Carolina Law Review* 60: 574–615.

Ahlfeldt, Gabriel M., and Wolfgang Maennig. 2011. "Homeownership and NIMBYism: A Spatial Analysis of Airport Effects." Working Paper no. 0085. London: Spatial Economics Research Centre, London School of Economics.

Albright, Len, Elizabeth S. Derickson, and Douglas S. Massey. 2013. "Do Affordable Housing Projects Harm Suburban Communities? Crime, Property Values, and Taxes in Mount Laurel, NJ." *City and Community* 12 (2): 89–112.

Alesina, Alberto, and Eliana La Ferrara. 2002. "Who Trusts Others?" *Journal of Public Economics* 85 (2): 207–34.

Altman, Karen E. 1990. "Consuming Ideology: The Better Homes in America Campaign." *Critical Studies in Mass Communication* 7 (3): 286–307.

Ansell, Ben. 2014. "The Political Economy of Ownership: Housing Markets and the Welfare State." *American Political Science Review* 108 (2): 383–402.

Apgar, William C., and Mark Duda. 2003. "The Twenty-Fifth Anniversary of the Community Reinvestment Act: Past Accomplishments and Future Regulatory Challenges." *Economic Policy Review* 9 (2): 169–91.

Avramenko, Richard, and Richard Boyd. 2013. "Subprime Virtues: The Moral Dimensions of American Housing and Mortgage Policy." *Perspectives on Politics* 11 (1): 111–31.

Bagli, Charles V. 2013. *Other People's Money: Inside the Housing Crisis and the Demise of the Greatest Real Estate Deal Ever Made*. New York: Dutton.

Barnes, Marian, Janet Newman, Andrew Knops, and Helen Sullivan. 2003. "Constituting 'the Public' in Public Participation." *Public Administration* 81 (2): 379–99.

Barreto, Matt A., Mara A. Marks, and Nathan D. Woods. 2007. "Homeownership: Southern California's New Political Fault Line?" *Urban Affairs Review* 42 (3): 315–41.

Basolo, Victoria. 2007. "Explaining the Support for Homeownership Policy in US Cities: A Political Economy Perspective." *Housing Studies* 22 (1): 99–119.

Batchelder, Lily L., Fred T. Goldberg, Jr., and Peter R. Orszag. 2006. "Efficiency and Tax Incentives: The Case for Refundable Tax Credits." *Stanford Law Review* 59 (1): 23–76.

Bauman, John F., Roger Biles, and Kristin M. Szylvian. 2000. *From Tenements to the Taylor Homes: In Search of an Urban Housing Policy in Twentieth-Century America.* University Park: Pennsylvania State University Press.

Baxandall, Rosalyn, and Elizabeth Ewen. 2000. *Picture Windows: How the Suburbs Happened.* New York: Basic Books.

Beauregard, Robert A. 2006. *When America Became Suburban.* Minneapolis: University of Minnesota Press.

Been, Vicki, Ingrid Gould Ellen, Amy Ellen Schwartz, Leanna Stiefel, and Meryle Weinstein. 2011. "Does Losing Your Home Mean Losing Your School? Effects of Foreclosures on the School Mobility of Children." *Regional Science and Urban Economics* 41 (4): 407–14.

Been, Vicki, Josiah Madar, and Simon Thomas McDonnell. 2014. "Urban Land–Use Regulation: Are Homevoters Overtaking the Growth Machine?" *Journal of Empirical Legal Studies* 11 (2): 227–65.

Belsky, Eric S. 2013. "The Dream Lives On: The Future of Homeownership in America." Working Paper W13-1. Cambridge, MA: Joint Center for Housing Studies, Harvard University.

Belsky, Eric S., Christopher E. Herbert, and Jennifer H. Molinsky. 2014. *Homeownership Built to Last.* Washington, DC: Brookings Institution Press.

Bennett, Michael J. 1999. *When Dreams Came True: The GI Bill and the Making of Modern America.* Lincoln, NE: Potomac Books.

Blum, Terry C., and Paul William Kingston. 1984. "Homeownership and Social Attachment." *Sociological Perspectives* 27 (2): 159–80.

Boehm, Thomas P., and Alan Schlottmann. 2008. "Wealth Accumulation and Home-ownership: Evidence for Low-Income Households." *Cityscape* 10 (2): 225–56.

Bohman, James, and William Rehg. 1997. *Deliberative Democracy: Essays on Reason and Politics.* Cambridge, MA: MIT Press.

Bonastia, Christopher. 2010. *Knocking on the Door: The Federal Government's Attempt to Desegregate the Suburbs.* Princeton, NJ: Princeton University Press.

Bostic, Raphael W., and Kwan Ok Lee. 2008. "Mortgages, Risk, and Homeownership among Low- and Moderate-Income Families." *American Economic Review* 98 (2): 310–14.

Bostic, Raphael W., and Brian J. Surette. 2001. "Have the Doors Opened Wider? Trends in Homeownership Rates by Race and Income." *Journal of Real Estate Finance and Economics* 23 (3): 411–34.

Boyer, Paul S. 1992. *Urban Masses and Moral Order in America, 1820–1920.* Cambridge, MA: Harvard University Press.

Bradford, Calvin. 1979. "Financing Home Ownership: The Federal Role In Neighborhood Decline." *Urban Affairs Review* 14 (3): 313–35.

Brady, Henry E., Sidney Verba, and Kay Lehman Schlozman. 1995. "Beyond SES: A Resource Model of Political Participation." *American Political Science Review* 89 (2): 271–94.

Bricker, Jesse, Arthur B. Kennickell, Kevin B. Moore, and John Sabelhaus. 2012. "Changes in U.S. Family Finances from 2007 to 2010: Evidence from the Survey of Consumer Finances." *Federal Reserve Bulletin* 98 (2).

Briggs, Xavier de Souza. 1998. "Brown Kids in White Suburbs: Housing Mobility and the Many Faces of Social Capital." *Housing Policy Debate* 9 (1): 177–221.

Brooks, Richard R. W., and Carol M. Rose. 2013. *Saving the Neighborhood: Racially Restrictive Covenants, Law, and Social Norms*. Cambridge, MA: Harvard University Press.

Browning, Christopher R. 2009. "Illuminating the Downside of Social Capital: Negotiated Coexistence, Property Crime, and Disorder in Urban Neighborhoods." *American Behavioral Scientist* 52 (11): 1556–78.

Brunner, Eric, and Jon Sonstelie. 2003. "Homeowners, Property Values, and the Political Economy of the School Voucher." *Journal of Urban Economics* 54 (2): 239–57.

Bucchianeri, Grace Wong. 2011. "The American Dream or the American Delusion? The Private and External Benefits of Homeownership for Women." Unpublished manuscript. Wharton School of Business, University of Pennsylvania.

Capozzola, Christopher. 2008. *Uncle Sam Wants You: World War I and the Making of the Modern American Citizen*. New York: Oxford University Press.

Carliner, Michael S. 1998. "Development of Federal Homeownership 'Policy.'" *Housing Policy Debate* 9 (2): 299–321.

Charles, Camille Zubrinsky. 2009. *Won't You Be My Neighbor? Race, Class, and Residence in Los Angeles*. New York: Russell Sage Foundation.

Chellman, Colin C., Ingrid Gould Ellen, Brian J. McCabe, Amy Ellen Schwartz, and Leanna Stiefel. 2011. "Does City-Subsidized Owner-Occupied Housing Improve School Quality?" *Journal of the American Planning Association* 77 (2): 127–41.

Clapp, John M., Anupam Nanda, and Stephen L. Ross. 2008. "Which School Attributes Matter? The Influence of School District Performance and Demographic Composition on Property Values." *Journal of Urban Economics* 63 (2): 451–66.

Clark, Clifford Edward. 1986. *American Family Home, 1800–1960*. Chapel Hill: University of North Carolina Press.

Clarke, Susan E. 2008. "Community and Problematic Citizenship." *Political Geography* 27 (1): 22–28.

Clayton, Richard, and Jonas Pontusson. 1998. "Welfare-State Retrenchment Revisited: Entitlement Cuts, Public Sector Restructuring, and Inegalitarian Trends in Advanced Capitalist Societies." *World Politics* 51 (1): 67–98.

Colton, Kent W. 2003. *Housing in the Twenty-First Century: Achieving Common Ground*. Cambridge, MA: Harvard University Press.

Conley, Dalton. 1999. *Being Black, Living in the Red: Race, Wealth, and Social Policy in America*. Berkeley: University of California Press.

Conley, Dalton, and Brian Gifford. 2006. "Home Ownership, Social Insurance, and the Welfare State." *Sociological Forum* 21 (1): 55–82.

Costa, Dora L., and Matthew E. Kahn. 2003. "Civic Engagement and Community Heterogeneity: An Economist's Perspective." *Perspectives on Politics* 1 (1): 103–11.

Coulson, N. Edward, and Herman Li. 2013. "Measuring the External Benefits of Homeownership." *Journal of Urban Economics* 77: 57–67.

Cox, Kevin R. 1982. "Housing Tenure and Neighborhood Activism." *Urban Affairs Review* 18 (1): 107–29.

Cronon, William. 1991. *Nature's Metropolis: Chicago and the Great West.* New York: Norton.

Crossney, Kristen B., and David W. Bartelt. 2005. "The Legacy of the Home Owners' Loan Corporation." *Housing Policy Debate* 16 (3–4): 547–74.

Crossney, Kristen B., and David W. Bartelt. 2005. "Residential Security, Risk, and Race: The Home Owners' Loan Corporation and Mortgage Access in Two Cities." *Urban Geography* 26 (8): 707–36.

Danielson, Michael N. 1976. "The Politics of Exclusionary Zoning in Suburbia." *Political Science Quarterly* 91 (1): 1–18.

Danielson, Michael N. 1976. *The Politics of Exclusion.* New York: Columbia University Press.

Dean, John P. 1945. *Home Ownership: Is It Sound?* New York: Harper.

Dear, Michael. 1992. "Understanding and Overcoming the NIMBY Syndrome." *Journal of the American Planning Association* 58 (3): 288–300.

DeFilippis, James. 2001. "The Myth of Social Capital in Community Development." *Housing Policy Debate* 12 (4): 781–806.

Dehring, Carolyn A., Craig A. Depken II, and Michael R. Ward. 2008. "A Direct Test of the Homevoter Hypothesis." *Journal of Urban Economics* 64 (1): 155–70.

Delfani, Neda, Johan De Deken, and Caroline Dewilde. 2014. "Home-Ownership and Pensions: Negative Correlation, but No Trade-Off." *Housing Studies* 29 (5): 657–76.

Denton, Nancy A. 1999. "Half Empty or Half Full: Segregation and Segregated Neighborhoods 30 Years after the Fair Housing Act." *Cityscape* 4 (3): 107–22.

Desmond, Matt. 2012. "Eviction and the Reproduction of Urban Poverty." *American Journal of Sociology* 118 (1): 88–133.

DeSilva, Sanjaya, and Yuval Elmelech. 2012. "Housing Inequality in the United States: Explaining the White-Minority Disparities in Homeownership." *Housing Studies* 27 (1): 1–26.

Deth, Jan W. van, and Sonja Zmerli. 2010. "Introduction: Civicness, Equality, and Democracy—A 'Dark Side' of Social Capital?" *American Behavioral Scientist* 53 (5): 631–39.

Di, Zhu Xiao, Eric Belsky, and Xiaodong Liu. 2007. "Do Homeowners Achieve More Household Wealth in the Long Run?" *Journal of Housing Economics* 16 (3–4): 274–90.

Dickerson, Mechele. 2009. "The Myth of Home Ownership and Why Home Ownership Is Not Always a Good Thing." *Indiana Law Journal* 84: 189–237.

Dickerson, Mechele. 2014. *Homeownership and America's Financial Underclass: Flawed Premises, Broken Promises, New Prescriptions*. New York: Cambridge University Press.

Dietz, Robert D., and Donald R. Haurin. 2003. "The Social and Private Micro-level Consequences of Homeownership." *Journal of Urban Economics* 54 (3): 401–50.

DiPasquale, Denise, and Edward L. Glaeser. 1999. "Incentives and Social Capital: Are Homeowners Better Citizens?" *Journal of Urban Economics* 45 (2): 354–84.

Doling, John, and Nick Horsewood. 2010. "Home Ownership and Pensions: Causality and the Really Big Trade-off." *Housing, Theory and Society* 28 (2): 166–82.

Doling, John, and Richard Ronald. 2010. "Home Ownership and Asset-Based Welfare." *Journal of Housing and the Built Environment* 25 (2): 165–73.

Downing, Andrew Jackson. 1969. *The Architecture of Country Houses: Including Designs for Cottages, and Farmhouses, and Villas, with Remarks on Interiors, Furniture, and the Best Modes of Warming and Ventilating*. New York: Dover.

Downing, Andrew Jackson, and Robert Twombly. 2012. *Andrew Jackson Downing: Essential Texts*. New York: Norton.

Drew, Rachel Bogardus. 2013. "Constructing Homeownership Policy: Social Constructions and the Design of the Low-Income Homeownership Policy Objective." *Housing Studies* 28 (4): 616–31.

Drew, Rachel Bogardus, and Christopher E. Herbert. 2013. "Post-recession Drivers of Preferences for Homeownership." *Housing Policy Debate* 23 (4): 666–87.

Duany, Andres, Elizabeth Plater-Zyberk, and Jeff Speck. 2001. *Suburban Nation: The Rise of Sprawl and the Decline of the American Dream*. New York: Macmillan.

Duke, Joanna. 2010. "Exploring Homeowner Opposition to Public Housing Developments." *Journal of Sociology and Social Welfare* 37 (1): 49–74.

Dumenil, Lynn. 1995. *The Modern Temper: American Culture and Society in the 1920s*. New York: Hill and Wang.

Eggers, Frederick J. 2001. "Homeownership: A Housing Success Story." *Cityscape* 5 (2): 43–56.

Engelhardt, Gary V., Michael D. Eriksen, William G. Gale, and Gregory B. Mills. 2010. "What Are the Social Benefits of Homeownership? Experimental Evidence for Low-Income Households." *Journal of Urban Economics* 67 (3): 249–58.

Engels, Friedrich. 1979 [1873]. *Housing Question*. New York: Firebird.

Essene, Ren, and William Apgar. 2009. "The 30th Anniversary of the CRA: Restructuring the CRA to Address the Mortgage Finance Revolution." In *Revisiting the CRA: Perspectives on the Future of the Community Reinvestment Act*, edited by Prabal Chakrabarti, David Erickson, Ren S. Essene, Ian Galloway, and John Olson, 12–29. San Francisco: Federal Reserve Bank of San Francisco.

Ewen, Elizabeth. 2001. *Picture Windows: How the Suburbs Happened*. New York: Basic Books.

Finnigan, Ryan. 2014. "Racial and Ethnic Stratification in the Relationship between Homeownership and Self-Rated Health." *Social Science and Medicine* 115: 72–81.

Fiorina, Morris. 1999. "Extreme Voices: A Dark Side of Civic Engagement." In *Civic Engagement in American Democracy*, edited by Theda Skocpol and Morris Fiorina, 395–425. New York: Russell Sage Foundation.

Fischel, William A. 2001. *The Homevoter Hypothesis: How Home Values Influence Local Government Taxation, School Finance, and Land-Use Policies*. Cambridge, MA: Harvard University Press.

Fischel, William A. 2001. "Why Are There NIMBYs?" *Land Economics* 77 (1): 144–52.

Fischer, Claude S. 2002. "Ever-More Rooted Americans." *City and Community* 1 (2): 177–98.

Fish, Gertrude Sipperly. 1979. *The Story of Housing*. New York: Macmillan.

Fishbein, Allen J. 1992. "The Community Reinvestment Act after Fifteen Years: It Works, but Strengthened Federal Enforcement Is Needed." *Fordham Urban Law Journal* 20: 293–310.

Flanagan, Richard M. 1997. "The Housing Act of 1954: The Sea Change in National Urban Policy." *Urban Affairs Review* 33 (2): 265–86.

Foley, Donald L. 1980. "The Sociology of Housing." *Annual Review of Sociology* 6: 457–78.

Follain, James R., David C. Ling, and Gary A. McGill. 1993. "The Preferential Income Tax Treatment of Owner-Occupied Housing: Who Really Benefits?" *Housing Policy Debate* 4 (1): 1–24.

Foote, Christopher L., Kristopher Gerardi, Lorenz Goette, and Paul S. Willen. 2008. "Just the Facts: An Initial Analysis of Subprime's Role in the Housing Crisis." *Journal of Housing Economics* 17 (4): 291–305.

Forrest, Ray, and Ade Kearns. 2001. "Social Cohesion, Social Capital and the Neighbourhood." *Urban Studies* 38 (12): 2125–43.

French, David M. 1941. "The Contest for a National System of Home-Mortgage Finance." *American Political Science Review* 35 (1): 53–69.

Fung, Archon. 2006. *Empowered Participation: Reinventing Urban Democracy*. Princeton, NJ: Princeton University Press.

Fung, Archon, and Erik Olin Wright. 2003. *Deepening Democracy: Institutional Innovations in Empowered Participatory Governance*. London: Verso.

Fung, Archon, and Erik Olin Wright. 2001. "Deepening Democracy: Innovations in Empowered Participatory Governance." *Politics and Society* 29 (1): 5–41.

Gabriel, Stuart A., and Stuart S. Rosenthal. 2011. "Homeownership Boom and Bust 2000 to 2009: Where Will the Homeownership Rate Go from Here?" Working Paper no. 11-03. Washington, DC: Research Institute for Housing America.

Gabriel, Stuart A., and Stuart S. Rosenthal. 2005. "Homeownership in the 1980s and 1990s: Aggregate Trends and Racial Gaps." *Journal of Urban Economics* 57 (1): 101–27.

Gainsborough, Juliet. 2001. *Fenced Off: The Suburbanization of American Politics*. Washington, DC: Georgetown University Press.

Galster, George C. 1987. *Homeowners and Neighborhood Reinvestment*. Durham, NC: Duke University Press.

Galster, George C. 1983. "Empirical Evidence on Cross-tenure Differences in Home Maintenance and Conditions." *Land Economics* 59 (1): 107–13.

Gans, Herbert J. 1982. *The Levittowners*. New York: Columbia University Press.

Garb, Margaret. 2011. *City of American Dreams: A History of Home Ownership and Housing Reform in Chicago, 1871–1919*. Chicago: University of Chicago Press.

Garon, Sheldon. 2011. *Beyond Our Means: Why America Spends While the World Saves*. Princeton, NJ: Princeton University Press.

Gibson, Timothy A. 2005. "NIMBY and the Civic Good." *City and Community* 4 (4): 381–401.

Gilderbloom, John I., and John P. Markham. 1995. "The Impact of Homeownership on Political Beliefs." *Social Forces* 73 (4): 1589–1607.

Glaeser, Edward L. 2011. "Rethinking the Federal Bias toward Homeownership." *Cityscape* 13 (2): 5–37.

Glaeser, Edward L. 2010. "Housing Policy in the Wake of the Crash." *Daedalus* 139 (4): 95–106.

Glaeser, Edward L., David I. Laibson, José A. Scheinkman, and Christine L. Soutter. 2000. "Measuring Trust." *Quarterly Journal of Economics* 115 (3): 811–46.

Glaeser, Edward L., and Jesse M. Shapiro. 2002. "The Benefits of the Home Mortgage Interest Deduction." Working Paper no. 9284. Cambridge, MA: National Bureau of Economic Research.

Glynn, Carroll J., Carole A. Lunney, and Michael E. Huge. 2009. "Public Perceptions of the U.S. Residential Housing Market before, during, and after the Housing Bubble (1990–2009)." *Public Opinion Quarterly* 73 (4): 807–32.

Goetz, Edward G., and Mara Sidney. 1994. "Revenge of the Property Owners: Community Development and the Politics of Property." *Journal of Urban Affairs* 16 (4): 319–34.

Gordon, Adam. 2005. "The Creation of Homeownership: How New Deal Changes in Banking Regulation Simultaneously Made Homeownership Accessible to Whites and Out of Reach for Blacks." *Yale Law Journal* 115 (1): 186–226.

Gotham, Kevin Fox. 2000. "Racialization and the State: The Housing Act of 1934 and the Creation of the Federal Housing Administration." *Sociological Perspectives* 43 (2): 291–317.

Gotham, Kevin Fox. 2000. "Separate and Unequal: The Housing Act of 1968 and the Section 235 Program." *Sociological Forum* 15 (1): 13–37.

Gould, Lewis L. 2001. *America in the Progressive Era, 1890–1914*. New York: Longman.

Green, Richard K., and Patric H. Hendershott. 2001. "Home-ownership and Unemployment in the US." *Urban Studies* 38 (9): 1509–1520.

Green, Richard K., and Susan M. Wachter. 2005. "The American Mortgage in Historical and International Context." *Journal of Economic Perspectives* 19 (4): 93–114.

Greif, Meredith. 2014. "The Intersection of Homeownership, Race and Neighbourhood Context: Implications for Neighbourhood Satisfaction." *Urban Studies* 52 (1): 50–70.

Grinstein-Weiss, Michal, Clinton Key, Shenyang Guo, Yeong Hun Yeo, and Krista Holub. 2013. "Homeownership and Wealth among Low- and Moderate-Income Households." *Housing Policy Debate* 23 (2): 259–79.

Grinstein-Weiss, Michal, Yeong Yeo, Katrin Anacker, Shannon Van Zandt, Elizabeth B. Freeze, and Roberto G. Quercia. 2011. "Homeownership and Neighborhood Satisfaction among Low- and Moderate-Income Households." *Journal of Urban Affairs* 33 (3): 247–65.

Grinstein-Weiss, Michal, Yeong Hun Yeo, Kim R. Manturuk, Mathieu R. Despard, Krista A. Holub, Johanna K. P. Greeson, and Roberto G. Quercia. 2013. "Social Capital and Homeownership in Low- to Moderate-Income Neighborhoods." *Social Work Research* 37 (1): 37–53.

Guest, Avery M., and Susan K. Wierzbicki. 1999. "Social Ties at the Neighborhood Level: Two Decades of GSS Evidence." *Urban Affairs Review* 35 (1): 92–111.

Habermas, Jürgen. 1991. *The Structural Transformation of the Public Sphere: An Inquiry into a Category of Bourgeois Society.* Cambridge, MA: MIT Press.

Hacker, Jacob S. 2008. *The Great Risk Shift: The New Economic Insecurity and the Decline of the American Dream.* New York: Oxford University Press.

Hames, Carl M. 1978. *Hill Ferguson, His Life and Works.* Birmingham: University of Alabama Press.

Hanchett, Thomas W. 2000. "Financing Suburbia: Prudential Insurance and the Post–World War II Transformation of the American City." *Journal of Urban History* 26 (3): 312–28.

Hanson, Andrew, Ike Brannon, and Zackary Hawley. 2014. "Rethinking Tax Benefits for Home Owners." *National Affairs* 19: 40–54.

Harkness, Joseph, and Sandra Newman. 2003. "Differential Effects of Homeownership on Children from Higher- and Lower-Income Families." *Journal of Housing Research* 14 (1): 1–19.

Harkness, Joseph, and Sandra Newman. 2003. "Effects of Homeownership on Children: The Role of Neighborhood Characteristics and Family Income." *Economic Policy Review* 9 (2): 87–107.

Harris, Dianne. 2013. *Second Suburb: Levittown, Pennsylvania.* Pittsburgh: University of Pittsburgh Press.

Harris, Richard. 1992. "The End Justified the Means: Boarding and Rooming in a City of Homes, 1890–1951." *Journal of Social History* 26 (2): 331–58.

Harris, Richard. 1990. "Working-Class Home Ownership in the American Metropolis." *Journal of Urban History* 17 (1): 46–69.

Haurin, Donald R., Robert D. Dietz, and Bruce A. Weinberg. 2003. "The Impact of Neighborhood Homeownership Rates: A Review of the Theoretical and Empirical Literature." *Journal of Housing Research* 13 (2): 119–52.

Haurin, Donald R., Patric H. Hendershott, and Susan M. Wachter. 1996. "Expected Home Ownership and Real Wealth Accumulation of Youth." Working paper no. 5629. Cambridge, MA: National Bureau of Economic Research.

Hayden, Dolores. 1986. *Redesigning the American Dream*. New York: Norton.

Herbert, Christopher E., Daniel T. McCue, and Rocio Sanchez-Moyano. 2013. "Is Homeownership Still an Effective Means of Building Wealth for Low-Income and Minority Households?" In *Homeownership Built to Last*, edited by Eric S. Belsky, Christopher E. Herbert, and Jennifer H. Molinsky, 50–98. Washington, DC: Brookings Institution Press.

Hendershott, Patric H., and Kevin E. Villani. 1985. "Direct Intervention in the Mortgage Market." In *Federal Housing Policy and Programs: Past and Present*, edited by Paul J. Mitchell, 123–41. New Brunswick, NJ: Center for Urban Policy Research.

Hilber, Christian A. L., and Yingchun Liu. 2008. "Explaining the Black–White Homeownership Gap: The Role of Own Wealth, Parental Externalities and Locational Preferences." *Journal of Housing Economics* 17 (2): 152–74.

Hillier, Amy E. 2003. "Redlining and the Home Owners' Loan Corporation." *Journal of Urban History* 29 (4): 394–420.

Hoff, Karla, and Arijit Sen. 2005. "Homeownership, Community Interactions, and Segregation." *American Economic Review* 95 (4): 1167–89.

Hoover, Herbert. 1952. *The Memoirs of Herbert Hoover*. New York: Macmillan.

Hornstein, Jeffrey M. 2005. *A Nation of Realtors: A Cultural History of the Twentieth-Century American Middle Class*. Durham, NC: Duke University Press.

Howard, Christopher. 1997. *The Hidden Welfare State*. Princeton, NJ: Princeton University Press.

Howard, Timothy. 2013. *The Mortgage Wars: Inside Fannie Mae, Big-Money Politics, and the Collapse of the American Dream*. New York: McGraw-Hill.

Humes, Edward. 2006. *Over Here: How the G.I. Bill Transformed the American Dream*. New York: Harcourt.

Hunt, D. Bradford. 2009. *Blueprint for Disaster: The Unraveling of Chicago Public Housing*. Chicago: University of Chicago Press.

Hutchison, Janet. 1997. "Building for Babbitt: The State and the Suburban Home Ideal." *Journal of Policy History* 9 (2): 184–210.

Hutchison, Janet. 1993. "Better Homes and Gullah." *Agricultural History* 67 (2): 102–18.

Hutchison, Janet. 1986. "The Cure for Domestic Neglect: Better Homes in America, 1922–1935." *Perspectives in Vernacular Architecture* 2: 168–78.

Hyman, Louis. 2013. *Debtor Nation: The History of America in Red Ink*. Princeton, NJ: Princeton University Press.

Immergluck, Daniel. 2004. *Credit to the Community: Community Reinvestment and Fair Lending Policy in the United States*. New York: M. E. Sharpe.

Jackson, Kenneth T. 1987. *Crabgrass Frontier: The Suburbanization of the United States*. New York: Oxford University Press.

Jackson, Kenneth T. 1980. "Race, Ethnicity, and Real Estate Appraisal: The Home Owners Loan Corporation and the Federal Housing Administration." *Journal of Urban History* 6: 419–52.

Johnson, Heather Beth. 2014. *The American Dream and the Power of Wealth: Choosing Schools and Inheriting Inequality in the Land of Opportunity.* New York: Routledge.

Joint Center for Housing Studies at Harvard University. 2008. "The State of the Nation's Housing, 2008." Joint Center for Housing Studies, Harvard University.

Joseph, Miranda. 2002. *Against the Romance of Community.* Minneapolis: University of Minnesota Press.

Kan, Kamhon. 2007. "Residential Mobility and Social Capital." *Journal of Urban Economics* 61 (3): 436–57.

Katz, Alyssa. 2009. *Our Lot: How Real Estate Came to Own Us.* New York: Bloomsbury.

Katz, Michael B., Michael J. Doucet, and Mark J. Stern. 1982. *The Social Organization of Early Industrial Capitalism.* Cambridge, MA: Harvard University Press.

Kelly, Barbara M. 1993. *Expanding the American Dream.* Albany: State University of New York Press.

Kemeny, Jim. 2005. "'The Really Big Trade-Off' between Home Ownership and Welfare: Castles' Evaluation of the 1980 Thesis, and a Reformulation 25 Years On." *Housing, Theory and Society* 22 (2): 59–75.

Kemeny, Jim. 2001. "Comparative Housing and Welfare: Theorising the Relationship." *Journal of Housing and the Built Environment* 16 (1): 53–70.

Kemeny, Jim. 1992. *Housing and Social Theory.* New York: Routledge.

Kemeny, Jim. 1982. *Myth of Home Ownership: Private versus Public Choices in Housing Tenure.* New York: Routledge, Kegan and Paul.

Kemeny, Jim. 1980. "Home Ownership and Privatization." *International Journal of Urban and Regional Research* 4 (3): 372–88.

Kennedy, David M. 2001. *Freedom from Fear: The American People in Depression and War, 1929–1945.* New York: Oxford University Press.

Keyssar, Alexander. 2009. *The Right to Vote: The Contested History of Democracy in the United States.* New York: Basic Books.

Kingston, Paul William, John L. P. Thompson, and Douglas M. Eichar. 1984. "The Politics of Homeownership." *American Politics Research* 12 (2): 131–50.

Kitts, James A. 1999. "Not in Our Backyard: Solidarity, Social Networks, and the Ecology of Environmental Mobilization." *Sociological Inquiry* 69 (4): 551–74.

Klinenberg, Eric. 2003. *Heat Wave: A Social Autopsy of Disaster in Chicago.* Chicago: University of Chicago Press.

Kohn, Margaret. 2002. "Review: Panacea or Privilege? New Approaches to Democracy and Association." *Political Theory* 30 (2): 289–98.

Krueckeberg, Donald A. 1999. "The Grapes of Rent: A History of Renting in a Country of Owners." *Housing Policy Debate* 10 (1): 9–30.

Kuebler, Meghan, and Jacob S. Rugh. 2013. "New Evidence on Racial and Ethnic Disparities in Homeownership in the United States from 2001 to 2010." *Social Science Research* 42 (5): 1357–74.

Kushner, David. 2009. *Levittown*. New York: Walker Books.

Lake, Robert W. 1996. "Volunteers, NIMBYs, and Environmental Justice: Dilemmas of Democratic Practice." *Antipode* 28 (2): 160–74.

Lake, Robert W. 1993. "Planners' Alchemy: Transforming NIMBY to YIMBY: Rethinking NIMBY." *Journal of the American Planning Association* 59 (1): 87–93.

Landis, John D., and Kirk McClure. 2010. "Rethinking Federal Housing Policy." *Journal of the American Planning Association* 76 (3): 319–48.

Lands, LeeAnn. 2009. *The Culture of Property: Race, Class, and Housing Landscapes in Atlanta, 1880–1950*. Athens: University of Georgia Press.

Lands, LeeAnn. 2008. "Be a Patriot, Buy a Home: Re-imagining Home Owners and Home Ownership in Early 20th Century Atlanta." *Journal of Social History* 41 (4): 943–65.

Lang, Robert E., and Rebecca R. Sohmer. 2000. "Legacy of the Housing Act of 1949: The Past, Present, and Future of Federal Housing and Urban Policy." *Housing Policy Debate* 11 (2): 291–98.

Lareau, Annette. 2014. "Schools, Housing and the Reproduction of Inequality." In *Choosing Homes, Choosing Schools*, edited by Annette Lareau and Kimberly A. Goyette, 169–206. New York: Russell Sage Foundation.

Lareau, Annette, and Kimberly A. Goyette. 2014. *Choosing Homes, Choosing Schools*. New York: Russell Sage Foundation.

Larsen, Larissa, Sharon L. Harlan, Bob Bolin, Edward J. Hackett, Diane Hope, Andrew Kirby, Amy Nelson, Tom R. Rex, and Shaphard Wolf. 2004. "Bonding and Bridging: Understanding the Relationship between Social Capital and Civic Action." *Journal of Planning Education and Research* 24 (1): 64–77.

Lea, Michael J. 1996. "Innovation and the Cost of Mortgage Credit: A Historical Perspective." *Housing Policy Debate* 7 (1): 147–74.

Lee, Caroline W., Michael McQuarrie, and Edward T. Walker. 2015. *Democratizing Inequalities: Dilemmas of the New Public Participation*. New York: New York University Press.

Lewis, Michael. 2011. *The Big Short: Inside the Doomsday Machine*. New York: Norton.

Lim, Chaeyoon. 2008. "Social Networks and Political Participation: How Do Networks Matter?" *Social Forces* 87 (2): 961–82.

Lindblad, Mark R., Kim R. Manturuk, and Roberto G. Quercia. 2013. "Sense of Community and Informal Social Control among Lower Income Households: The Role of Homeownership and Collective Efficacy in Reducing Subjective Neighborhood Crime and Disorder." *American Journal of Community Psychology* 51 (1–2): 123–39.

Lindblad, Mark R., and Roberto G. Quercia. 2015. "Why Is Homeownership Associated with Nonfinancial Benefits? A Path Analysis of Competing Mechanisms." *Housing Policy Debate* 25 (2): 263–88.

Lloyd, Robert E. 1994. "Government-Induced Market Failure: A Note on the Origins of FHA Mortgage Insurance." *Critical Review* 8 (1): 61–71.

Lochner, Kimberly A., Ichiro Kawachi, Robert T. Brennan, and Stephen L. Buka. 2003. "Social Capital and Neighborhood Mortality Rates in Chicago." *Social Science and Medicine* 56 (8): 1797–1805.

Logan, John R., and Harvey L. Molotch. 1988. *Urban Fortunes: The Political Economy of Place.* Berkeley: University of California Press.

Long, James E., and Steven B. Caudill. 1992. "Racial Differences in Homeownership and Housing Wealth, 1970–1986." *Economic Inquiry* 30 (1): 83–100.

Luken, Paul C., and Suzanne Vaughan. 2006. "Standardizing Childrearing through Housing." *Social Problems* 53 (3): 299–331.

Luken, Paul C., and Suzanne Vaughan. 2005. "'… Be a Genuine Homemaker in Your Own Home': Gender and Familial Relations in State Housing Practices, 1917–1922." *Social Forces* 83 (4): 1603–25.

Maki, Dean M. 2001. "Household Debt and the Tax Reform Act of 1986." *American Economic Review* 91 (1): 305–19.

Manturuk, Kim, Mark Lindblad, and Roberto G. Quercia. 2012. "Homeownership and Civic Engagement in Low-Income Urban Neighborhoods: A Longitudinal Analysis." *Urban Affairs Review* 48 (5): 731–60.

Manturuk, Kim, Mark Lindblad, and Roberto G. Quercia. 2010. "Friends and Neighbors: Homeownership and Social Capital among Low- to Moderate-Income Families." *Journal of Urban Affairs* 32 (4): 471–88.

Manturuk, Kim, Mark Lindblad, and Roberto G. Quercia. 2009. "Homeownership and Local Voting in Disadvantaged Urban Neighborhoods." *Cityscape* 11 (3): 213–30.

Manzi, Tony, and Bill Smith-Bowers. 2005. "Gated Communities as Club Goods: Segregation or Social Cohesion?" *Housing Studies* 20 (2): 345–59.

Marsico, Richard D. 1994. "Fighting Poverty through Community Empowerment and Economic Development: The Role of the Community Reinvestment and Home Mortgage Disclosure Acts." *New York Law School Journal of Human Rights* 12: 281–309.

Martinez, Sylvia C. 2000. "The Housing Act of 1949: Its Place in the Realization of the American Dream of Homeownership." *Housing Policy Debate* 11 (2): 467–87.

Mason, David. 2004. *From Buildings and Loans to Bail-outs: A History of the Savings and Loan Industry, 1831–1989.* New York: Cambridge University Press.

Massey, Douglas S. 2005. "Racial Discrimination in Housing: A Moving Target." *Social Problems* 52 (2): 148–51.

Massey, Douglas S., Len Albright, Rebecca Casciano, Elizabeth Derickson, and David N. Kinsey. 2013. *Climbing Mount Laurel: The Struggle for Affordable Housing and Social Mobility in an American Suburb.* Princeton, NJ: Princeton University Press.

Massey, Douglas S., and Nancy A. Denton. 1993. *American Apartheid: Segregation and the Making of the Underclass.* Cambridge, MA: Harvard University Press.

Mayorga-Gallo, Sarah. 2014. *Behind the White Picket Fence: Power and Privilege in a Multiethnic Neighborhood.* Durham, NC: University of North Carolina Press.

McAdam, Doug, and Ronnelle Paulsen. 1993. "Specifying the Relationship between Social Ties and Activism." *American Journal of Sociology* 99 (3): 640–67.

McCabe, Brian J. 2014. "When Property Values Rule." *Contexts* 13 (1): 38–43.

McCabe, Brian J. 2013. "Are Homeowners Better Citizens? Homeownership and Community Participation in the United States." *Social Forces* 91 (3): 929–54.

McCabe, Brian J. 2012. "Homeownership and Social Trust in Neighbors." *City and Community* 11 (4): 389–408.

McClaughry, John. 1975. "Troubled Dream: The Life and Times of Section 235 of the National Housing Act." *Loyola University of Chicago Law Journal* 6: 1–35.

McClymont, Katie, and Paul O'Hare. 2008. "'We're Not NIMBYs!' Contrasting Local Protest Groups with Idealised Conceptions of Sustainable Communities." *Local Environment* 13 (4): 321–35.

McGerr, Michael E. 1986. *The Decline of Popular Politics: The American North, 1865–1928.* New York: Oxford University Press.

McKenzie, Evan. 2005. "Planning through Residential Clubs: Homeowners' Associations." *Economic Affairs* 25 (4): 28–31.

McKenzie, Evan. 1996. *Privatopia: Homeowner Associations and the Rise of Residential Private Government.* New Haven: Yale University Press.

Meltzer, Rachel. 2013. "Do Homeowners Associations Affect Citywide Segregation? Evidence from Florida Municipalities." *Housing Policy Debate* 23 (4): 688–713.

Meltzer, Rachel, and Ron Cheung. 2014. "How Are Homeowners Associations Capitalized into Property Values?" *Regional Science and Urban Economics* 46: 93–102.

Mettler, Suzanne. 2005. *Soldiers to Citizens: The G.I. Bill and the Making of the Greatest Generation.* New York: Oxford University Press.

Milan, Atif, and Amir Sufi. 2015. *House of Debt: How They (and You) Caused the Great Recession, and How We Can Prevent It from Happening Again.* Chicago: University of Chicago Press.

Miller, Brian J. 2008. "The Struggle over Redevelopment at Cabrini-Green, 1989–2004." *Journal of Urban History* 34 (6): 944–60.

Milligan, Kevin, Enrico Moretti, and Philip Oreopoulos. 2004. "Does Education Improve Citizenship? Evidence from the United States and the United Kingdom." *Journal of Public Economics* 88 (9–10): 1667–95.

Mitchell, J. Paul. 1985. *Federal Housing Policy and Programs: Past and Present.* New Brunswick, NJ: Center for Urban Policy Research.

Mitchell, J. Paul. 1985. "Historic Overview of Federal Policy: Encouraging Homeownership." In *Federal Housing Policy and Programs: Past and Present,* edited by J. Paul Mitchell, 39–46. New Brunswick, NJ: Center for Urban Policy Research.

Modell, John, and Tamara K. Hareven. 1973. "Urbanization and the Malleable Household: An Examination of Boarding and Lodging in American Families." *Journal of Marriage and Family* 35 (3): 467–79.

Molinsky, Jennifer H., Eric S. Belsky, and Christopher E. Herbert. 2014. "Introduction: Balancing Access, Affordability, and Risk after the Housing Crisis." In *Homeownership Built to Last*, edited by Eric S. Belsky, Christopher E. Herbert, and Jennifer H. Molinsky, 1–28. Washington, DC: Brookings Institution Press.

Morenoff, Jeffrey D., Robert J. Sampson, and Stephen W. Raudenbush. 2001. "Neighborhood Inequality, Collective Efficacy, and the Spatial Dynamics of Urban Violence." *Criminology* 39 (3): 517–58.

Morton, Joseph E. 1956. *Urban Mortgage Lending: Comparative Markets and Experience*. Princeton, NJ: Princeton University Press.

Murray, Melissa. 2008. "When War Is Work: The G.I. Bill, Citizenship, and the Civic Generation." *California Law Review* 96 (4): 967–98.

Newton, Kenneth. 2001. "Trust, Social Capital, Civil Society, and Democracy." *International Political Science Review* 22 (2): 201–14.

Nguyen, Mai Thi. 2005. "Does Affordable Housing Detrimentally Affect Property Values? A Review of the Literature." *Journal of Planning Literature* 20 (1): 15–26.

Nicolaides, Becky M. 2002. *My Blue Heaven: Life and Politics in the Working-Class Suburbs of Los Angeles, 1920–1965*. Chicago: University of Chicago Press.

Oates, Wallace E. 1969. "The Effects of Property Taxes and Local Public Spending on Property Values: An Empirical Study of Tax Capitalization and the Tiebout Hypothesis." *Journal of Political Economy* 77 (6): 957–71.

Oliver, J. Eric. 2001. *Democracy in Suburbia*. Princeton, NJ: Princeton University Press.

Oliver, J. Eric, Shang E. Ha, and Zachary Callen. 2012. *Local Elections and the Politics of Small-Scale Democracy*. Princeton, NJ: Princeton University Press.

Oliver, Melvin L., and Thomas M. Shapiro. 1997. *Black Wealth/White Wealth: A New Perspective on Racial Inequality*. New York: Routledge.

Oswald, Andrew. 2009. "The Housing Market and Europe's Unemployment: A Nontechnical Paper." In *Homeownership and the Labour Market in Europe*, edited by Casper van Ewijk and Michiel van Leuvensteijm, 43–52. New York: Oxford University Press.

Oswald, Andrew J. 1996. "A Conjecture on the Explanation for High Unemployment in the Industrialized Nations: Part 1." Working paper no. 475. Coventry, England: Department of Economics, University of Warwick.

Passy, Florence, and Marco Giugni. 2001. "Social Networks and Individual Perceptions: Explaining Differential Participation in Social Movements." *Sociological Forum* 16 (1): 123–53.

Pattillo, Mary. 2013. "Housing: Commodity versus Right." *Annual Review of Sociology* 39 (1): 509–31.

Pattillo, Mary. 2007. *Black on the Block: The Politics of Race and Class in the City*. Chicago: University of Chicago Press.

Paxton, Pamela. 1999. "Is Social Capital Declining in the United States? A Multiple Indicator Assessment." *American Journal of Sociology* 105 (1): 88–127.

Peek, Gina. 2011. "Better Citizens? The Relationship between Home Ownership and Religious and Political Volunteerism in the United States." *International Journal of Home Economics* 4 (1): 39–54.

Perin, Constance. 1977. *Everything in Its Place: Social Order and Land Use in America.* Princeton, NJ: Princeton University Press.

Pierson, Paul. 1996. "The New Politics of the Welfare State." *World Politics* 48 (2): 143–79.

Pierson, Paul. 1994. *Dismantling the Welfare State? Reagan, Thatcher and the Politics of Retrenchment.* New York: Cambridge University Press.

Pietila, Antero. 2010. *Not in My Neighborhood: How Bigotry Shaped a Great American City.* Chicago: Rowman and Littlefield.

Polletta, Francesca, and James M. Jasper. 2001. "Collective Identity and Social Movements." *Annual Review of Sociology* 27: 283–305.

Poterba, James, and Todd Sinai. 2008. "Tax Expenditures for Owner-Occupied Housing: Deductions for Property Taxes and Mortgage Interest and the Exclusion of Imputed Rental Income." *American Economic Review* 98 (2): 84–89.

Prasad, Monica. 2012. *The Land of Too Much: American Abundance and the Paradox of Poverty.* Cambridge, MA: Harvard University Press.

Purcell, Mark. 2001. "Neighborhood Activism among Homeowners as a Politics of Space." *Professional Geographer* 53 (2): 178–94.

Putnam, Robert D. 2001. *Bowling Alone: The Collapse and Revival of American Community.* New York: Simon and Schuster.

Radford, Gail. 1997. *Modern Housing for America: Policy Struggles in the New Deal Era.* Chicago: University of Chicago Press.

Reid, Carolina. 2014. "To Buy or Not to Buy? Understanding Tenure Preferences and the Decisionmaking Processes of Lower-Income Households." In *Homeownership Built to Last,* edited by Eric S. Belsky, Christopher E. Herbert, and Jennifer H. Molinsky, 143–71. Washington, DC: Brookings Institution Press.

Reingold, David A. 1995. "Public Housing, Home Ownership, and Community Participation in Chicago's Inner City." *Housing Studies* 10 (4): 445–69.

Retsinas, Nicolas P., and Eric S. Belsky. 2002. *Low-Income Homeownership: Examining the Unexamined Goal.* Washington, DC: Brookings Institution Press.

Riley, Sarah F., HongYu Ru, and Roberto G. Quercia. 2009. "The Community Advantage Program Database: Overview and Comparison with the Current Population Survey." *Cityscape* 11 (3): 247–56.

Rohe, William M., and Victoria Basolo. 1997. "Long-Term Effects of Homeownership on the Self-Perceptions and Social Interaction of Low-Income Persons." *Environment and Behavior* 29 (6): 793–819.

Rohe, William M., and Michael A. Stegman. 1994. "The Effects of Homeownership: On the Self-Esteem, Perceived Control and Life Satisfaction of Low-Income People." *Journal of the American Planning Association* 60 (2): 173–84.

Rohe, William M., and Michael A. Stegman. 1994. "The Impact of Home Ownership on the Social and Political Involvement of Low-Income People." *Urban Affairs Review* 30 (1): 152–72.

Rohe, William M., and Leslie S. Stewart. 1996. "Homeownership and Neighborhood Stability." *Housing Policy Debate* 7 (1): 37–81.

Rohe, William M., Shannon Van Zandt, and George McCarthy. 2002. "Home Ownership and Access to Opportunity." *Housing Studies* 17 (1): 51–61.

Rohe, William M., and Harry L. Watson. 2007. *Chasing the American Dream: New Perspectives on Affordable Homeownership.* Ithaca, NY: Cornell University Press.

Rolnik, Raquel. 2013. "Late Neoliberalism: The Financialization of Homeownership and Housing Rights." *International Journal of Urban and Regional Research* 37 (3): 1058–66.

Ronald, Richard. 2008. *The Ideology of Home Ownership: Homeowner Societies and the Role of Housing.* New York: Palgrave Macmillan.

Ronald, Richard, and John Doling. 2012. "Testing Home Ownership as the Cornerstone of Welfare: Lessons from East Asia for the West." *Housing Studies* 27 (7): 940–61.

Roland, Richard, and Marja Elsigna. 2011. *Beyond Home Ownership: Housing, Welfare and Society.* New York: Routledge.

Ross, Catherine E., and Sung Joon Jang. 2000. "Neighborhood Disorder, Fear, and Mistrust: The Buffering Role of Social Ties with Neighbors." *American Journal of Community Psychology* 28 (4): 401–20.

Rossi, Peter H., and Eleanor Weber. 1996. "The Social Benefits of Homeownership: Empirical Evidence from National Surveys." *Housing Policy Debate* 7 (1): 1–35.

Rotolo, Thomas, John Wilson, and Mary Elizabeth Hughes. 2010. "Homeownership and Volunteering: An Alternative Approach to Studying Social Inequality and Civic Engagement." *Sociological Forum* 25 (3): 570–87.

Saegert, Susan, Desiree Fields, and Kimberly Libman. 2009. "Deflating the Dream: Radical Risk and the Neoliberalization of Homeownership." *Journal of Urban Affairs* 31 (3): 297–317.

Sampson, Robert J., Jeffrey D. Morenoff, and Thomas Gannon-Rowley. 2002. "Assessing 'Neighborhood Effects': Social Processes and New Directions in Research." *Annual Review of Sociology* 28: 443–78.

Sampson, Robert J., Stephen W. Raudenbush, and Felton Earls. 1997. "Neighborhoods and Violent Crime: A Multilevel Study of Collective Efficacy." *Science* 277 (5328): 918–24.

Sanders, Anthony. 2008. "The Subprime Crisis and Its Role in the Financial Crisis." *Journal of Housing Economics* 17 (4): 254–61.

Saunders, Peter. 1990. *A Nation of Home Owners.* London: Unwin Hyman.

Saunders, Peter. 1978. "Domestic Property and Social Class." *International Journal of Urban and Regional Research* 2: 233–51.

Scally, Corianne Payton. 2013. "The Nuances of NIMBY Context and Perceptions of Affordable Rental Housing Development." *Urban Affairs Review* 49 (5): 718–47.

Scanion, Edward. 1998. "Low-Income Homeownership Policy as a Community Development Strategy." *Journal of Community Practice* 5 (1–2): 137–54.

Schively, Carissa. 2007. "Understanding the NIMBY and LULU Phenomena: Reassessing Our Knowledge Base and Informing Future Research." *Journal of Planning Literature* 21 (3): 255–66.

Schlozman, Kay Lehman, Sidney Verba, and Henry E. Brady. 2012. *The Unheavenly Chorus: Unequal Political Voice and the Broken Promise of American Democracy.* Princeton, NJ: Princeton University Press.

Schwartz, Alex F. 2010. *Housing Policy in the United States.* New York: Routledge.

Schwartz, Amy Ellen, Ingrid Gould Ellen, Ioan Voicu, and Michael H. Schill. 2006. "The External Effects of Place-Based Subsidized Housing." *Regional Science and Urban Economics* 36 (6): 679–707.

Schwartz, Herman. 2012. "Housing, the Welfare State, and the Global Financial Crisis: What Is the Connection?" *Politics and Society* 40 (1): 35–58.

Schwartz, Herman. 2009. *Subprime Nation: American Power, Global Capital, and the Housing Bubble.* Ithaca, NY: Cornell University Press.

Schwartz, Herman, and Leonard Seabrooke. 2008. "Varieties of Residential Capitalism in the International Political Economy: Old Welfare States and the New Politics of Housing." *Comparative European Politics* 6 (3): 237–61.

Shapiro, Thomas M. 2006. "Race, Homeownership and Wealth." *Washington University Journal of Law and Policy* 20: 53–74.

Shapiro, Thomas, Tatjana Meschede, and Sam Osoro. 2013. "The Roots of the Widening Racial Wealth Gap: Explaining the Black-White Economic Divide." Working paper. Waltham, MA: Institute on Assets and Social Policy, Brandeis University.

Shiller, Robert J. 2015. *Irrational Exuberance.* Princeton, NJ: Princeton University Press.

Shlay, Anne B. 2006. "Low-Income Homeownership: American Dream or Delusion?" *Urban Studies* 43 (3): 511–31.

Smith, David Horton. 1994. "Determinants of Voluntary Association Participation and Volunteering: A Literature Review." *Nonprofit and Voluntary Sector Quarterly* 23 (3): 243–63.

Staeheli, Lynn A. 2008. "Citizenship and the Problem of Community." *Political Geography* 27 (1): 5–21.

Stern, Stephanie M. 2011. "Reassessing the Citizenship Virtues of Homeownership." *Columbia Law Review* 11 (4): 890–938.

Stern, Stephanie M. 2009. "Residential Protectionism and the Legal Mythology of Home." *Michigan Law Review* 107 (7): 1093–1144.

Stolle, Dietlind. 1998. "Bowling Together, Bowling Alone: The Development of Generalized Trust in Voluntary Associations." *Political Psychology* 19 (3): 497–525.

Stolle, Dietlind, Stuart Soroka, and Richard Johnston. 2008. "When Does Diversity Erode Trust? Neighborhood Diversity, Interpersonal Trust and the Mediating Effect of Social Interactions." *Political Studies* 56 (1): 57–75.

Subramanian, S. V., Daniel J. Kim, and Ichiro Kawachi. 2002. "Social Trust and Self-Rated Health in US Communities: A Multilevel Analysis." *Journal of Urban Health* 79 (1): S21–S34.

Sugrue, Thomas J. 2005. *The Origins of the Urban Crisis: Race and Inequality in Postwar Detroit*. Princeton, NJ: Princeton University Press.

Taub, Jennifer. 2014. *Other People's Houses: How Decades of Bailouts, Captive Regulators and Toxic Bankers Made Home Mortgages a Thrilling Business*. New Haven: Yale University Press.

Taylor, John, and Josh Silver. 2008. "The Community Reinvestment Act at 30: Looking Back and Looking to the Future." *New York Law School Law Review* 53: 203–25.

Teaford, Jon C. 2000. "Urban Renewal and Its Aftermath." *Housing Policy Debate* 11 (2): 443–65.

Temkin, Kenneth, and William M. Rohe. 1998. "Social Capital and Neighborhood Stability: An Empirical Investigation." *Housing Policy Debate* 9 (1): 61–88.

Theiss-Morse, Elizabeth, and John R. Hibbing. 2005. "Citizenship and Civic Engagement." *Annual Review of Political Science* 8 (1): 227–49.

Tocqueville, Alexis de. 2003 [1835]. *Democracy in America*. London: Penguin Classics.

Torgersen, Ulf. 1987. "Housing: The Wobbly Pillar under the Welfare State." *Scandinavian Housing and Planning Research* 4: 116–26.

Toussaint, Janneke, and Marja Elsinga. 2009. "Exploring 'Housing Asset–Based Welfare': Can the UK Be Held Up as an Example for Europe?" *Housing Studies* 24 (5): 669–92.

Turner, Tracy M., and Heather Luea. 2009. "Homeownership, Wealth Accumulation and Income Status." *Journal of Housing Economics* 18 (2): 104–14.

United States Housing and Home Finance Agency. *Handbook of Information on Provisions of the Housing Act of 1949 and Operations under the Various Programs*. Washington, DC: Housing and Home Finance Agency, Office of the Administrator, 1950.

United States National Advisory Commission on Civil Disorders. 1968. *Report of the National Advisory Commission on Civil Disorders*. Washington, DC: U.S. Government Printing Office.

Upton, Dell. 1984. "Pattern Books and Professionalism: Aspects of the Transformation of Domestic Architecture in America, 1800–1860." *Winterthur Portfolio* 19 (2–3): 107–50.

Uslaner, Eric M., and Richard S. Conley. 2003. "Civic Engagement and Particularized Trust: The Ties That Bind People to Their Ethnic Communities." *American Politics Research* 31 (4): 331–60.

Vale, Lawrence J. 2007. "The Ideological Origins of Affordable Homeownership Efforts." In *Chasing the American Dream: New Perspectives on Affordable Homeownership*, edited by William M. Rohe and Harry L. Watson, 15–40. Ithaca, NY: Cornell University Press.

Venkatesh, Sudhir. 2002. *American Project: The Rise and Fall of a Modern Ghetto.* Cambridge, MA: Harvard University Press.

Ventry, Dennis J. 2010. "The Accidental Deduction: A History and Critique of the Tax Subsidy for Mortgage Interest." *Law and Contemporary Problems* 73: 233–84.

Verba, Sidney, Kay Lehman Schlozman, and Henry Brady. 1995. *Voice and Equality: Civic Voluntarism in American Politics.* Cambridge, MA: Harvard University Press.

Verberg, Norine. 2000. "Homeownership and Politics: Testing the Political Incorporation Thesis." *Canadian Journal of Sociology* 25 (2): 169–95.

Vesselinov, Elena. 2008. "Members Only: Gated Communities and Residential Segregation in the Metropolitan United States." *Sociological Forum* 23 (3): 536–55.

Voicu, Ioan, and Vicki Been. 2008. "The Effect of Community Gardens on Neighboring Property Values." *Real Estate Economics* 36 (2): 241–83.

von Hoffman, Alexander. 2004. *House by House, Block by Block: The Rebirth of America's Urban Neighborhoods.* New York: Oxford University Press.

von Hoffman, Alexander. 2000. "A Study in Contradictions: The Origins and Legacy of the Housing Act of 1949." *Housing Policy Debate* 11 (2): 299–326.

Wells, Katie J. 2015. "A Housing Crisis, a Failed Law, and a Property Conflict: The US Urban Speculation Tax." *Antipode* 47 (4): 1043–1061.

Wexler, Mark N. 1996. "A Sociological Framing of the NIMBY (Not-in-My-Backyard) Syndrome." *International Review of Modern Sociology* 26 (1): 91–110.

White, Brett. 2010. "Underwater and Not Walking Away: Shame, Fear and the Social Management of the Housing Crisis." *Wake Forest Law Review* 45: 971–1024.

Wiebe, Robert H. 1967. *The Search for Order, 1877–1920.* New York: Hill and Wang.

Williamson, Thad. 2011. *Sprawl, Justice, and Citizenship: The Civic Costs of the American Way of Life.* New York: Oxford University Press.

Winter, Ian. 1995. *Radical Home Owner: Housing Tenure and Social Change.* Basel: Gordon and Breach Science Publishers.

Wolff, Edward N. 2007. "Recent Trends in Household Wealth in the United States: Rising Debt and the Middle-Class Squeeze." Working paper no. 589. Annandale-on-Hudson, NY: Levy Economics Institute, Bard College.

Wolff, Edward N. 1998. "Recent Trends in the Size Distribution of Household Wealth." *Journal of Economic Perspectives* 12 (3): 131–50.

Wright, Gwendolyn. 1983. *Building the Dream: A Social History of Housing in America.* Cambridge, MA: MIT Press.

Yamamura, Eiji. 2011. "How Do Neighbors Influence Investment in Social Capital? Homeownership and Length of Residence." *International Advances in Economic Research* 17 (4): 451–64.

Yamashita, Takashi. 2008. "The Effect of the GI Bill on Homeownership of World War II Veterans." Unpublished working paper. Portland, OR: Department of Economics, Reed College.

Yinger, John. 1997. *Closed Doors, Opportunities Lost: The Continuing Costs of Housing Discrimination.* New York: Russell Sage Foundation.

Yinger, John. 1999. "Sustaining the Fair Housing Act." *Cityscape* 4 (3): 93–106.

Yinger, John. 1986. "Measuring Racial Discrimination with Fair Housing Audits: Caught in the Act." *American Economic Review* 76 (5): 881–93.

Zmerli, Sonja. 2010. "Social Capital and Norms of Citizenship: An Ambiguous Relationship?" *American Behavioral Scientist* 53 (5): 657–76.

Zunz, Olivier. 1983. *The Changing Face of Inequality: Urbanization, Industrial Development, and Immigrants in Detroit, 1880–1920.* Chicago: University of Chicago Press.

INDEX

Figures and tables are indicated by "f" and "t" following page numbers.